Christopher Hibbert was born in Leicestershire in 1924 and educated at Radley and Oriel College, Oxford. He served as an infantry officer during the war, was twice wounded and was awarded the Military Cross in 1945. Described by Professor J.H. Plumb as 'a writer of the highest ability', he was, in the words of the *Times Educational Supplement*, 'perhaps the most gifted popular historian we have'. Christopher Hibbert was a Fellow of the Royal Society of Literature and an Hon. D. Litt. of Leicester University.

By Christopher Hibbert

The Destruction of Lord Raglan (*Heinemann Award for Literature 1962*)
Benito Mussolini
The Court at Windsor
The Making of Charles Dickens
London: The Biography of a City
The Dragon Wakes: China and the West 1793–1911
George IV
The Rise and Fall of the House of Medici
Edward VII: A Portrait
The Great Mutiny: India 1857
The French Revolution
The Personal History of Samuel Johnson
Garibaldi and His Enemies
Rome: The Biography of a City
The Virgin Queen: The Personal History of Elizabeth I
Nelson: A Personal History
Wellington: A Personal History
King Mob: Lord George Gordon and the Riots of 1780
The Roots of Evil: A Social History of Crime and Punishment
The Grand Tour
The English: A Social History
Venice: The Biography of a City
Florence: The Biography of a City
Charles I
George IV
George III: A Personal History
The Marlboroughs
Queen Victoria
Napoleon: His Wives and Women
Redcoats and Rebels: The War for America
The Story of England

AS EDITOR
The Recollections of Rifleman Harris
A Soldier of the 71st
The Wheatley Diary
The London Encyclopaedia (*McColvin Medal*)
An American in Regency England

GREAT BATTLES SERIES
Agincourt
Corunna
Arnhem

Arnhem

CHRISTOPHER HIBBERT

A Windrush Press Book

First published in Great Britain in 1962
by B.T. Batsford Ltd

This paperback edition published in 1998
in association with The Windrush Press
by Weidenfeld & Nicolson
an imprint of The Orion Publishing Group Ltd,
Carmelite House
50 Victoria Embankment
London EC4Y 0DZ

An Hachette UK Company

Reissued in 2022

3 5 7 9 10 8 6 4

A CIP catalogue record for this book
is available from the British Library.

ISBN mmp: 978 1 4746 2635 4
ISBN ebook: 978 1 4746 2636 1
ISBN audio: 978 1 4746 2634 7

Typeset at The Spartan Press Ltd,
Lymington, Hants

Printed in the UK by Clays Ltd,
Elcograf S.p.A.

MIX
Paper from
responsible sources
FSC® C104740

www.orionbooks.co.uk
www.weidenfeldandnicolson.co.uk

CONTENTS

LIST OF ILLUSTRATIONS, MAPS AND DIAGRAMS

A Dutch nurse tending the wounded
by permission of The Trustees of the Imperial War Museum, London
Wounded British prisoners

ACKNOWLEDGEMENTS

The author wishes to express his gratitude to the authors and publishers of the following books and articles for permission to quote from them:

A Full Life by Lieutenant-General Sir Brian Horrocks (Wm. Collins Sons & Co. Ltd); *Arnhem* by Major-General R.E. Urquhart (Cassell and Company Ltd); *Arnhem Lift* by Louis Hagen (Hammond, Hammond & Company, Limited); *Buch der Tapferkeit* by Erich Kern (Duffel Verlag, Leoni am Starnberger See); *Cloud over Arnhem* by Kate A. ter Horst (Allan Wingate Ltd); *Crusade in Europe* by Dwight D. Eisenhower (Doubleday and Company, Inc., New York); *Freely I Served* by Stanislaw Sosabowski (William Kimber & Co. Limited); *Lease of Life* by Andrew Milbourne (Museum Press Ltd); *My Three Years with Eisenhower* by Harry C. Butcher (William Heinemann Ltd; Simon and Schuster, Inc., New York); *Nine Days* by Ronald Gibson (Stockwell Ltd); *Normandy to the Baltic* by Field-Marshal Montgomery (Hutchinson & Co. Ltd; Houghton Mifflin Company, Boston); *Operation Victory* by Major-General Sir Francis de Guingand (Hodder & Stoughton Ltd); *Return Ticket* by Anthony Deane-Drummond (Wm. Collins Sons & Co. Ltd); *Straight On* by Robert Collis (Methuen & Co. Ltd); *The Battle Round the Bridge at Arnhem* by M. Heijbroek (The Airborne Museum, Kasteel de Doorwerth); *The Eighty-Five Days by* R.W. Thompson (Hutchinson & Co. Ltd); *The 43rd Wessex Division at War 1944–1945* by Major-General H. Essame (William Clowes & Sons Ltd); *The Second World War* by Winston S. Churchill (Cassell and Company Ltd);

The Silent War by Allard Martens (Hodder & Stoughton Ltd); *The Struggle for Europe* by Chester Wilmot (Wm. Collins Sons & Co. Ltd); *Top Secret* by Ralph Ingersoll (Harcourt, Brace & World, Inc., New York); *War as I knew it* by General George S. Patton (Houghton Mifflin Company, Boston); *With the Red Devils at Arnhem* by Marek Sweicicki (Max Love).

'Airborne Operation' by Alexander Johnson *(Services and Territorial Magazine);* 'Arnhem Diary' by Lieutenant J. Stevenson, Postscript by Sergeant F. Winder and Intelligence Officer's Report *(Reconnaissance Journal);* 'Arnhem from the Other Side' by Colonel-General Kurt Student *(An Cosantoir);* 'Arnhem 17–26 September' by Major H.S. Cousens *(Sprig of Shillelagh),* 'Do You Remember?' by J.A.G. *(Pegasus);* 'Do You Remember?' by D.O.C. *(Pegasus);* 'The Airborne Operation in Holland' by Major C.F.O. Breeze *(The Border Magazine);* 'The Battle of Arnhem Bridge' by Major E.M. Mackay *(Blackwood's Magazine);* 'The Evacuation of the First Airborne Division from Arnhem' *(Royal Engineers Journal);* 'With the RAMC at Arnhem' by Robert Smith *(Stand-To).*

PREFACE

'There has been no single performance by any unit that has more greatly inspired me or more highly excited my admiration', wrote General Eisenhower to the Commander of the 1st British Airborne Division when the battle of Arnhem was over, 'than the nine-day action of your Division between September 17 and 26.'

The battle was, indeed, one of the great epic tragedies which ennoble the history of the British Army. It was planned in the light of Intelligence which proved to be false; it was characterised by a succession of miscalculations and disasters; it ended in surrender and retreat. Out of nearly 9,000 men who had landed scarcely more than 2,000 returned; but it was a victory for the human spirit. It has a special quality, a flavour almost of *mystique*. Men who were there — Germans, Poles and Dutchmen as well as British soldiers — talk of it as though it were fought yesterday. It is, for many reasons, unique.

It is impossible for me to catalogue here the names of the many people in England, Holland and Germany who have spoken to me about the battle, or who have written to me about it, and to whom I am so grateful for the trouble they have taken on my behalf; but there are some who have been good enough to help me in a specially valuable way by providing me with information which I could not have obtained elsewhere or by letting me make use of personal documents and diaries from which I have quoted in my book. I want, therefore, particularly to thank Lieutenant-Colonel Th. A. Boeree, Lieutenant-General

Sir Frederick Browning, K.C.V.O., K.B.E., C.B., D.S.O., Mr R.H. Cain, V.C., Mr Fred Davis, Mr David Dawson, Brigadier Anthony Deane-Drummond, D.S.O., M.C., Major-General H. Essame, C.B.E., D.S.O., M.C., Herr Otto Felder, Major-General J.D. Frost, D.S.O., M.C., Major-General G. de Gex, O.B.E., Mevrouw Ida Goch, Lieutenant-Colonel C.F.H. Gough, M.C., T.D., M.P., Lieutenant-General J.W. Hackett, C.B., C.B.E., D.S.O., M.C., Mr John Harris, Oberst Walter Harzer, Mijnheer P. Houten, Major Anthony Hibbert, M.C., Air Commodore W.N. Hibbert, Mijnheer Paul de Jong, General Sir Gerald Lathbury, K.C.B., D.S.O., M.B.E., Brigadier J.E.F. Linton, D.S.O., Colonel R.T.H. Lonsdale, D.S.O., M.C., Brigadier Charles Mackenzie, D.S.O., O.B.E., Major-General R.J. Moberly, C.B., O.B.E., Brigadier E.C.W. Myers, C.B.E., D.S.O., Major John North, Lieutenant-Colonel Henry Preston, Mr Cyril Ray, Major C.G. Sheriff, D.S.O., Mr Eric Spence, Brigadier W.F.K. Thompson, O.B.E., Major Brian Urquhart, Major-General R.E. Urquhart, C.B., D.S.O., Mijnheer A.A. Van Beelen, Mijnheer J.D. Waarde, Colonel G.M. Warrack, D.S.O., O.B.E., The Rev. R. Talbot Watkins, M.C., and Mr Clifford Williams.

I want also to thank Lieutenant-Colonel P.St.C. Harrison of the Regimental Headquarters of the King's Own Scottish Borderers; Major D.M. Mayfield, T.D., of the Regimental Headquarters of the Parachute Regiment; Lieutenant-Colonel O.G.W. White, D.S.O., O.B.E., and the staff of the Dorset Regiment Museum, Dorchester; Lieutenant-Colonel J.K. Windeatt, O.B.E., of the Regimental Headquarters of the Devonshire and Dorset Regiment; and Mejuffrouw Greta Barmes of the Royal Netherlands Embassy.

For their help in my researches I want to thank Mr D.W. King, O.B.E., the War Office Librarian and his staff; the staff of the Imperial War Museum; Brigadier H.B. Latham of the Historical Section of the War Office; Mr L.A. Jackets and Mr W. Mervyn Mills of the Air Historical Branch of the Air

Ministry; Mr L.W. Burnett of the War Office Records Centre; Sergeant D. Wrigley of the Airborne Forces Museum, Aldershot; Mr Richard Wiener; Miss Frances Ryan; Mrs St George Saunders of Writers' and Speakers' Research; Lieutenant-Colonel Roderick A. Stamey, Jr, of the office of the Chief of Military History, Department of the Army, Washington; Mr Sherrod East, Chief Archivist, World War II Records Division of the National Archives and Record Service of the Central Services Administration, Washington; and the Staffs of the *Bundesarchiv,* Koblenz and the *Militärgeschichtliches Forschungsamt,* Freiburg im Breisgau.

For having read the proofs, in whole or in part, and for having made valuable suggestions for their improvement I am grateful to Brigadier Deane-Drummond, Brigadier Thompson, General Hackett, General Lathbury, Colonel Lonsdale, General Moberly, General Essame, Colonel Warrack, Brigadier Myers, General Urquhart and Oberst Walter Harzer.

C.H.

PART ONE

The Plan

'The Most Momentous Error of the War'

'One powerful full-blooded thrust across the Rhine and into the heart of Germany, backed by the whole of the resources of the Allied Armies, would be likely to achieve decisive results.'

Field-Marshal Sir Bernard Montgomery

On the evening of August 8th, 1944, ten days before he committed suicide, Günther von Kluge, Hitler's Commander-in-Chief in the West, telephoned General Hausser of the 7th German Army. 'A breakthrough such as we have never seen', he told him urgently, 'has occurred south of Caen.'

A fortnight later the Allied armies were streaming across France. Soon after dawn on August 25th, French and American armoured columns rattled down the Champs-Élysées and into the Boulevard St Germain. The people of Paris rushed out to greet them with flowers and wine, shouting and cheering, clapping their hands, reaching up to touch the unshaven, friendly faces. Paris was French again; the Germans were in full retreat; there was a feeling in the air that the war was as good as over.

With their armies rolling east before them, on an irregular front which stretched and looped for hundreds of miles across northern France, the Allied commanders could not feel such confidence. To maintain this rate of advance on so broad a front was impossible. The armies must either slow down or the already strained resources of administration and supply must be concentrated behind a single thrust into Germany. This was the inevitable choice.

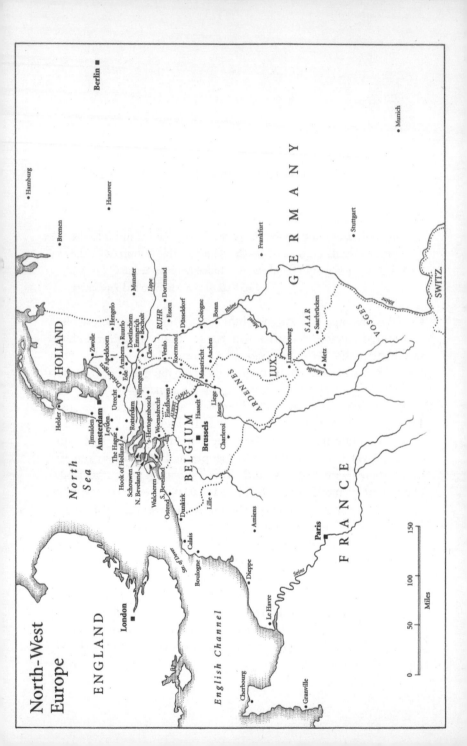

North-West Europe

Sir Bernard Montgomery left no room for doubt as to what he thought should be done. He had already suggested to General Omar Bradley, commanding the US 12th Army Group, that after crossing the Seine his own 21st Army Group and Bradley's 12th 'should keep together as a solid mass of 40 divisions, which would be so strong that it need fear nothing. This force should advance northwards.'

Bradley recognised the merit of Montgomery's plan; but Eisenhower, as Supreme Commander, could not agree to it. His reasons could be made to appear entirely military, but there were other reasons which he could not so readily give, both political and characteristic. On the day that Montgomery's advice of a thrust in the north was offered to Eisenhower through Bradley, the principal New York newspapers made public the disturbing fact that Bradley's Army Group, comprising General Patton's 3rd US Army and General Hodges's 1st US Army, was still under Montgomery's 'operational control'. While this may have been reluctantly acceptable to American opinion during the Normandy landings and initial operations – which were, as Eisenhower himself said, 'a single battle requiring the supervision of a single battleline commander' – it was not at all acceptable now.

Unlike Alexander, for whom Eisenhower had already stated a preference before the Normandy landings, Montgomery was not a popular figure with Americans in general, still less so with American Army officers in particular. 'Montgomery was a general we did not like', wrote Ralph Ingersoll, the American war correspondent. 'We found him arrogant to the point of bumptiousness, bad-mannered and ungracious.' And in August after the news of Bradley's subordination to Montgomery had created such an uproar in the American Press, General Marshall, Chief of Staff in Washington, wrote urgently to Eisenhower telling him that in view of the 'severe editorial reaction' to the news of Montgomery's continued influence, he should immediately 'assume and exercise direct command of the ground forces' himself. Eisenhower, well aware of the feeling amongst his staff at SHAEF, irrespective of what had appeared in the American newspapers, took Marshall's advice and on August 23rd informed Montgomery that he intended to take over direct control of Allied operations as from September 1st. He said at the same time that he intended to continue the advance on a broad front as it was necessary not only to push forward in the north to secure a good sea port for an eventual thrust towards the Ruhr, but also to press on in the south so that General Patton's 3rd US Army could link up with the French and American armies coming up from the Mediterranean. It was, in fact, this 'necessity' of advancing on extended and even diverging lines of operation that Eisenhower gave to Montgomery as his reasons for assuming overall control.

Eisenhower's method of attack appeared to Montgomery both unimaginative and dangerous. 'Administratively we haven't the resources to maintain both Army Groups at full pressure', Montgomery insisted with the determination and single-mindedness of an obdurate man who knows when he is right. 'The only policy is to halt the right and strike with the left, or halt the left and strike with the right. We must decide on one thrust and put all the maintenance to support it. If we split the maintenance and advance on a broad front, we shall be so weak everywhere we'll have no chance of success.'

He had not, he tried to make clear, a personal axe to grind. He was quite prepared to serve under Bradley if that should be considered advisable as, in his view, operations could only be successfully controlled by a single ground commander. He was, however, satisfied that the administrative resources available for a broad-front policy 'would not stand up to the strain', but that, on the other hand, 'one powerful full-blooded thrust across the Rhine and into the heart of Germany, backed by the whole of the resources of the Allied armies, would be likely to achieve decisive results'. He was obsessed, he was later to confess, by the thought that the impetus of the Allied advance might not be maintained after the crossing of the Seine. Whatever happened, he told Eisenhower, the Germans must not be allowed time to reorganise and oppose in strength a crossing of the next and far greater obstacle, the Rhine. He felt sure that if the enemy were kept on the run, the Allies could cross the Rhine quickly, make north-west for the Ruhr and so draw the Germans into a fight on the north German plains which would give the Allied armour the advantage of a chosen battle-ground. Otherwise 'the enemy would be given time to recover and we should become involved in a long winter campaign'.

It was a persuasive argument but Eisenhower held firm. There was, he insisted, one decisive factor which Montgomery did not appreciate. Even if it were agreed that his plan was strategically sound and logistically possible, this problem remained: the deep thrust in the north, which the British proposed, would entail his having to hold back George Patton's 3rd US Army in the south. 'The American public', he told Montgomery, 'would never stand for it.'

He may well have been right. Patton's short sturdy figure, his tough little face under the star-splashed helmet, his flamboyant poses and well-known independence, the famous pearl-handled revolver in its open, cowboy's holster and his undoubted success, were all a part of the American ideal of the 'little old fighting general', at once tough and emotional. Nor was Patton's success a fortuitous one; he was a very good general and an expert in the art of military exploitation.

Eisenhower, not only as an American but as a diplomatist, a Supreme Commander and a realist in matters of this kind, felt that Patton must not be stopped. The public, he repeated, 'would never stand for it; and public opinion wins war.'

'Victories win wars', Montgomery snapped with impatient logic, dismissing public opinion in a statement symptomatic both of his greatness and the limits of his vision. 'Give people victory and they won't care who won it.'

Patton and public opinion were not, of course, the only

considerations. Eisenhower felt confident that what he was later to term Montgomery's 'pencil-like thrust into the heart of Germany' would meet nothing but certain destruction. Apart from this, neither the British nor the Canadians had yet proved themselves capable of the verve and dash that Patton's men were so splendidly displaying to an admiring world. It would be safer and wiser in the circumstances, he thought, for the whole Allied force to advance to the Rhine, obtain bridgeheads where possible and, when the dangerously long lines of communication had been shortened by the capture of the Channel ports and Antwerp and when the whole matter of supply and reinforcements had been re-established on a firmer base, to attack either in the north towards the Ruhr or along the southern axis through the Saar and Frankfurt or perhaps on both lines simultaneously, dependent upon conditions. Montgomery was accordingly given orders to secure Antwerp and push on towards that part of the Siegfried Line which covered the Ruhr, while Patton was authorised to continue east towards the Saar. The broad-front policy was confirmed.

Eisenhower was, however, prepared to give some priority to Montgomery; for the capture of the Channel ports and Antwerp was an essential prerequisite to the successful development of any attack into Germany. And so the advance into Belgium of Montgomery's 21st Army Group – comprising the British 2nd Army under General Dempsey and the 2nd Canadian Army under General Crerar – was to be supported by the 1st US Army which was to 'establish itself in the general area Brussels–Maastricht–Liège–Charleroi'. Later on, 'up to and including the crossing of the Rhine', Montgomery was, in addition, to have the support of the Allied Airborne Army which had recently been formed under the command of an American, Lieutenant-General Lewis H. Brereton.

On August 29th Montgomery's advance was resumed. His commanders were instructed to be 'swift and relentless . . . Any tendency to be sticky or cautious must be stamped on ruthlessly.'

If Patton could exploit an advantage, Montgomery was determined to show that he could too.

He was brilliantly served. By noon the following day the
commander of his XXX Corps, the brave and gifted Lieutenant-
General Brian Horrocks, had sent the 11th Armoured Division
racing for Amiens. At dawn on the 31st, after driving all night in
the teeming rain, the leading tanks rumbled into the cobbled
town and took over the Somme bridges from the Resistance.
The command post of the German 7th Army Headquarters was
overrun and General Hans Eberbach was captured as he drove
away, still in his pyjamas, in a Volkswagen. Two days later the
Guards Armoured Division reached the Belgian border near
Lille and two American divisions crossed it further south. On the
afternoon of September 3rd the Guards drove into Brussels and
by the evening of the next day Antwerp, too, had fallen. The 15th
German Army was isolated in Flanders; the 7th had been routed.

Montgomery hoped that Eisenhower would surely recognise,
at last, the chance for a final blow that lay within his grasp. The
chance had been clear a fortnight before; now it was unmistak-
able. He sent a signal suggesting that the time was ideal for that
'one powerful thrust' he had already advocated. 'We have now
reached a stage', he insisted, 'where a really powerful and full-
blooded thrust towards Berlin is likely to get there and thus end
the war.'

The successes of the past few days, however, seem to have
indicated to Eisenhower that a continued advance by all his
forces, 'to keep the enemy stretched everywhere', would not only
be safer but more rewarding. At the end of August he had spoken
of the certainty of 'one major battle before we break into
Germany' and of the necessity of not being 'too optimistic
about an early end of the war'; and after the war was over he
wrote of his anxiety lest the enemy's 'considerable reserve' in
Germany would bring a single thrust to ruin. But at this period
he seems to have believed that the whole defence of Germany's
West Wall was crumbling. 'The defeat of the German armies',

he wrote on September 5th, 'is now complete.' A week later, Captain Harry Butcher, one of his staff officers at SHAEF, noted in his diary: 'He felt for some days it had been obvious that our military force could advance almost at will, subject only to supply.' And despite the growing difficulties of supply and administration Eisenhower still, even then, apparently hoped that the British drive to the Ruhr and the American drive to the Saar could be supported simultaneously. 'We shall soon have captured the Ruhr and the Saar and the Frankfurt area', Montgomery was surprised to read in a letter from Eisenhower addressed to himself and Bradley and written as late as September 15th, 'and I would like your views as to what we should do next.' But, in fact, by now the Supreme Commander was already engaged in a process of compromise and adjustment that was to bring both drives to a halt.

Urged by Montgomery to give priority to a northern thrust to the Ruhr, he was now increasingly badgered by Patton, supported by Bradley, to give more supplies to the Americans further south. Patton bitterly complained that he had already been held up for two days on the Meuse through lack of gasoline, and if he was to secure crossings over the Moselle he must have more. 'My men can eat their belts', he said. 'But my tanks have gotta have gas.'

They were given it. On September 5th Bradley authorised Patton's continued advance and the 3rd US Army went forward to the Moselle. The 1st US Army, ordered by Eisenhower to support the British on its left, was therefore obliged to help the advancing Americans on its right. And the British, having outrun their administrative resources, were forced to halt.

Within the following 10 days the Germans, suddenly relieved from the pressing force that had sent them hurtling back since August 30th, were able to reform and recover their strength. On September 4th there was only one weak division, together with a battalion of Dutch SS and a few *Luftwaffe* detachments, facing the spearheads of the 2nd Army. A fortnight later there was a formidable defensive line.

There was by then, too, a formidable force facing Patton who, also hamstrung by administrative difficulties, was compelled to slow down. 'I believe', wrote Ralph Ingersoll with a tendentious simplification of Eisenhower's political problems that gives an unqualified but nevertheless not readily dismissible reason for this sad position, 'that in August 1944 a Supreme Allied Commander . . . not necessarily a brilliant one but a bold and forceful man making at least good horse sense – could have ended the war by decisively backing either Montgomery or Bradley. But there was no such Supreme Allied Commander. There was no strong hand at the helm, no man in command. There was only a conference, presided over by a chairman – a shrewd, intelligent, tactful, careful chairman.'

Patton, as certain as Montgomery that he could push his way to victory if given the supplies and transport to do it, was understandably bitter when he discovered the predicament in which Eisenhower's compromise was eventually to place him. It was, he afterwards commented, 'the most momentous error of the war'. Montgomery, similarly discomfited, had reason to agree with him.

2

Operation Market Garden

'Ike has decided that a northern thrust toward the Ruhr under Montgomery is not at the moment to have priority over other operations.'

Captain Harry C. Butcher

As the Allied armies slowly closed up towards the frontiers of the Reich, the enemy resistance stiffened.

Hitler had refused to accept as a possibility Eisenhower's confident belief that the defeat of the German armies was complete. Garrison and training battalions, officer-cadet training schools, youth organisations, convalescent and invalid establishments had been hastily converted into infantry units and sent to the defence of the Siegfried Line. Goering added to these battalions, six paratroop regiments which, unknown to the Army General Staff were in process of re-equipment, and two other paratroop regiments made up of men in convalescent depots; he also promised to organise 10,000 men of the *Luftwaffe*, who had been grounded through lack of petrol, into army units. Determined and heroic as these efforts were, however, they did not much impress British Intelligence.

'Both as regards quality and diversity,' one of its officers reported sardonically, 'the enemy force opposing us shows the effects of the recent measures in Germany to step up the national effort. Paratroops and pilots, policemen and sailors, boys of 16 and men with duodenal ulcers' had all been taken prisoner during the past few days; and now 'some deep sea

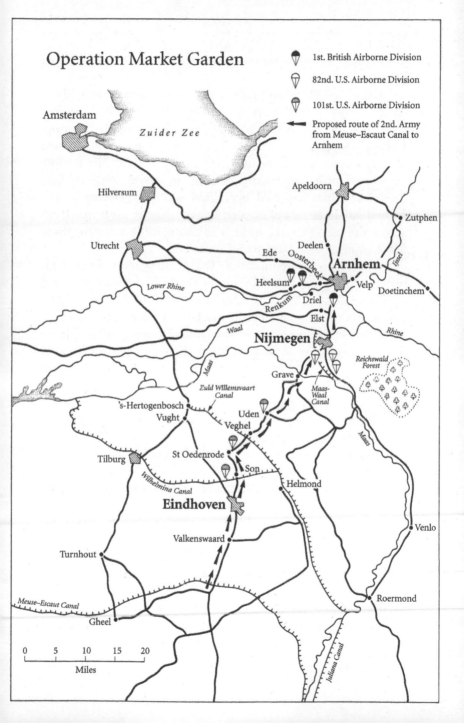

divers' had been captured. The depths had 'indeed been plumbed'.

Diverse and ill-trained, callow and seedy as they were, these hastily formed units were, nevertheless, putting up so determined a defence that the Allied advance was unmistakably faltering. General Dempsey directing the operations of the 2nd Army was already aware of a hardening German resistance. His leading units were being repeatedly held up by young Nazi soldiers defending what they had been told was the gateway to the Fatherland. In groups of isolated houses, from streams which cut across the sandy heath, hidden in inaccessible swamps, these fierce youths fought back with frantic bravery.

It was in these circumstances that Montgomery formed his plan of quickly breaking through the crust of German opposition after a series of airborne landings by the Allied Airborne Army which Eisenhower had made available to him. By seizing a succession of bridges between the Dutch frontier and the Neder Rijn, he hoped to be able to make the way clear for a rapid advance by the 2nd Army through Holland and on to the north German plains before the enemy had time to reorganise. He was, as he himself repeated often enough, 'deeply impressed with the magnitude of the military problems of fighting an opposed crossing over the great water barriers of the Maas and the Rhine' and wanted to avoid it at all costs. He hoped that if he could launch the 2nd Army in a fast and successful attack which would establish it on an extended line facing east between Arnhem and Zwolle, with a deep bridgehead across the Ijssel, he would be in a strong position from which to advance eastwards across the German frontier and threaten the Ruhr from the north. He felt convinced that once he had got as far as this Eisenhower could not but agree to give him the resources to complete the stroke upon which he had set his heart.

Although the intended route through Holland involved the crossing of several canals and rivers and was a circuitous approach to the Ruhr, it had three advantages. It was an unlikely route and the Germans might, therefore, be taken by surprise; it would outflank the Siegfried defences which ended in the area of the Reichswald; and the preliminary airborne operations could be carried out within reasonable distance of English bases.

There were admittedly five major water obstacles to cross – the Wilhelmina Canal about 20 miles beyond the Dutch frontier; the Zuid Willemsvaart canal 10 miles further north; then three roughly parallel rivers; the Maas (the Meuse), the Waal (the main channel of the Rhine) and the Neder Rijn (the Lower Rhine). But these would not be serious obstacles if bridges across them could be secured intact by the three divisions of the Airborne Army. One division could land in the 20-mile stretch between Eindhoven and Uden to capture bridges across the Wilhelmina and Zuid Willemsvaart canals and open up the road between them; a second division could land further north to capture the bridges over the Maas at Grave and over the Waal at Nijmegen; while a third division could land at Arnhem to secure the most northerly bridges over the 150-yards-wide Neder Rijn. As soon as all these bridges and the roads which linked them were in the hands of the Airborne Army, the British 2nd Army could roll forward to the Zuider Zee, cutting off all the Germans in western Holland and opening up the way to the Reich.

It was a bold plan, but a good one. General Bradley, although he spoke disdainfully of 'a 60-mile salient to be driven up a side-alley route to the Reich' and felt more strongly than Montgomery did that the operation would open up a dangerous gap between the 2nd Army and the already heavily committed 1st US Army, had to agree that it was highly imaginative. It came to be known as OPERATION MARKET GARDEN – MARKET for the airborne operation, GARDEN for the follow-through by the 2nd Army. Its success depended upon speed of execution and concentrated administrative support.

And no one was more clearly aware of the need for speed and concentration than the commander of the British 2nd Army. Indeed General Dempsey doubted that OPERATION MARKET

GARDEN would succeed. His Intelligence staff reported mounting German activity in central Holland, with 'considerable railway activity at Arnhem and Nijmegen'. Heavy and light flak 'was increasing very considerably'. Dutch Resistance sources reported 'that battered Panzer formations had been sent to Holland to refit' and mentioned Eindhoven and Nijmegen as the reception areas. Now that the Americans were fully committed further south and so unable to offer much support, Dempsey thought it might be better to hold a firm line along the Dutch frontier, close to which there had already been heavy fighting along the Albert Canal, and strike out alongside the Americans in an easterly direction towards the Rhine at Wesel rather than in a northerly direction alone. He discussed this plan with Montgomery who seemed doubtful that it was a wise one, for both the RAF and the USAAF were afraid that their unarmed transport aircraft would suffer heavily in supplying armies advancing across the Rhine so close to the thick flak defences covering the Ruhr.

General Dempsey, nevertheless, believed that the dangers involved might well prove less than those encountered by 'going off at a tangent into Holland'; and, on September 10th, he went to see Montgomery to press his point of view. But Montgomery told him that he had just had a signal from the War Office asking what could be done to capture or cut off the bases near the Hague from which the V2s, which had landed on London two days before, were launched. After this there could be no further discussion; the northern attack must be made.

That afternoon Montgomery flew to Brussels airfield to meet Eisenhower who was due to fly in from his headquarters at Granville. Montgomery was determined that his ideas for a single thrust in the north should prevail and, disdaining the uses of tact even in his moods of careful restraint, he behaved now in a manner which was scarcely less than insolent. His first request was that Eisenhower's Chief Administrative Officer – Lieutenant-General Sir Humphrey Gale – should leave the aircraft in which the discussion was to take place, but that his own – Major-

General Miles Graham – should remain. Eisenhower, conciliatory as always, agreed. Montgomery then and there, without further social preliminaries, told Eisenhower that he completely disagreed with his proposed method of advance; and, picking up a file of signals and messages he had had from the Supreme Commander, he pulled them each in turn to pieces. 'He vehemently declared', Eisenhower wrote later, 'that all he needed was adequate supply to go directly into Berlin . . . If we would support his 21st Army Group with all supply facilities available he would rush right on to Berlin and, he said, end the war.'

Fluently and with fine disparagement of his critics Montgomery spoke for several minutes until, during a brief pause, Eisenhower leant forward, put his hand on his knee and said, 'Steady, Monty! You can't speak to me like that. I'm your boss.'

Exercising a self-control which years of dedicated training had made it possible for him immediately to achieve when he felt it to be necessary, Montgomery said quietly, 'I'm sorry, Ike.'

And after this gentle rebuke and designedly gracious apology the two men came together in friendship if not in understanding. The discussion then continued without bitterness; but without agreement either. Montgomery pleaded his case for his 'single powerful full-blooded thrust'; and had no success. Eisenhower reiterated his determination to advance on a broad front to the line which was 'needed for temporary security'; and received no sympathy. All that the Supreme Commander would approve was Montgomery's plan for OPERATION MARKET GARDEN. He had seemed at first reluctant even about this for it involved the withdrawal of transport planes from supplying purposes and, as he wrote afterwards, 'it was difficult to determine whether greater results could be achieved by continuing the planes in supply activity. Unfortunately the withdrawal of planes from other work had to precede an airborne operation by several days to provide time for refitting equipment and for briefing and retraining of crews.' In any event, he insisted, OPERATION

MARKET GARDEN was merely an extension of his own strategic concept of a general eastward advance. Apparently he still hoped that a move towards the Ruhr need not have precluded a simultaneous move towards the Saar. Montgomery, on the other hand, was becoming more and more convinced that a successful assault on the Ruhr could only be made if he were given priority over all other operations. Already all the transport reserves of 21st Army Group were in use; new transport companies were promised from England but had not yet arrived; even tank transporters, with lengths of airfield track welded to their sides, were conveying essential supplies; most of the 2nd Army's heavy artillery and anti-aircraft guns had consequently been grounded for some time. In order to get them on the move again, Patton's Army would have to be held back. Moreover, unless orders were given to stop Patton's advance there would be no possibility of Montgomery's thrust to the Ruhr being supported by the American 1st Army under General Hodges which was already over-extended in the wide gap between them.

Eisenhower steadfastly refused to agree. He was still thinking, Captain Harry Butcher wrote in his diary the following day, 'in terms of advancing on a wide front to take advantage of all existing lines of communication. He expects to go through the Aachen gap in the north and the Metz gap in the south'; to advance, in fact, against both the Ruhr and the Saar simultaneously. He told Montgomery that his Chief Intelligence Officer had provided him with information which suggested that the Germans would not be able to gather together more than 20 divisions all told for the defence of the West Wall within the month and that the Wall could not 'be held with this amount, even when supplemented by many oddments and large amounts of flak'. He refused, therefore, to give Montgomery priority over Patton who was, in fact, already extending his front even further south and would soon, if undisturbed, have firm contact with the 6th US Army Group coming up from the Mediterranean. All that Eisenhower would concede was the promise of a 'limited priority' which would involve some additional supplies and transport being granted from American sources to help the operations of the Airborne Army in Holland.

'Ike', Montgomery wrote that evening to the Vice-Chief of the Imperial General Staff in London, 'came to see me to-day. He is lame and cannot walk and we talked in the plane . . . I gave him my opinion on need to concentrate on one selected thrust. He did not (repeat not) agree . . . He said he did not mean priority for Ruhr and northern route to be absolute priority and could not scale down the Saar thrust in any way.'

Although Montgomery did not appreciate at the time how deep it had gone, a rankling resentment had already been caused amongst the Americans by Eisenhower's decision that even a 'limited priority' should be given to the northern thrust. They had begun to feel strongly that their allies were getting the lion's share. For the British had been given not only the use of the whole Airborne Army, (including two American divisions) and the support of the 1st US Army, but they were now promised supplies and transport which the American armies could not possibly spare. While the Americans thought that he had got too much, however, Montgomery continued strongly to insist that he had not got enough. He was, nevertheless, to be disappointed. The Chief of the Imperial General Staff, understanding the political difficulties, replied to Montgomery's complaint of September 10th to say that although it was viewed sympathetically, 'It would be difficult to interfere with Eisenhower on combined Chiefs of Staff level. Indeed it would probably do more harm than good.'

The promise of American help was, in any event, not enough to set Dempsey's mind at rest; for so long as Patton was pushing forward with the 3rd US Army, the 1st US Army in the gap between himself and Patton could not adequately support and protect the advance of XXX Corps which was to lead his own army's attack. Support would have to be provided, therefore, from within the 2nd Army by bringing up VIII Corps to the right of XXX Corps. Most of the transport of VIII Corps, however, was already in use by other units of 2nd Army, and the additional transport promised by Eisenhower would not be enough to make up the deficiency. Accordingly, on the day after the meeting at Brussels airfield, Montgomery told Eisenhower that OPERATION MARKET GARDEN could not take place as planned by September 17th. He would be obliged to postpone the attack until September 21st at the soonest and, because of this delay, 'stronger resistance and slower progress' must be expected.

As the whole success of the operation so largely depended upon its being executed with speed before the Germans gathered strength in Holland, the Americans reacted quickly to Montgomery's disappointing estimate. Having allowed what he called 'the attractive possibility of quickly turning the German north flank' to lead him to approve a 'temporary delay in freeing the vital port of Antwerp' (the approaches to which were still blocked by German troops firmly dug in along the banks of the Scheldt estuary), Eisenhower was now desperately anxious to get OPERATION MARKET GARDEN under way. For until Antwerp – the third greatest port in the world – was usable, it was difficult to see, at least so long as the Channel ports held out as well, how any thrust into Germany could be satisfactorily maintained.*

* In his well-argued book, *The 85 Days*, R.W. Thompson has discussed this problem at length. 'It is surprising', he has written, 'how few in those days seemed to understand the undoubted plain truth that the price of the Arnhem gamble, win, lose or draw, must be Antwerp.' He suggests that Montgomery had his eye so firmly fixed on the Rhine that he tended to lose sight of what both Eisenhower and Churchill realised was the vital importance to the Allies of this great port. Sir Brian Horrocks in his book, *A Full Life*, has admitted that he, for his part, had his eyes 'fixed entirely on the Rhine and everything else seemed of subsidiary importance'. He goes on to confess: 'It never entered my head that the Scheldt would be mined and that we should not be able to use Antwerp port until the channel had been swept and the Germans cleared from the coast-line on either side.' The town should have been by-passed on the east, he thinks, and then by advancing 'only 15 miles north-west towards Woensdrecht we should have blocked the Beveland isthmus and cut the main German escape route'.

And so, the day after Montgomery's warning about the dangers of delay due to inadequate facilities for supply was received at SHAEF, General Bedell Smith – Eisenhower's Chief of Staff – flew to Montgomery's headquarters with the promise of several American truck companies and an American delivery of 1,000 tons of supplies a day to Brussels. Bedell Smith also said that the drive to the Saar would be stopped and that most of the American 12th Army Group's supplies would be allocated to its 1st Army so that Montgomery could be adequately supported on his right. In addition, three American divisions were to be grounded. Hearing these assurances Montgomery supposed that Eisenhower had given way at last and had decided that his broad-front policy was unworkable. He felt relieved and delighted and suggested in a signal to London that the war might now be won 'reasonably quickly'.

Bradley – the 12th Army Group's commander – seems also to have had the impression that Eisenhower had given way to the British. On the day that Bedell Smith and Montgomery met in Belgium, Bradley spoke to Patton in France. Told that the British plan had been accepted by Eisenhower and that he would probably be asked to assume the defensive, Patton's reply was characteristic. He would get so inextricably committed beyond the Moselle, he confided to Bradley, that no one would be able to stop him. According to Patton, Bradley agreed to this artful proposal and gave him 'until the night of the fourteenth' to carry it out.

Patton, as usual, was successful. By the agreed date he was heavily engaged and in a directive issued by Eisenhower on September 15th he saw further opportunities for the prosecution of his thrust in the south. For, although Eisenhower directed that the first 'priority in all forms of logistical support' – after Patton's Army was established in position across the Moselle, and until the Rhine bridgeheads were won – was to be the operation in the north, at the same time he authorised Patton to advance 'far enough for the moment so as to hold adequate bridgeheads over the Moselle and thus create a constant threat'. Thereafter Patton was authorised to carry out 'a continuous reconnaissance'.

The loophole was enough. It gave Patton the excuse he needed to pursue what he liked to call his 'rock soup method'. He could now, he himself frankly admitted, 'pretend to re-connoitre, then reinforce the reconnaissance and finally put in an attack – all depending on what gasoline and ammunition we could secure'. And, as one of his officers commented, they 'secured plenty'. Already the capture of over 100,000 gallons of petrol from the Germans had been concealed from Eisenhower; now Patton's ordnance officers went so far as to represent themselves as 'members of the 1st Army' and secured 'quite a bit of gasoline from one of the dumps of that unit'. This was the kind of enterprise that delighted George Patton's heart. It might not be war, he commented without embarrassment, 'but it was magnificent.' Bradley tacitly supported him. And so the 12th Army Group's supplies, instead of being allocated with priority to General Hodges's 1st US Army, and thus to the support of Montgomery as Eisenhower had directed, continued to be divided between Hodge's 1st Army and Patton's 3rd.

Montgomery, accordingly, received far less American support for OPERATION MARKET GARDEN than Eisenhower had in-tended. The support, indeed, soon became negligible; for on September 11th Hodges crossed the German frontier near Prum and met the same defiant defenders that Patton had already encountered beyond the Moselle. All the resources of the 1st US Army were needed now in support of its own operations and the British would have to look out for themselves.

The day after the 1st US Army invaded Germany, Eisenhower reminded Bradley that Hodges must be given priority over Patton who must be stopped. When given these orders again, Patton realised that in order to 'avoid such an eventuality', it was evident that his own Army 'should get deeply involved at once'. 'I asked Bradley', he confessed, 'not to call me until after dark on the nineteenth.' The next day he attacked Metz and was sharply repulsed; by September 18th he found himself heavily engaged with units of the recently reformed German 5th Panzer Army under command of the brilliant General Hasso von Manteuffel.

Patton had committed himself more deeply than even he could have hoped; and Eisenhower was worried. For not only along the Moselle but along the whole of the Allied lines, German resistance was growing stronger day by day. The situation which Montgomery had feared was unmistakably taking shape.

Although on September 4th Field-Marshal Model, Kluge's successor as Commander-in-Chief in the West, had informed the Führer that 'the unequal struggle cannot long continue', he was not now feeling so depressed. The *Wehrmacht* was getting quickly back on its feet again. OPERATION MARKET GARDEN was already in jeopardy.

3

'The Toughest and Most Advanced Assignment'

'I think we might be going a bridge too far.'
Lieutenant-General F.A.M. Browning

On September 10th, the day that Montgomery met Eisenhower at Brussels airport, Major-General R.E. Urquhart, the commander of the 1st British Airborne Division, was summoned to his corps commander, Lieutenant-General F.A.M. Browning, whose head-quarters was in the clubhouse on Moor Park Golf Course. With a few characteristically direct words General Browning gave Urquhart his orders for OPERATION MARKET GARDEN. He drew a circle north of Eindhoven to show him where the 101st US Airborne Division was to land; another further north round Nijmegen to indicate the dropping area of the 82nd US Airborne Division and then, with what Urquhart called 'a grand sweep of the hand', Browning drew a third large circle on the talc-covered map. 'Arnhem Bridge', he said, 'and hold it.'

Urquhart walked slowly back to his caravan from General Browning's barely furnished room, his mind already at work. To plan his part in the largest airborne operation that had ever yet taken place, he had the dangerously short time of six days. There were two principal and immediate problems, Browning had told him: the shortage of aircraft, and the belief that the flak in the Arnhem area was too heavy for a landing immediately around the bridge and on both sides of the river.

The RAF had allocated to his Division 10 squadrons of 38 Group and six squadrons of 46 Group to tow in his gliders, and the USAAF were to make available the Dakotas of the 9th US Troop Carrier Command for his parachutists. It was far from enough. He calculated that he would need at least 130 aircraft for each of his brigades and accordingly told Browning that he must have another 40 planes. Browning said that he could not hope to get 'even a proportion of them'. There were just not that number of planes available, and Urquhart must make plans based on his original allocation. The Americans could not spare any more aircraft as the parachutists of the 82nd and 101st US Divisions were both being taken in in one lift, owing to the necessity of capturing the bridges over the Maas and the Waal before the 2nd Army could advance to the Neder Rijn, and all available planes would be needed for these essential operations. Priority must be given to the two American divisions, Browning said, as it had 'got to be bottom to top'. There would obviously be no point in the British Division capturing and holding the bridges at Arnhem if the 2nd Army never got there. Urquhart's only course, then, was to send his division into Arnhem in three separate lifts. The danger of this was obvious; for the first lift would have the double duty of seizing the bridges and of protecting the dropping and landing zones which were to be used by the men who were to follow; and, if the Germans were stronger than Intelligence supposed, there might not be enough men for either task.

It was certain that even if a surprise attack could be made by the first lift, by the time the second lift arrived the enemy would have had time to make preparations to resist the subsequent landings. To offset this danger it was suggested that the available aircraft should make two trips to Holland on the same day; but this was rejected by the troop-carrier commanders on the grounds that 'there would be insufficient time between missions for spot maintenance, repair of battle damage and rest for the crews'. The RAF's 38 Group then suggested that the first lift should be taken in before dawn which would give time for a second lift the same day. This was a suggestion which was

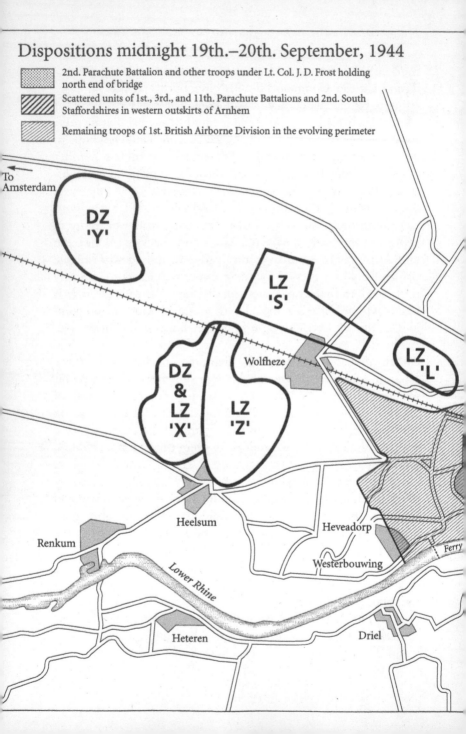

Dispositions midnight 19th.–20th. September, 1944

2nd. Parachute Battalion and other troops under Lt. Col. J. D. Frost holding north end of bridge

Scattered units of 1st., 3rd., and 11th. Parachute Battalions and 2nd. South Staffordshires in western outskirts of Arnhem

Remaining troops of 1st. British Airborne Division in the evolving perimeter

To Amsterdam

DZ 'Y'

LZ 'S'

LZ 'L'

DZ & LZ 'X'

LZ 'Z'

Wolfheze

Heelsum

Heveadorp

Renkum

Westerbouwing

Ferry

Lower Rhine

Heteren

Driel

welcomed at the British Airborne Headquarters as it had become recognised there that night landings, with the opportunities they provided of surprising the enemy and of causing confusion by diversionary tactics, such as the dropping of dummy parachutists, were 'vital factors in the successful employment of airborne assault'. But the idea could not be adopted because the American crews, who were to fly in the parachutists, had not had sufficient training in night work and on two previous occasions – in Sicily and the Cotentin Peninsula – when they had operated at night, the results had been alarming. Furthermore, as the official report said later:

> The period from 17 September onwards was a new-moon period and night landings on a large scale were therefore impossible. It had always been considered that daylight landings unless attended by overwhelming air support against fighters, together with the achievement of complete surprise, would be too expensive. These conditions appeared, however, for the first time in the history of airborne forces, to be possible of achievement. Moreover, daylight landings would greatly increase the chances of accuracy and would give the attacking troops a better opportunity of concentrating quickly and taking advantage of the surprise achieved. The Commanding General, First Allied Airborne Army, decided to utilise daylight.

The dangers of dropping the British Division in three stages might have been less great, had the chosen landing zones been nearer the town. But the RAF, after having carried out several reconnaissance flights which confirmed the impression of bomber crews who flew by that route on their way to the Ruhr, was insistent that the flak likely to be encountered in the Arnhem area made dropping close to the main road bridge out of the question. The RAF feared, too, that if the unwieldy, unarmed glider-towing tugs – which were without self-sealing tanks and had not been designed for low flying in daylight over enemy country – came in as far as Urquhart would have liked, they would either run into more flak over Deelen airfield on making a homeward turn to the north or would become entangled with the American tugs over Nijmegen on turning to the south. Apart from the heavy flak which, the RAF warned, would be 'almost prohibitive' near the town, there was an additional hazard involved in a landing close to it: the expanse of flat land around the main bridge south of the river, which appeared ideal from the air photographs, was, in fact, said to be quite unsuitable as either a dropping ground or landing zone. Intelligence officers and Dutch Resistance reports agreed that it was low-lying swampy polderland, very exposed and cut up by deep ditches, unsuitable for both glider landings and the quick deployment of troops. Dutch officers who had been on manoeuvres in the area, which had frequently been used by the Dutch Army for field exercises before the war, supported this view.

An alternative dropping ground was the open heath about four miles north of Arnhem. It was screened from the town by woods and the sandy ground was hard and dry. But although suitable as a dropping ground for parachutists it was not only too broken up by dunes and scrub but also too constricted for use as a landing zone by any considerable number of gliders which, even when heavy risks are accepted, still need a large area for landing.

The only possible area left was the more spacious tract of open country west of the town. It was a long way from the bridge at its nearest point, and the second and third lifts, which might have to advance into the town against rapidly mounting opposition, would inevitably be in danger of being prevented from linking up on the final objective with the men who had landed earlier. The dangers of the Division being split up by the enemy would also be increased by the inevitable necessity of leaving some units of the first lift behind to protect the landing and dropping grounds until the whole force had landed. But at least it was firm ground 250 feet above sea level and was screened by belts of woodland; and certainly here a close and tidy landing could be made.

So Urquhart decided that he had no choice and marked his map accordingly. Five zones were drawn in to the west of Arnhem – three of them to the north of the Arnhem to Utrecht railway line on Ginkel heath, two others to the south of it on Renkum heath. These areas were marked (see pages 26–7) DZ & LZ 'X', LZ 'Z', LZ 'S', LZ 'L', and DZ 'Y'. On Dropping Zone 'X', and Landing Zone 'S', at two hours before H-hour, 12 Stirlings of 38 Group RAF were to drop the men of 21st Independent Parachute Company who would then mark out all the zones with coloured strips of nylon tape. At H-hour on Dropping Zone 'X', 149 Dakotas of IX United States Troop Carrier Command would drop the main body of 1st Parachute Brigade. Simultaneously, 130 Dakotas of 46 Group RAF and 23 aircraft of 38 Group RAF would release their 153 Horsa gliders, carrying elements of 1st Airlanding Brigade, over Landing Zone 'S'; and over Landing Zone 'Z', 167 aircraft of 38 Group RAF would release 154 Horsa and 13 Hamilcar gliders carrying other elements of 1st Airlanding Brigade and divisional troops.

On the second day of the operation IX United States Troop Carrier Command would drop most of the 4th Parachute Brigade on Dropping Zone 'Y'; and the RAF would release the remaining gliders (257 Horsas, 15 Hamilcars and 4 Hadrians) of 1st Airlanding Brigade over Landing Zones 'X' and 'S' and drop supplies on Landing Zone 'L'. Supplies would subsequently be dropped on Supply Dropping Point 'V'.

A sixth zone, despite the objections which had been raised to its suitability by Intelligence, was marked on the polder south of the bridge. This dropping zone (DZ 'K') was allocated to the 1st Polish Parachute Brigade which was to be dropped there by the Americans on the third day of the operation. Although the difficulties of landing in what was supposed to be swampy polderland could not be discounted, when these orders were given to General Sosabowski he could at least be assured that by the time his men landed the flak batteries near the bridge, against which the RAF had warned so strongly, should have been put out of action. By then, too, the whole of the British Division would have already landed – Brigadier G.W. Lathbury's 1st Parachute Brigade and most of Brigadier P.H.W. Hick's 1st Airlanding Brigade on the first day and Brigadier J.W. Hackett's 4th Parachute Brigade, with the rest of the Airlanding Brigade, on the second day. The Poles' landing would accordingly be well covered from the ground. General Sosabowski did not, however, listen to the reassurances of the British officers with much conviction. He was haunted by the knowledge – as indeed, although less disconcertingly, were they – that, even if the weather held and all the planned flights could take place, it would be three whole days before the entire force could be landed. And if the weather did not hold, Urquhart's only hope of success would lie in a quick drive by the 2nd Army to relieve him, combined with a slow reaction by the Germans. Fortunately there seemed at this stage good reason to hope that German reactions would not in fact be quick and that, in any event, the enemy forces in the area were by no means formidable.

Facing Horrocks's XXX Corps, the waiting spearhead of the 2nd Army along the Dutch border, there were – it was believed – no more than six infantry battalions supported by 25 guns and only 20 tanks. Behind this weak front line, in the Nijmegen area, Dutch Resistance agents reported six further battalions of low medical category and beyond these, in the Arnhem area, a few battered armoured units being reorganised and refitted. The enemy was also supposed not only to be weak in numbers but weak in morale. On September 12th the Intelligence Summary of the 21st Army Group, which made no reference to troops in the Arnhem area, said that the German retreat had been both disorderly and dispirited. It quoted orders from the German command intended to restore failing discipline, end rumour-mongering and enforce the rigid conservation of equipment. 'Every hand grenade,' the Germans were reported as having insisted, 'every rifle, every gallon of petrol is now needed to arm the new line to receive our troops. These are more important

than suitcases or useless loot.' 'Several hundred thousand
soldiers are moving backwards,' the Intelligence Summary
continued, 'among them there stream along, together with now
superfluous headquarters, columns which have been routed,
which have broken out from their front and which for the
moment have no firm destination and no clear orders.'

Six days later 21st Army Group's Intelligence staff were still
maintaining this optimistic note. Their Summary issued that
week reported:

North and South Holland are very thinly held at present.
Probably only the fortress areas of the Hook, Ijmuiden and the
Helder are seriously held . . . 4 SS Training and Replacement
Battalion was at Ede, northwest of Arnhem and had a strength at
the beginning of August of 2,000 to 2,500 men of whom at least
600 were known to have been drafted since to France. 12 SS
Training and Replacement Battalion, according to a prisoner
who left for France on August 8th, had seven companies in the
area of Leyden, and a convalescent company, March Company
and HQ Company at Arnhem.

Despite the earlier warning tone of their reports which had
disturbed Dempsey at the time of Eisenhower's meeting with
Montgomery at Brussels on September 10th, 2nd Army Intelligence now shared 21st Army Group's optimism.* When Dutch
Resistance groups reported SS troops with a number of tanks

* General Horrocks cannot therefore be blamed for appearing to a senior officer
on the staff of the Airborne Division, who visited him during this week, to be
'completely hopeful'. He gave the impression that he believed XXX Corps would
be in Arnhem almost as soon as the Airborne Division itself. Discounting the
possibility of failure, he said, 'You'll be landing on top of our heads.'

Although Horrocks's aversion to what the Army calls 'belly-aching' frequently
seemed to his divisional and brigade commanders, as one of them has said, to
be 'an unwillingness to face up to realities', it should be added that no corps
commander was more capable of infusing – without hint of inner personal doubt
– both optimism and enthusiasm into any orders which it was his duty to transmit.

east of the Ijssel and close to Arnhem they doubted that the report was reliable; no other source confirmed it and although it was known that the area north of Apeldoorn was the main training ground in the West for Tiger tanks, no tanks could be seen on the reconnaissance photographs. And although it was known also that gangs of forced labour, including 12-year-old Dutch children, were constructing defences west of the Reichswald where the land, rising to over 600 feet is the highest in Holland and where the canal connecting the Maas and the Waal and these rivers themselves form a naturally defensive position, it was not supposed that these defences were 'either strong or well defended'. The belief of an intelligence officer at SHAEF that these reported armoured units might be the 9th (Hohenstaufen) and 10th (Frundsberg) SS Panzer Divisions of the *II SS Panzer Korps*, which had been pulled out of the Normandy beachhead so as to escape the final rout, was discredited at 2nd Army and at this time by 21st Army Group also. It was not, in fact, until after OPERATION MARKET GARDEN had begun that the 21st Army Group Intelligence Summary mentioned the presence in Holland of the 9th SS Division which had been 'entrusted with the task of clearing up Arnhem'.

During the previous 10 days Intelligence officers at Airborne Headquarters had been trying to piece together a reliable guide to German strength in the Arnhem area from the scraps of information which came to them. Basing their views on the generally encouraging reports which were sent from more senior headquarters, they had come to the conclusion by September 12th that German strength in Arnhem could be estimated as being 'nothing larger than a brigade with a few guns and tanks'.

And at this stage of the war a brigade was not likely to number more than about 3,000 men. By September 17th the estimate had not greatly altered. Lieutenant-Colonel Tasker, G.I. Intelligence officer at 1st Airborne Army Headquarters, collecting information from 21st Army Group, 2nd Army, XXX Corps and elsewhere, concluded that there was 'no direct evidence that the area Arnhem–Nijmegen' was 'manned by much more than the considerable flak defences already known to exist'. There were 'rather fragmentary Dutch reports' which confirmed that there were 20,000 German troops 'in the Hengolo–Bocholt–Cleve area where tanks had previously been reported' but this was well away to the east. General Browning, having heard a report that a Panzer battle group which was on its way to Germany to refit had been halted in Holland, referred the matter to 21st Army Group but was assured that the battle group was 'no longer a threat' on the British front. A Dutch Resistance radio message sent to London on September 15th which said that 'SS Div Hohenstruff [obviously Hohenstaufen] along Ijssel, sub-units observed between Arnhem and Zutphen–Apeldoorn road', was not passed on to the 1st Airborne Division until September 20th, long after the paratroopers had learned this distressing information for themselves.

The Chief Intelligence Officer at Corps Headquarters, Major Brian Urquhart, was, however, convinced that the general optimism was unjustified and dangerous. He felt sure that SHAEF was right and that there was, in fact, a large concentration of armour in the Arnhem area. Reports from Dutch agents confirmed it and oblique-angle photographs which he had seen clearly showed the presence of numbers of tanks. Indeed, the previous week when a plan for another operation with similar objectives to those of OPERATION MARKET GARDEN had been briefly discussed, reports of the presence of a German Panzer Corps in the Arnhem area had been passed to the Airborne Division. At subsequent conferences these reports were not mentioned. Although a highly intelligent man, Brian Urquhart was, however, both young and emotional and he pressed his views at Corps Headquarters not merely with conviction but with a passion that seemed, to those anxious to get into the fight whatever the hazards, to be almost hysterical. He was told that he was suffering from nervous exhaustion and sent home.

But, even if Brian Urquhart's categoric warnings had been accepted by Corps Headquarters and had consequently led to modifications in the British Division's plans, they would not have affected the determination of most of its officers and men to go to war. The Division, as a whole, was relieved beyond measure that the opportunity of joining the armies on the Continent seemed really to have come at last. 'The men were truly and deeply thankful', one of its officers said. 'They'd had to wait too long.' And if, as another officer thought, 'those responsible for planning were determined that we should see something of the party before it was too late, and were not too particular as to how or where we made our entrance', at least most of the Division were not too particular either.

Their rivals of the 6th Airborne Division had been chosen for the Normandy landings and since then 17 different operations varying from the possible to the wildly impracticable had been planned for them only to be abruptly cancelled, sometimes because of the weather, sometimes because their impracticability had been admitted, or more often because the Allied armoured columns had been so successful that by the time the operation had been fully planned the need for it had gone. Four times the men had been briefed and the aircraft loaded up and then at the very last moment the operation had been cancelled. By the beginning of September these recurrent cancellations had, so the Division's chief administrative officer says, 'produced in the officers a sort of weary cynicism and in the men a desire to find an outlet in other directions'. Public-house brawls, fights with Americans and air crews and attacks, in alliance with Americans, on military policemen, had become almost common-place in the 4th Brigade and were becoming more frequent in the others. There was, also, a sharply rising venereal-disease rate. The Division was, in fact, as its commander put it, 'battle-hungry to a degree which only those who have commanded large forces of trained soldiers can fully comprehend'. Both officers and men were 'ready for anything'. 'The British', so Eisenhower told

Captain Butcher, 'had voluntarily insisted that their airborne division take the toughest and most advanced assignment.' They would accordingly, as Urquhart himself admits, have readily agreed to an operation risking the flak at Arnhem and the supposed dangers of landing close to the bridge and on both sides of the river if they had not been advised so strongly against it. It is one of the great tragedies of the battle of Arnhem that – in addition to the British misapprehension of German strength in the area – both the RAF's estimate of the amount of flak which would be encountered there and the Intelligence reports on the state of the polder to the south of the river were to be proved wrong.

Several officers at the Order Group held on the afternoon of Tuesday, September 12th looked in surprise at the map of the Arnhem area and the circles which indicated the dropping and landing zones drawn so far from both the main road bridge in Arnhem and the railway bridge south of Oosterbeek which they had been ordered to capture. One of them thought that, despite the RAF's warnings, Urquhart was 'over-concerned about a safe approach and a tidy drop', and several others wondered why, if a mass landing closer to the bridge was impracticable, no plans had been made for a *coup de main* force to be dropped there. The brigadiers, however, appeared to Urquhart, 'not unhappy with the tasks confronting' them.

They were all men of great experience and talent. In command of the 1st Parachute Brigade, whose task it would be to make the initial drive for Arnhem, was Brigadier Gerald Lathbury. Later to become a General, a K.C.B. and Quartermaster-General, he had already had a distinguished career. Commissioned into the Oxfordshire and Buckinghamshire Light Infantry in 1926, he had passed through the Staff College just before the war and soon afterwards had been given command of the 3rd Parachute Battalion. Two years later he was given a brigade and had been wounded while commanding it in Sicily. He was a tall, loose-limbed man of 38 with the slow voice and indolent movements which so often conceal a perceptive and forceful intellect. He had, in addition, as one of his fellow-brigadiers said, 'a most engaging sense of the ridiculous'. His brigade was composed of veterans from the North Africa and Sicily campaigns and was considered to be one of the finest in the whole Army.

In striking contrast to Lathbury was the small and vital commander of the 4th Parachute Brigade. Born in Australia where his Irish father had set up newspapers in the West, J.W. Hackett was not only a man of dynamic presence and limitless courage, he was also a scholar. He had come from Geelong Grammar School to New College Oxford, where he had read Greats hoping to become a don. But after two years he changed his mind and decided that he would become a soldier instead. For the time being, however, he remained at Oxford, took his degree in Greats and then, having also passed the Final Schools in Modern History, joined the 8th King's Royal Irish Hussars in 1931. As a subaltern he spent his free time on mediaeval research and for a thesis presented on the Third Crusade he was given the research degree of Bachelor of Letters. Highly intelligent, self-confident, direct, argumentative and determined, it was clear that he would have been successful whatever career he had chosen. Although his academic cleverness and alert and some-times sardonic sense of humour were occasionally regarded with suspicion, he had been rapidly promoted. He was still only 34 and had been twice wounded and twice decorated. His future seemed bright and assured and his early promise has been fulfilled. He had formed his brigade from various units in the Middle East and India. Most of his men had been abroad a long time (he had been abroad himself for 10 years) and the brigade was consequently, as he put it, 'both independent and very closely knit'.

The third brigadier, Philip Hicks, in command of the 1st Airlanding Brigade was considerably older than Hackett. This difference in age combined with Urquhart's unfortunate regard for what he took to be Hackett's sensitivity, was to lead to a potentially dangerous quarrel at the height of the battle. As a 19-year-old subaltern in the Royal Warwickshire Regiment, Hicks had fought in the First World War and was now nearly 49. He had been at Dunkirk, in Africa, in Sicily and in Italy. Although neither as brilliant nor dashing an officer as Hackett, nor as dedicated a one as Lathbury, he had proved himself as brave as either of them. Reserved, kind, thoughtful and rather sad, he gave the impression of a man who had earned a more comfortable job near his family and would have welcomed it. His brigade was more like a normal infantry brigade than Hackett's with strong regimental rivalry and distinctions. His men respected him deeply.

Major-General Robert Urquhart, himself, was a big, good-looking, brave and talented Scotsman, the son of a doctor, and an officer of great energy and popularity. He was fairly new to the Division, having been given its command only about nine months previously. He suffered badly from air sickness, had never made a parachute landing and being so heavy was not expected to do so. He felt 'very much like a new boy at school' when he joined the Division and was conscious of a certain initial resentment which his gifts and charm overcame sooner than his modesty allowed him to believe.

It had been expected that Brigadier Lathbury would be given the command and there was no doubt that many of the Division's officers would have preferred a general who had had experience of airborne operations and was 'one of themselves'. A feeling had grown up amongst paratroops that there was a certain *mystique* in the specialities of their profession, a kind of esoteric quality which only the initiates of airborne combat could acquire. The conception was false, of course, for – as Urquhart tried to persuade himself – once paratroops have landed the ordinary rules of infantry fighting have only to be modified by common sense and ingenuity and the constant awareness that a parachute division can only be lightly armed. But it was a strong conception and Urquhart was impressed by the persuasive influence of those who clung to it.

His own instincts and intelligence had told him that he should refuse to accept the RAF's ruling against the proximity of the bridge as a landing ground and, in fact, unsuccessful representations were made to the RAF in an attempt to persuade them to drop or land at least some of his troops south of the river. The landings of the British 6th Airborne Division commanded by Major-General R.B. Gale in Normandy had demonstrated the advisability, if not the necessity, of landing on to or close to the objective. And the brilliant American general, James M. Gavin, later his country's Ambassador in Paris, who commanded the 82nd US Airborne Division has given it as his opinion that 'it is in general better to take landing losses and land on the objective than to have to fight after landing in order to reach the objective'.

The British Division, however, had suffered heavily in Sicily where it had made a poor choice of landing zones; and Urquhart was understandably concerned to get it down in Holland 'all in one piece and able to function immediately on landing', particularly as he would be 'functioning some 60 or 70 miles away from our nearest troops'.

The RAF's warnings about the strong flak defences in Arnhem were, accordingly, taken to heart; and although, as Lord Montgomery says, the difficulties of having to march some eight miles into Arnhem placed the Division 'at a great disadvantage', the officers at Urquhart's Order Group, acknowledging that an airborne operation is an air force responsibility until the troops have been landed, accepted these difficulties – if with mental reservations – without spoken complaint. After all, OPERATION COMET which had been so recently planned and cancelled had envisaged the British Division doing on its own what the whole Corps was now to do. Surely what had been supposed as possible for one division would not, despite these difficulties, prove too hard a task for three?

Urquhart showed on the map the areas which would be marked, with strips of red and orange nylon tape, by the men of the Independent Company who would land first. Then he explained that Lathbury's Brigade, led by Major C.F.H. Gough's 1st Airborne Reconnaissance Squadron which would land next, had the job of making a dash for the railway bridge south of Oosterbeek, the main road bridge in Arnhem and the pontoon bridge which was believed to be about half a mile west of it. In execution of this plan Lathbury decided that the 2nd Battalion of his brigade, commanded by Lieutenant-Colonel J.D. Frost, should advance into Arnhem on the most southerly of the roads which led towards the town from the west. This road passed through Heelsum and then curving down towards the river led into the town south of Oosterbeek. When he reached the bridge Colonel Frost was to relieve Major Gough, whose Reconnaissance Squadron should already have arrived there, and then take up a defensive position on both banks. The 3rd Battalion, under Lieutenant-Colonel J.A.C. Fitch was to advance on the 2nd Battalion's left by a more northerly road which led through the village of Oosterbeek and then, having reached the bridge in Arnhem, was to take up a defensive position on its north-eastern side. The 1st Battalion, commanded by Lieutenant-Colonel D.T. Dobie was initially to be held in reserve and then, if the situation developed as expected, to make for the high ground north of Arnhem and close the route leading into the town from Apeldoorn and Zutphen. Lathbury's plan was based on the assumption that opposition outside the town would be light and that the dangers of advancing on a wide front, without an adequate reserve, would be offset by the advantages of speed in reaching the objectives. It was, of course, a perfectly valid assumption in the light of the Intelligence reports that he had seen.

The landing and dropping zones would, in any event, as Urquhart went on to say at the Order Group, be protected by Hick's Airlanding Brigade which would remain there until the landing of Hackett's Brigade on the second day. Only after Hackett's Brigade had arrived would Hicks move into the western suburbs of Arnhem to form the left sector of the bridgehead. The northern sector would simultaneously be formed by Hackett whose brigade was to advance into the northern suburbs of the town to link up with Colonel Dobie's battalion of Lathbury's Brigade on the Arnhem to Apeldoorn road. On the third day, when the Polish Brigade landed on the south bank of the Neder Rijn, the main bridge would be in Lathbury's hands so that the Poles could march across it and then out into the eastern suburbs of the town to close the bridgehead on that last side also. Thus the bridges would be taken on the first day and, by the end of the third day, four brigades of infantry would be formed up in a box-shaped perimeter on the outskirts of Arnhem holding a bridgehead for the 2nd Army advancing from the south.

It was a simple plan and – so it seemed – a sound one. Urquhart finished explaining it. General Stanislaw Sosabowski,* the gallant and extremely gifted commander of the Polish Brigade, looked morosely about him. He was over 50 and had been in the army before some of these men were born. Touchy, imperious, violently patriotic, tactless and obstinate, he was inclined to regard his command as an independent one and more than once threatened to refuse to obey an order which seemed unreasonable. Understandably concerned that his glider-borne units carrying his main reserve of ammunition were to land on D-day +1 and D-day +2 on the north bank of the river, while his parachutists were to land on the south bank,

* 'Sosabowski and I used to sit together at conferences', General Hackett tells me. 'A grim and dedicated fighting man with a warm heart and an explosive sense of humour', he had 'enough experience to know the form'. Occasionally he could not bear the agony of an impractical plan being seriously discussed without making a violent protest. At the conference for the last projected operation before OPERATION MARKET GARDEN, Hackett heard him 'bubbling away until he could bear it no longer. "But the *Germans*, General, the *Germans*" he finally burst out in his deep voice.'

he did not hide the fact that he considered the whole operation extremely hazardous. He had read an article by a military expert in a Swiss newspaper which suggested that Arnhem was vital to the Germans and that the Germans realised this; and yet the British seemed to disregard this fundamental fact. On previous occasions when airborne operations had been planned he considered that his allies had disregarded not only the likely reactions of the Germans but even their very presence.

But only Brigadier Hackett, who afterwards warned his battalion commanders that they could expect heavy casualties, now seemed to share his concern.

'Do you realise, General,' Sosabowski asked Urquhart later, 'that your defence perimeter is 10 miles round in a wooded and inhabited area?'

'I quite agree', Urquhart replied with a confidence which he was far from feeling but which struck Sosabowski as foolhardy. 'But there will be no heavy German resistance and it is a risk we can afford to take.'

For the moment, however, Sosabowski said nothing. At the end of the Order Group, Urquhart asked, 'Any questions?'

'Not one brigadier or unit commander spoke', Sosabowski wrote afterwards, 'I looked round but most of them sat nonchalantly with legs crossed, looking rather bored and waiting for the conference to end.'

Eventually one officer asked how long they were expected to hold the bridgehead.

General Browning had asked Montgomery the same question a few days before; and Montgomery had said, 'Two days. They'll be up with you by then.'

'We can hold it for four', Browning had replied, and then, casting a shadow across Montgomery's brisk confidence, he added, 'But I think we might be going a bridge too far.'

It was a prophetic observation.

4

'The Saviour of the Eastern Front'

'Model was a very good tactician . . . He had a knack of gauging
what troops could do and what they could not do.'

General Hasso von Manteuffel

Two miles west of Arnhem on the road to Utrecht is the small
suburban town of Oosterbeek.

In the Tafelberg Hotel, Field-Marshal Model, commander of
German Army Group B, had his headquarters. He was a harsh,
forceful, energetic man of 54 who had shown himself a master of
defensive action in Russia and Poland. Hitler himself had called
him 'the saviour of the Eastern Front' and he had been sent to
the West to stem the tide on that front also.

He gave Hitler his political support and in return was allowed
much more freedom of action than other German generals
had the courage to demand. General Hasso von Manteuffel,
the great tank commander who had given Patton such trouble
on the Moselle, said that 'Model was a very good tactician and
better in defence than in attack. He had a knack of gauging what
troops could do and what they could not do.' His 'manner was
rough and his methods were not always acceptable in the higher
quarters of the German Army, but they were both to Hitler's
liking. Model stood up to Hitler in a way that hardly anyone else
dared to, and even refused to carry out orders with which he
disagreed.'

Efficient and ruthless, impatient and peremptory, with a
monocle fixed in the Prussian manner to a scarred and sternly

handsome face, Model presented the appearance of a supposedly typical senior officer of the *Wehrmacht*. He was not, however, a member of the military caste; and had risen to the rank of field-marshal at the age of 54 by virtue of intellect, ambition and Hitler's patronage rather than through the influence of the old, traditionally military families.

Hitler had no hesitation in appointing him Commander-in-Chief in the West when von Kluge killed himself, and although he had now been superseded in this appointment by the old and respected von Runstedt this had been a political rather than a military move. Von Runstedt's appointment was no more than a sop to the conservative officer corps and Model remained as commander of Army Group B and the main hope of the defenders of Germany's West Wall.

He had under his command a more formidable force than all but the most realistic British Intelligence officers had supposed. Facing the 2nd Army in their bridgeheads over the Meuse-Escaut canal along the Dutch frontier was Colonel-General Kurt Student's 1st Parachute Army, hastily formed on September 4th after the fall of Antwerp on orders telephoned from the Führer's Headquarters in East Prussia to Student who was then at Berlin Wannsee. Kurt Student, the originator and commander of the German parachute forces, had led the attack on Rotterdam and the invasion of Crete and was a man of strong nerves and quick decisions. His command included the German Army forces already in Holland together with the parachute regiments and *Luftwaffe* battalions which had been formed into infantry units. Most of his units were ill-equipped and ill-trained but they were fighting hard to carry out their orders to halt the Allied advance on the Albert and Meuse-Escaut canals and to 'advance deep into the American east flank regardless of local losses'. In addition Student's command was being hourly increased by scattered but formidable remnants of the 15th German Army, which for several days had been edging past the slowly extending pincers of the Allies along the Belgian frontier and had been crossing the Scheldt Estuary north-east of Antwerp. These were more formidable troops than the low medical category 'ear and stomach battalions' of the *Wehrkreis* and the heterogeneous 'Wall defence forces' which British Intelligence had suggested composed the main defensive force in southern Holland.

Although the town of Antwerp had been taken on September 4th, not for a fortnight – owing partly to the exhaustion of the British troops after their furious advance, partly to the difficulties of making supplies available for an extended operation beyond the port to open up its approaches, but mainly, perhaps, because the eyes of the British commanders were so 'firmly fixed on the Rhine' – was any major action taken to close the gap between Antwerp and the base of the Beveland isthmus through which over 60,000 German troops escaped into Holland. This failure to seal the remains of the 15th German Army in the lowlands north of Antwerp was one of the main reasons why Model and Student were able to put up that determined defence in Holland which was to contribute so much to the tragedy of Arnhem.

It was, in addition, a cruel chance that the two men most capable of successfully wrecking the Allied plans could scarcely have been better placed to do so. Model's Headquarters at Oosterbeek close to the British dropping zones near Arnhem, and Student's at Vught between the American zones at Nijmegen and Eindhoven were ideally situated to deal with the coming emergency. Nor were these two the only alert and capable German generals in this constricted area. For in the neighbourhood of Arnhem, as SHAEF had feared and Dutch Resistance had reported were two SS Panzer Divisions. These were the 9th and 10th of the *II SS-Panzer Korps* under the command of General Willi Bittrich.

Tall, stiff, handsome and highly intelligent, Bittrich was one of the most respected *Waffen SS* Generals in the German army. Unlike most of them he had a cultivated taste, a kindly manner, and a pleasant sense of humour. Although by then an ambitious officer, he had once wanted to be a musician and had studied at one of Germany's leading academies of music where he had shown great talent as a conductor. He was a Nazi, but he despised the Party sycophants and in particular Goering with whom he had once served in the *Luftwaffe*. His courage was legendary. In June 1953, after eight years in prison, he was tried for war crimes by a French court at Marseilles and was acquitted.

In the area for which he was responsible at this time were the 2nd and 116th Panzer Divisions as well as the 9th and 10th. The 2nd and 116th were in action along the frontier near Aachen; the 9th, commanded by *SS Brigadeführer und General Major der Waffen SS* Sylvester Stadler (until he was wounded and replaced by his Chief of Staff *Obersturmbannführer* Walter Harzer) was being prepared for a move back into Germany for refitting; and the 10th commanded by *SS Brigadeführer und General Major der Waffen SS* Heinz Harmel, was being reorganised for a counter-attack. By the end of the second week in September, however, only a few men of *II Panzer Korps* had left Holland. Both the 9th Division whose main *Unterkunftsraum* (bivouac area) was around Zutphen and the 10th whose *Unterkunftsraum* was between Zutphen and Ruurloo had several units in the villages to the east of Arnhem. And in the suburbs of the town, the woods and Dutch Army barracks to the north of it and in the open fields beside the Nijmegen road, other units of these two crack divisions – comparable only to the Hermann Goering and Alpine Divisions – were being reformed and regrouped. Camouflaged beneath green and khaki nets, concealed under tarpaulin, hidden from view in railway sheds and garages, were their *Schützen-panzerwagen* tanks and their self-propelled guns (*Sturmgeschütze*). Although both divisions had been in action continuously in France since June 29th, 1944 and had not received any replacements in either men or material between then and September 17th, and although almost all their armoured vehicles were under repair they were both still fighting formations with several excellent mortar platoons which were almost intact. The 9th had one complete armoured infantry regiment, one artillery battalion, two assault gun batteries, an armoured reconnaissance battalion, an armoured company equipped with Panther-type tanks and elements of an engineer battalion and of an anti-aircraft battalion.

The Division was particularly well equipped with armour, for *Obersturmbannführer* Harzer, using methods which would have delighted George Patton, ignored an order from Berlin to hand over all his serviceable tanks and vehicles to the 10th Division. Instead he had the tracks and guns taken off several of his tanks so that they appeared to be disabled and he described them as such in his returns. The 10th Division, already rather weaker than the 9th, having lost most of its vehicles in the Falaise pocket, could still nevertheless muster a partially motorised armoured infantry regiment, two artillery battalions, an engineer battalion, an anti-aircraft battalion and an armoured reconnaissance battalion. And like the 9th, it had received specialised training in opposing airborne landings.

In addition to these two divisions there were also in Holland at this time two *ersatz* battalions of SS troops under *Sturmbannführers* Kraft and Eberwein, a training battalion of *SS Unteroffizier* cadets under Colonel Lippert, a battalion of Dutch quislings under Lieutenant-Colonel Helle and various *Schiffstamm* detachments made up of men from abandoned coastal defence units and airfields. One of these units, the SS battalion commanded by *Sturmbannführer* Sepp Kraft, was actually stationed just outside Arnhem on September 17th.

'Depleted as we were,' one of its officers afterwards said, 'we knew that we were Germany's last hope. We knew in our hearts that the war had already been lost, but we had the desperate courage of despair. We wanted to make you suffer for your victory.'

PART TWO

The Operation

5

Sunday

By nine o'clock on Sunday, September 17th the morning fog had cleared and the weather was fit for take-off. At eight British and 14 United States airfields, stretching from Dorset to Lincolnshire, the troops were waiting to climb aboard the aircraft. Most of the men had been at some sort of party the night before and many of them felt, as one soldier said afterwards, 'a little fuzzy'. 'We had grasped our pints', he remembers, 'and sung until we were hoarse a host of paratroop songs, including "Three cheers for the next man to die".' They were grateful when the canteen vans came round for they were thirsty; and even those who were not, drank tea. It gave them something to do. They did not talk much.

Lieutenant-Colonel John Frost, of the Parachute Brigade's 2nd Battalion, was suddenly conscious of that apprehension which all men who enjoy life feel when they come near to the danger of leaving it. Earlier that morning he had hopefully asked his batman to put his gun and cartridges and golf clubs in the staff car which would arrive in Holland later with the heavier baggage. Now, standing on the runway by his Dakota, he thought of death. 'As every second ebbed by, a sneaking wish for a last-minute cancellation or even a further postponement' grew more urgent in his mind. He thought of 'one more day or even, perhaps, two doing all the pleasant things that now seemed

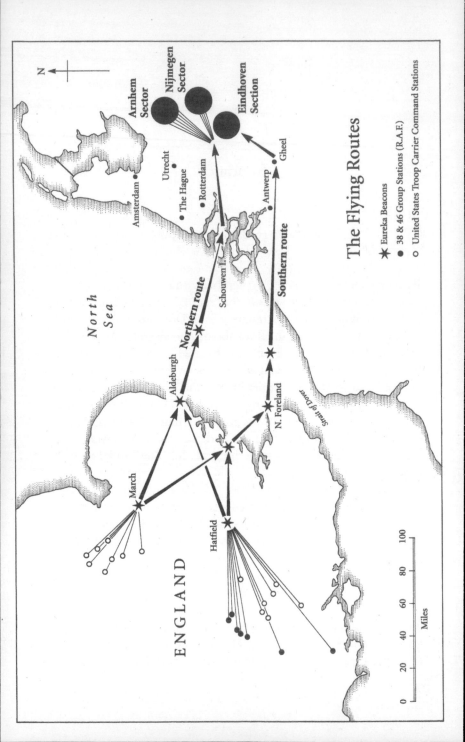

The Flying Routes

★ Eureka Beacons
● 38 & 46 Group Stations (R.A.F.)
○ United States Troop Carrier Command Stations

so precious. But another thought persisted, a more strident, vigorous one – "Come on! Let's get away. We've been too long already".'

The plans for taking the 1st Airborne Division to Holland had been laid with great care by the joint planning staff of 38 Group RAF and IX United States Troop Carrier Command at Eastcote, where it had been decided that the base airfields for the complete operation should form two distinct groups. Aircraft from bases in the southern group should form up over Hatfield in Hertfordshire and those in the northern group over March in Cambridgeshire. From the rendezvous over Hatfield the aircraft were to continue their flight, in three parallel streams one and a half miles apart, towards the North Fenland and then due east across the Channel to Gheel, turning north there for Eindhoven. From the rendezvous over March the aircraft were to fly to a second rendezvous over Aldeburgh and then east-south-east across Schouwen Island towards a final rendezvous above s'Hertogenbosch where the streams would diverge and make for the respective targets at Grave, Nijmegen and Arnhem (see opposite).

The routes would be marked by Eureka beacons and occults at all rendezvous and turning-points; by further Eureka beacons and coded Holophane lights on ships in mid-Channel; and by ground strips, coloured smoke signals and Verey lights, as well as Eureka beacons, on the dropping and landing zones. Air cover was to be provided during the flight by VIII United States Army Air Force which, assisted by fighters of Air Defence Great Britain, would also attack all flak positions along the route both before the operation and in the course of it; while, after the landings, cover would be maintained over the target areas by IX United States Air Force by day and by fighters of Air Defence Great Britain by night. At the same time aircraft of Coastal Command would carry out diversionary missions beyond the operational area and 2nd Tactical Air Force would carry out armed reconnaissance around the dropping and landing zones. Already on the previous day aircraft of Bomber Command had attacked enemy fighter airfields and flak positions and that night were to drop dummy parachutes west of Utrecht, at Emmerich and east of Arnhem. Shortly before H-hour (13.00 hours) aircraft of 2 Group RAF were to attack barracks in the area of the dropping and landing zones, completing their missions at 25 minutes before H-hour.

No aspect of the operation appeared to have been overlooked and no danger discounted. It was believed that, although the route had been carefully chosen to avoid the heaviest flak areas, flak would nevertheless be extremely heavy and losses of up to 40 per cent of the gliders and transport planes involved were predicted. The anti-flak precautions taken were accordingly sound and comprehensive. The dangers caused by the shortage of aircraft, which necessitated the airborne movement to the Arnhem area being extended over three days, were also fully realised. But on Saturday, September 16th a very favourable weather forecast for the next five days was issued and there seemed, therefore, no reason to suppose that the second and third lifts on Monday and Tuesday would not be able to fly in as planned, nor that the subsequent operations to supply the troops would not be successful.

Certainly when the first aircraft took off at a quarter to ten on Sunday morning the weather was as forecast. Winds were light, visibility was good, the few patches of stratus cloud had lifted by 10 o'clock. Of the 359 gliders detailed for the main lift only one was damaged before it reached the take-off point. Looking down from his Dakota, Major Anthony Deane-Drummond, second-in-command of the divisional signals, thought how peaceful everything looked. 'We could see the streets of the villages we passed over thronged with people looking upwards and an occasional handkerchief could be seen waving a farewell. It was midday when we crossed the coast and flew out across the North Sea, which for once was like a mill-pond with scarcely a ripple to disturb its brown-looking water. The men in my plane were nearly all asleep.'

By the time the convoy passed the Dutch coast 30 gliders had been lost in the clouds, mainly through broken tow ropes. But flak was not nearly as heavy as had been predicted and the few Focke-Wulfs and Messerschmitts that were seen, attacked the high fighter cover but did not interfere with the main formations. It was, one of the Stirling pilots said afterwards, 'no trouble at all – a piece of cake'.

As his glider was towed over the North Sea and approached the continental coastline, Lieutenant-Colonel W.F.K. Thompson, commanding the 1st Airlanding Light Regiment, saw that the low, broken clouds had completely dispersed and 'it was easy to see: first the air–sea rescue craft; then the coast defences of Holland, apparently abandoned, and the flooded land at the mouth of the Scheldt. And then quite suddenly', he noticed, 'the air photographs we had so carefully studied came to life and we were fast approaching our landing zone.'

Alexander Johnson, a glider pilot with E squadron, thought to himself, 'Holland looks very pretty from the air. It's hard to think there are Germans down there thinking evil thoughts about us.'

Below him, in a little village on the banks of the Maas, Willem Haart on his way back from Sunday school heard the roar of aircraft and pulling the brakes on his bicycle he looked up into the blue sky, shading the sun from his eyes, one foot on the road. He had never seen so many aeroplanes all at once before. There were hundreds of them, 'thousands perhaps'. For a long time he looked at them listening to the roar of the engines, wishing he was old enough to fly. Then he rode back fast to his grandfather to ask him where they were going.

'I don't know', the old man said. 'But it looks like the end of the war.'

A few minutes later the roaring streams of aircraft passed over Vught where Colonel-General Kurt Student was working at his desk.

He had been aware for some days that an attack by the British on his 1st Parachute Army was imminent. Only the day before he had reported to Model at Oosterbeek that 'a heavy attack must be expected very shortly'. Reports of increased motor activity behind the British lines and preparations for the movement of armour had been confirmed by his Intelligence officers. And on that same day, September 16th, these reports had been given an additional weight by the appearance at his headquarters of a Dutchman, Cristiaan Antonius Lindemans, who had come through the Allied lines from Brussels.

Lindemans was a big, uncouth, 31-year-old man with an insatiable appetite for women, drink and self-dramatisation. Because of his size and rough manners and his shambling gait he was known as King Kong, a nickname which he took pains to encourage. He had been a resistance worker until the end of the previous year when his younger brother, Henk, and his mistress, Veronica, had been arrested by the Gestapo, and his colleagues, fearing that these arrests and Christiaan's drunken boasts and sexual extravagances would lead to their betrayal, suggested that he should go over to England for a rest. Irritated by this suggestion and persuaded by a friend who had a German wife that he could arrange for the release of his younger brother and his mistress provided he agreed to work for the Gestapo himself, Lindemans went to see Lieutenant-Colonel H.J. Giskes, chief of the *Abwehr*'s counter-espionage organisation in Holland.

Giskes agreed to employ him and instructed him first of all to betray the organisers of the Spanish escape route, on the Dutch end of which he had been working, and then to infiltrate into the Belgian resistance. In both these missions Lindemans was successful and impressed Giskes with his reliability. At the beginning of September 1944, when the Allies' advance made the evacuation of his headquarters in Brussels essential, Giskes asked him to come to see him and told him that the Germans were withdrawing to Driebergen but that Lindemans must remain in Brussels and use his contacts with the Belgian underground to get attached to an Allied regiment. By September 5th Lindemans had managed to ingratiate himself with a Canadian Intelligence officer who eight days later, having made some not very revealing enquiries as to his reliability, instructed him to take a message through the German lines to Eindhoven warning the Dutch underground there to keep quiet for the time being and to call a halt to rail sabotage in view of the imminence of a British attack. By September 15th Lindemans had succeeded in getting through the British lines and was at General Student's Headquarters in Mijnheer van Beuninghen's country cottage at Vught, where he said that he had important information to give to Colonel Giskes at Driebergen. Giskes, in fact, had left the *Abwehr* Headquarters in Driebergen to take up another appointment, but his successor, Major Kiesewetter, told Lindemans that he could make his report to him instead. Kiesewetter listened quietly as Lindemans gave him several details about Allied units he had seen on his way back into Holland and told him that the 2nd British Army would launch its attack on September 17th. All this the German either knew or suspected, but when Lindemans added that the attack would be supported by an airborne landing beyond Eindhoven he was frankly sceptical. If parachutists were to be used at all, he thought, they would be dropped east of the Rhine, somewhere in the Ruhr area. Eventually Kiesewetter decided to pass on Lindemans' report to the *Sicherheitsdienst* with the warning that it should be treated with caution. 'Major Kiesewetter of IIIF. Intelligence Service of the German Army gave information to me about King Kong on 17 September, 1944', the chief of the Nazi Secret Service told a Dutch Commission of Enquiry after the war was over. 'Kiesewetter said that King Kong had brought him a report about Arnhem . . . At the moment when the first report that the attack in the Arnhem sector came in, Kiesewetter said to the officers who were with him, "This proves that the information from King Kong is correct after all".'

At the time, however, Kiesewetter was not convinced. Lindemans was suspected of being an agent for the Allies as well as for the Germans and it was thought that the information he was providing 'might well prove a blind'. If this supposedly dubious report was ever passed on to the *Wehrmacht* by the *Sicherheitsdienst* it was certainly discounted by the enemy commanders.*

For when General Student heard the roar of aircraft above his head on that Sunday morning he was, as he himself admits, taken 'completely by surprise'. He had 'never considered the possibility' of an airborne attack in his area. 'Actually, it was really obvious to use airborne troops in this situation in order to gain possession of bridges before their demolition. However, both the command and the troops, particularly my staff and I, were all so overtaxed and under such severe strain in the face of our difficult and many-sided mission that we thought only in terms of ground operations.'

During the morning of September 17th the front line had been quiet, he remembers:

But in the late hours of the morning, the enemy air activity suddenly increased considerably, particularly that of fighter bombers. From my command post at Vught I was able to observe numerous enemy planes and to hear the sounds of bombardments and the firing of aircraft, machine-guns and flak quite nearby . . . At about noon I was disturbed at my desk by a roaring in the air

---

* On September 16th at a meeting at Hitler's headquarters in East Prussia the possibility of an airborne landing in Holland was also mentioned. But here too it was not considered an immediate threat. Denmark and Germany were suggested as being just as likely targets and General Jodl thought that if a landing were to be made in Holland it would probably be made in West Frisia. At midnight on September 17th, however, when the news of the landings was the subject of anxious discussion at Rastenburg, Hitler told his staff that the situation in the West was now 'much more serious than in the East'. There were no divisions which could be sent to Holland immediately and unless the attack could be held for a few days it might be disastrous. The narrowness of Model's escape also disturbed Hitler. 'If such a thing happened here,' he said, 'where I sit with my whole supreme command, it would certainly be a worthwhile catch. Personally I would not hesitate to use two parachute divisions if by so doing I could lay my hands on the whole of the German command.'

which increased in intensity so that finally I left my desk and went on to the balcony. Wherever I looked I could see aircraft, troop-transports and large aircraft towing gliders. They flew both in formation and singly. It was an immense stream which passed quite low over the house. I was greatly impressed by the spectacle and I must confess that during these minutes the danger of the situation never occurred to me. I merely recalled with some regret my own earlier airborne operations, and when my Chief of Staff joined me on the balcony I could only remark, 'Oh, how I wish that I had ever had such a powerful force at my disposal.'

Any delay that his surprise or envy may have caused, however, was soon amply compensated by a remarkable discovery.

Soon after the gliders had streamed over his cottage, one of them was hit by anti-aircraft fire just north of it. The glider, one of its wings badly damaged, plummeted into a field and the American troops inside it were killed instantaneously. A platoon of one of Student's units rushed across the field to inspect the damage and search the bodies of the dead. Hans Koch pushed one body over with his foot and undid the front of the jacket. In a breast pocket he found a sheaf of papers and pulled them out. He looked at them uncomprehendingly for a moment and then handed them to a sergeant.

'A few hours later', General Student says, 'the orders for the complete airborne operation were on my desk. The importance of this capture was immense for we learned at once of the enemy's strength and intentions and the speed and comparative success of our counteraction was to no small extent due to early knowledge of his hostile moves.'*

* 'The same thing happened in 1940 on the occasion of the first German airborne operation in Holland,' says General Student, 'when a German officer against strict orders had taken the attack orders along with him. This order fell into enemy hands thus enabling him to make a close study of German airborne tactics. This incident was the chief reason for the heavy German losses in *Fallschirm* troops on the island of Crete.'

Model had been as surprised by the airborne attack as Kurt Student. Only three days before a senior staff officer at his headquarters, in an attempt to consider the problems of a thrust into Germany from the Allied point of view, had composed an imaginary order by General Eisenhower.

The 2nd British Army [he had written] will assemble its units at the Maas-Scheldt and Albert Canals. On its right wing it will concentrate an attack force mainly composed of armoured units and, after forcing a crossing of the Maas, will launch operations to break into the Ruhr with its main attack through Roermond. On its left wing it will close the Waal crossing at Nijmegen so as to cover the northern flank of this drive into the Ruhr and to cut off the German forces in the Dutch coastal areas. In conjunction with these operations a large-scale airborne landing is planned for an as yet uncertain date north of the Lippe river in the area south of Munster.

Model accepted this as the most likely form which the forthcoming attack would take and considered his headquarters at Oosterbeek, 100 miles from Munster and separated from the enemy by three wide rivers, as safe as it could expect to be anywhere. Not all the German generals agreed with him. On the day after this imaginary order of General Eisenhower's was prepared by his staff – that is on September 15th – he received a visit from General Rauter, *Polizeiführer* in Holland. Rauter told Model that he thought an airborne landing in the area was a 'distinct possibility'. But neither Model nor his Chief of Staff, General Krebs, was convinced. Airborne forces were a precious commodity, they insisted, and Montgomery, 'tactically a very prudent man', would not use them on so reckless a mission; certainly not until the port of Antwerp was in use and the line of communications could be shortened. Besides, Arnhem was far too far in advance of the spearheads of the 2nd Army; an airborne force landed there would be almost certainly defeated

before these spearheads could get through to it. Model felt
quite secure, he assured General Rauter; his headquarters was
defended by 250 men of the Field Police and that was enough.

Although he was caught unawares by the airborne landings,
however, Model reacted to them with characteristic speed. As
soon as he was told that British parachutists were tumbling down
from the sky, he put down the glass of wine he was drinking as an
aperitif before lunch, gave rapid orders for the evacuation of the
Park Hotel at Hartenstein and his headquarters at The Tafelberg Hotel at Oosterbeek, and ran upstairs to his bedroom to
cram his belongings into a suitcase while his driver in the road
below nervously tooted the horn of his car. His officers, too,
grabbed what they could from their rooms before running out
into the road but they, like Model, were obliged to leave much
behind including several plans and many files of secret documents. As Model himself rushed into his waiting staff car at the
gate of his hotel, his suitcase burst open and his shirts and
shaving things spilled out on the street and had to be hastily re-
packed.

The convoy of cars raced out of Oosterbeek and down the
road towards Arnhem. It had covered less than a mile when it
overtook an SS major pedalling furiously towards Arnhem on a
bicycle.

'Which is the way to General Bittrich's headquarters?' Model
shouted from the front seat of the leading car, leaning over the
door in what the major enviously noticed was a brand new black
leather jacket.

'The Doetinchem road', the major shouted back and was
almost knocked into the ditch as the car accelerated past him.

In the town Field-Marshal Model told the driver to stop at the
headquarters of the garrison commander and to wait outside for
him while he conferred with the officer in charge. The garrison
commander, himself, had been killed in an air raid that morning
and Model found his staff in complete confusion. But shouting
orders at telephonists, despatch riders and wireless operators, he

managed to restore confidence to the headquarters before driving on to General Bittrich's *II Panzer Korps* Headquarters at Doetinchem.

Bittrich had already heard of the landings at Arnhem and Nijmegen through the *Luftwaffe* communications network. Many of the units under his command, due to leave for Germany that day, had been entrained during the morning or the night before and the men from several others had been granted a few hours' leave to enjoy the pleasant Sunday sunshine. Three goods trains had already left Arnhem Station that morning. The Corps Headquarters was thrown into sudden tumult as staff officers tried frantically to reassemble the equipment of the divisions and to get the men into battle order. There were about 8,500 men scattered around the area to dispose of,* and because much of the Corps's wireless equipment had been lost in the retreat through France and most of the Dutch operators of the telephone system were as slow as they dared to be, it was some time before General Bittrich's orders could take effect. Within an hour, however, a battle group of the 9th SS Panzer Division, in response to a message given to *Obersturmbannführer* Harzer by a breathless soldier on a bicycle, was on its way towards the landing zones with orders to 'destroy the enemy troops landed at Oosterbeek, west of Arnhem'. 'It is necessary to strike immediately', the order continued. 'The most important task is to occupy and secure the bridge with strong forces.'

Having despatched this order to the 9th Division, General Bittrich telephoned to General Harmel's 10th Division (Harmel himself was in Germany) and ordered it to 'proceed immediately south to Nijmegen, take firm control of the main bridge and defend the Nijmegen bridgeheads'. For Bittrich realised immediately that the spearheads of the 2nd Army would try to advance on Arnhem through Nijmegen and it was as important

---

* 3,500 of them, Colonel Harzer tells me, were from his own Division and 5,000 from the 10th.

to prevent this link-up as to destroy the airborne troops that had landed north of the Neder Rijn.

It was about three o'clock when Field-Marshal Model and General Krebs arrived at Bittrich's headquarters and learned what action had been taken. Although Bittrich's orders had removed almost half the strength of *II Panzer Korps* from the Arnhem area, they accepted his decision as a wise one, agreeing that the continued isolation of the airborne troops from the British 2nd Army was essential to their destruction, and sympathising with his estimate of the British soldier's character and capacities which had given his plan additional grounds for support.

'We must remember', Bittrich had said as he walked up and down outside his house, 'that British soldiers do not act on their own initiative when they are fighting in a town and when it consequently becomes difficult for officers to exercise control. They are amazing in defence but we need not be afraid of their capabilities in attack.'

He believed, too, that the British attack would be 'not too daring and not too widespread'; and accordingly hoped that while waiting for reinforcements he could ignore the areas not under immediate attack. He was greatly assured when the plan of operations was passed on to him by General Student and he saw that his immediate assumptions concerning Allied intentions had been correct. 'We shall soon be able to discount the threat of the British north of the Neder Rijn', he decided. 'The great problem is to ensure that the American parachutists and the British 2nd Army are prevented from linking up with them.'

Bittrich's whole plan was based on the hope that most of the British troops could be held west of Arnhem until reinforcements could be brought up from regrouped formations of Army Group B by Field-Marshal Model. The successful working of the plan rested, in fact, on the ability of *Obersturmbannführer* Harzer's 9th SS Division, whose troops were already concentrating to the west of the town, to check the initial advance of the British troops from the landing grounds; and, in particular, upon the ability of the local commander whose troops would bear the brunt of the first shock. *Sturmbannführer* Sepp Kraft of Panzer Grenadier Depot Battalion Number 16 was this commander. His men were already stationed between Oosterbeek and Wolheze and now consequently found themselves closer to the landing grounds than any other German unit.

Kraft was a brave and energetic officer of decided views, ideally suited to the command of the keen and fresh recruits, mostly between 17 and 19 years old, who comprised his battalion. They had arrived in the area only the day before and numbered no more than 422 men and 13 officers besides himself, but they were to put up a defence of remarkable courage and ingenuity.

'The only way to draw the teeth of an airborne landing with an inferior force', Kraft thought, 'is to drive right into it.' From a 'tactical point of view', he wrote in his battalion's War Diary,

it would be wrong to play a purely defensive role and let the enemy gather his forces unmolested. Whilst it is not the rule to attack far superior forces, there are occasions when this must be done. And in this present fight for existence by the German people there are occasions occurring every day when only a virile offensive spirit can lead to success. That is the opinion, often repeated, of our highest War Lord – the Führer – who calls to account any officer who shuns an enemy far superior to himself, particularly in a critical situation. Any commander who had led a battalion of first-class troops back to Arnhem, even if it had been intended to occupy the town and hold the bridge, would deserve to be summarily court-martialled.

With the determination of a man unhampered by doubt, Sepp Kraft on his own responsibility sent one company forward with orders to fight a delaying action, while the rest of the battalion were brought forward to a defensive line across the roads leading into Arnhem. Anxious to support him there as soon as possible,

Obersturmbannführer Harzer sent forward another battalion of Panzer grenadiers with armoured cars and light tanks to cover the roads which led into Arnhem from Ede and Heelsum, and a third battalion to the bridge. These units were soon reinforced by a combat group led by *Obersturmbannführer* Spindler the commander of the artillery battalion in the 9th Division.

Less than two hours after General Student had first heard the roar of approaching aircraft, these various units had succeeded in establishing a strong defensive ring across the approaches to Arnhem; and orders had gone out to four further battalions to concentrate in the area between Ede and Renkum so as to threaten the British troops from the east and if possible, to advance across the landing grounds. 'Almost before the British had touched the ground', General Bittrich commented afterwards with justifiable satisfaction 'we were ready to defeat them.'

To the men of Major Wilson's 21st Independent Parachute Company as they floated down towards the flat and gently swaying land, the scene below looked quiet and peaceful. The small neat buildings, the thin roads, the patch-work of woodland formed a familiar pattern. Far away to the east they could see the town, bigger than they had expected for most of them had never heard of it before; and curling past it and out of sight, the wide smooth river. 'Everything looked so peaceful', Major Wilson said. 'Not a sign of fighting or war. Not a glimpse of the enemy.'

As the ground grew closer – seeming, as it does to parachutists, to be coming up to meet them – its surface and the objects on it took on more definite shapes. Moving things were clearly seen now and figures on the roads: a bicyclist racing down a farmyard track; a group of men by a churchyard wall shading their eyes against the sun, their hands and faces white against their dark Sunday suits; cows grazing unconcernedly in the lush green grass by the water's edge.

Then there was a burst of rifle-fire and two of Major Wilson's men were hit just before they reached the ground, one in his ammunition pouches, the other in his haversack. But only one was hurt and the rest fell to the soft turf and quickly escaped from their harnesses. Wilson himself, an enterprising and unconventional soldier of 45, looked up into the face of a German soldier who already had his hands above his head. Wilson told him to take him to his comrades and without hesitation the frightened German took the English major to a slit trench where his nervous fellow-soldiers gave themselves up as readily as he had done. Wilson disdainfully told them to wait there as he hadn't time to take them prisoner yet; and keeping his eyes on them he called his three platoon commanders by wireless and gave them their orders. Then he ordered the release of his pigeons. Instead of flying back to London with news of his landing, however, they settled in a cluster on the roof of a farmhouse and had to be dislodged by a cascade of pebbles.

The coloured strips of nylon were unrolled across the fields without interference from anyone, the Eureka beacon was set up and the smoke signals and Verey lights prepared. Everything, so far, was going according to plan. The sun still shone in a clear sky and there was hardly any wind. From the pine woods there came a pleasant smell of resin, fresh and curiously strong. It was about a quarter past one.

Presently the distant roar of aircraft was heard and Wilson's men looked up to see the approaching Dakotas in an unclouded sky. In one of them Colonel Frost nodded at his men encouragingly. He noticed the 'transparent insincerity of their smiles and the furious last-minute puffing at their cigarettes', and felt acutely conscious of their tension and their fear. 'While the red light glowed I peered anxiously ahead at the dropping zone', he remembers. 'In front and below parachutists were falling and then I too was out. Once again the thrill of falling. The great relief of feeling the harness pulling and that highly satisfactory bounce as the canopy filled with air.' Soon the sky was filled with aircraft, parachutes, kitbags dropped by nervous men hurtling towards the earth, gliders skimming down to land or circling to find a clear run in.

By two o'clock the landing zones were littered with gliders and the long lines of trailing skid marks. Several gliders had skidded off the flat fields into the surrounding roads, others had overshot on landing runs which were down-wind and had crash-landed into clearings in the woods where the thin walls and flimsy plywood frames of many were broken and crushed. Two Hamilcars which had landed on soft ground had bogged their wheels, nosed in and overturned, and two 17-pounder guns had been lost. But 319 gliders had landed – a far higher proportion than had been predicted – and the loads of only a few were damaged. No more than seven aircraft had been hit by flak and not a single one had been shot down.

The loss, however, was much greater than these numbers imply. 'I went by glider with "A" Troop vehicles', Lieutenant J. Stevenson of the 1st Airborne Reconnaissance Squadron said afterwards. 'We got down about ten minutes before the parachute party. It took us four-and-a-half hours to unload and when I looked round for the remainder of the troop vehicles I found that, besides the Jeep from our glider, only two others had got down so far.' And it was not only 'A' Troop's vehicles which had failed to arrive. In fact nearly all the squadron's vehicles were in the missing gliders and Major Gough, the squadron's commander, was unable to make the race for the road and railway bridges on which so much depended.

As yet, however, this seemed of little consequence. Brigadier Lathbury's Brigade would soon be ready to move off and there appeared no cause for alarm or even, indeed, for hurry. There was a little scattered rifle and machine-gun fire but so far no other sign of the enemy.

There were scores of Dutch people, though. And they were a hindrance of a different sort. They were excited, friendly, talkative and pressing. They came out of their farmhouses in their best church clothes, they came running down the roads

from Wolfheze and Renkum and Heelsum and from villages
even further distant, for the news had travelled fast. They carried
trays of food and jugs of water and baskets of fruit and flowers.

At eleven o'clock that morning some of them, on their way to
church, had looked up at the air formations flying over their
heads. 'They were low, very low,' a Dutch girl, Mejuffrouw
Hogerzeil, remembered, 'unusually low. But the people were
quite used to the sight and did not take much notice.' Even when
the firing started, they stayed in church, loudly and defiantly
singing the *Wilhelmus,* their national anthem. They thought it
was another air-raid. And after church, in the early afternoon,
when an old farmer called through the Hogerzeils' kitchen
window that 'thousands, *millions* of Allied paratroops' were
dropping from the sky, nobody believed him.

But now there could be no doubt. Out of the woods from
a bombed mental hospital, already filled with Dutch civilians
wounded in the preliminary air-raids, came groups of bewil-
dered patients, smiling and lost, and their nurses, smiling with a
bewilderment so similar that a glider pilot thought it was 'rather
hard to tell who were the loonies and who were the nurses
helping them'. And across the railway lines scampered gangs of
little boys screaming in excitement. The holiday mood was so
infectious that some soldiers, waiting for the others to land, had
already lit fires and were making tea. 'We were violently attacked
by hordes of Dutch children who gave us dozens of apples', says
the glider pilot, Alexander Johnson. 'Peter [Major Peter Jackson]
and I were invited to tea by an elderly Dutch couple and we
accepted – so far, everything had been very gentlemanly and
unwarlike.'

The Dutch, indeed, made it seem impossible that a battle was
about to take place. They had 'turned out in force. Everyone was
wearing some garment or part of a garment in orange colours,
some with favours and some with coloured arm-bands.' Their
happiness and excitement were very moving. Little girls, laughing cheerfully, cut strips from the parachutes to make dresses for

their dolls and provident men came up with wheelbarrows to cart away the interesting debris on the landing zones. They waved at the soldiers as they passed and shook them by the hand. They had no doubt that now that the British had come, now that the British Liberation Army was at last in Holland, the war was won. The soldiers should not be blamed if they too felt so, and took no chances in their long march into Arnhem. Many men had got boot polish in their haversacks and contraceptives, too, and they wanted to be alive to use them when the Army entered the streets of a welcoming and liberated city for a few days' leave.

They were slow and cautious. Mevrouw Kate ter Horst, watching them file past her house which stands next to the little eighteenth-century church of Oosterbeek Laag, thought to herself 'they seem to be in no hurry, for they walk so calmly'. The leading man turned towards her and laughed 'from under his helmet, the net over it full of green strips, a grotesque sight'. He spread out his arms and called, 'Give me a kiss!'

We stare and stare [Mevrouw ter Horst wrote afterwards]. We are so accustomed to the noisy marching of the Germans. At an inaudible command they all kneel alongside the hedge . . . Is this a manoeuvre? There is surely no danger anywhere? They start walking again, and as they pass they have all kinds of pretty words for little Sophie. Big fellows in yellow coats with a countless number of pockets in them, which absorb quite a lot of the apples and tomatoes we offer them. Orange streamers and flags, flowers and cheering, people embracing each other in joy. Our own flag in the absence of the genuine village flag is run up on the spire of the church. Even a little bell which the Germans had accidentally overlooked begins to ring. Two enthusiasts are pushing the bell to and fro with their feet for there is no rope.

On the other roads, too, the scene was the same, as the British soldiers marched through the villages. They looked 'tired, sweaty, covered with grime', Mejuffrouw Hogerzeil said. 'The people were cheering and giving them fruit and flowers, looking at these soldiers curiously, listening to their strange, new language.'

The march, led by Colonel Frost's 2nd Battalion now that the Reconnaissance Squadron had lost most of its jeeps, began at about a quarter-to-three. The route which the Battalion had been ordered to take was by the most southerly of the roads that ran into Arnhem through Heelsum and south of the village of Oosterbeek; and it was, in fact, the only one that Harzer had largely ignored in the immediate dispositions which he had made in his attempt to bar the way into the town. Even so there were many delays. For these 'very friendly Dutch' people, one of the company commanders reported, kept on running up and offering his men cups of tea which they were too polite to refuse. 'Apples, pears and jugs of milk appeared', Colonel Frost remembered. 'Orange flowers were pressed upon us and one old gentleman asked me if I would like to use his car . . . They all seemed familiar rather than foreign. Certainly they impressed us very much by their bearing and generosity.' And as if in return for the courtesy of the Dutch, the soldiers deferentially asked permission to search houses for enemy ambushes in the line of advance. They were careful, too, not to step on flower-beds or to damage the high, wire-mesh fences which surrounded many of the neat gardens. This politeness and respect for property slowed up the advance as much as the soldiers' natural caution.

Then the maps which had been issued, so Major Digby Tatham-Warter, commanding 'A' Company, reported, 'showed few of the roads that actually existed'. Men got lost or dispersed and had to be 'rallied by bugle calls'.

After about half a mile the men of the leading platoon of 'A' Company, advancing in single file on each side of the road, came up against the first signs of serious opposition when a machine-gun opened fire on them from the high ground west of Heveadorp. They threw themselves to the ground and began operations to deal with the obstacle with an understandable circumspection which was to become typical of their advance. 'They were excessively cautious', a German officer said making no allowances for the psychological difference between attack and defence in built-up areas nor for the suitability of the country for a delaying action. 'They could easily be stopped with a few bursts from light automatics.' *Sturmbannführer* Sepp Kraft, agreed with him. Although the English were very skilful in house fighting, he thought, and their tree and ground snipers were the 'very devil', they 'lacked courage and resolution when advancing. If opposed they were inclined to withdraw rather than dig in . . . They should have pushed straight on into Arnhem instead of trying to wipe out the opposition around it.'

Colonel Frost's leading platoon stopped again at about four o'clock to the west of Oosterbeek and then for a third time, on the other side of the village, when an armoured car fired at them down the cobbled road forcing them to take cover until an anti-tank gun could be brought up to clear the way. The anti-tank gun was being placed in a shop window when General Urquhart drove up in a jeep to try to find Colonel Frost and tell him that his men would have to be instilled with a greater sense of urgency.

Urquhart was already in difficulties. Not only had he lost the vehicles of the Reconnaissance Squadron; he had for the time being lost the men too. Major Gough had taken the Squadron off somewhere, but no one at Headquarters knew where; and they could not find out for the communications within the Division had almost completely broken down.

The Division's Tactical Headquarters was on the edge of the wood to the east of the landing zones and the radio sets refused to function efficiently there. Even when taken out into the open there was an utter lack of sensitivity in the reception and no intelligible response from any of the operational units which Urquhart badly needed to contact. He had decided that there was, accordingly, no point in waiting at his headquarters where he could learn nothing of what was going on and had driven after Colonel Frost, with his signaller in the back of the jeep trying constantly and in vain to contact Gough on his Rover set.

When Urquhart reached the 2nd Battalion, Colonel Frost was with his leading platoon personally directing operations and Urquhart decided to leave a message at his Battalion Head-quarters urging him to make all possible speed. It would soon be dark and the Arnhem bridges were still a long way off.

The 3rd Battalion under Lieutenant-Colonel J.A.C. Fitch had started along the middle road, soon after Colonel Frost's men had left on the southern one. At about four o'clock the leading platoon under Captain Cleminson came up to a crossroads about two miles west of Oosterbeek. Most of Cleminson's men were across the junction when a heavily camouflaged Citroën staff car came racing down towards it from the village of Wolfheze. The driver almost drove into the parachutists and the tyres screeched on the surface as he pushed his foot on the brake and rammed the gear lever into reverse. The car was still skidding towards them when Cleminson's men opened up with Sten guns and rifles from both sides of the road at once. Its windows were smashed, its tyres flattened, an officer who tried to get out was killed as he opened the door, the driver was killed in his seat, an orderly and interpreter in the back were shot as they threw themselves out into the road. The officer was Major-General Kussin, *Feldkommandatur* of Arnhem. He was on his way back to his headquarters having paid a visit to the front to see for himself what was happening. He had run into Kraft's battalion and Kraft had advised him not to use that road but he had replied that he could not spare the time to take a safer one.

Leaving the bodies where they lay, Cleminson's men prepared to move on again. As they did so German mortars, over a mile away, began to fire on the crossroads where a large part of the 3rd Battalion was now concentrated. The men, many of them hearing for the first time the frightening and characteristically explosive crack of mortar bombs, ran for cover into the woods which line the road at this point and when General Urquhart, having been shot at several times as he raced down the road in his jeep after his visit to the 2nd Battalion, came up with them he found them under an increasingly heavy fire.

Bombs were bursting in the trees and as the fragments whined through the air many men, lying in the undergrowth, were hit in the back. Their screams of agony were unnerving. More fortunate men found slit trenches dug by Germans on a field exercise some months previously and were crouching there in relative safety as the mortar 'stonk' increased in intensity. For several minutes the 3rd Battalion remained in this dangerous and heavily-bombed locality. It would have been difficult to find a more unfortunate place to wait or rest. Eventually during a temporary lull in the bombardment, Brigadier Lathbury decided that they must get out of it and he gave Colonel Fitch orders to move on. He had no idea how the rest of his brigade was progressing. His wireless sets were working as erratically as those at Divisional Headquarters and he had lost touch with Colonel Dobie's 1st Battalion altogether and was only in the most uncertain contact with Colonel Frost of the 2nd. But he knew it would be 'suicide to stay any longer on that infernal crossroads'.

Before he moved off he told his signaller to try once more to make contact with the other two battalions of his brigade. At the same time General Urquhart went back to his jeep to make another attempt to get through to Divisional Headquarters. Before he reached it, the jeep was hit by a mortar bomb. The signaller was badly wounded and, although the Rover set was not damaged, Urquhart could not get anything from it but a low-pitched buzz. Brigadier Lathbury had no more luck with his set. Urquhart, as he afterwards confessed, realised now that he 'was losing control' of the battle. He anxiously wondered whether he should try and get back to his Headquarters where, for all he knew, wireless communications were still as bad as they were at the front or remain with the brigade which had been given the task of seizing the bridge. He cannot be blamed for deciding to remain with Lathbury, although the consequences of his decision were, for him, all but disastrous.

He followed after the 3rd Battalion in growing concern. It was getting late and the sun was going down.

Further down the road in front of him, Major Peter Waddy's company, still led by Captain Cleminson's platoon, had come under close-range fire from a self-propelled gun. As the men took cover Waddy crawled up to Cleminson to help him to decide how to deal with it. They decided that Cleminson should take a patrol to the right and Waddy one to the left and that they should attack the gun with Bren guns and Stens from the houses that lined both sides of the road. Before they moved off, however, a British six-pounder gun came up and both of them hoped that this would silence the self-propelled gun for them. They waited to see what would happen.

They watched in anxious alarm as the six-pounder's crew brought their gun round in what seemed 'the most casual manner' while the enemy gun was driven quickly down the road towards it and opened fire. The first German shot found its mark. The shell exploded in the road just in front of the six-pounder, putting it out of action and killing some of its crew. The self-propelled gun came on down the road and one of its crew jumped out and grabbed a wounded British anti-tank gunner and laid him across the front of the chassis beneath the barrel of the gun. With this human shield the vehicle tracked back in safety to its lines, for the British soldiers between the houses on either side of the road could not bring themselves to fire or to throw the gammon bombs they had loosened from their belts.

As soon as the gun had disappeared from view the advance began again, but within minutes other guns had come up and the 3rd Battalion was held up once more. Colonel Fitch now decided to send one of his companies – 'C' Company – down a side road to get round the self-propelled guns on their southern flank while the remaining companies with Battalion Headquarters, edged slowly forward along the original line of advance.

They had not gone far, however, when they were held up once more near the Park Hotel, Hartenstein, on the outskirts of Oosterbeek. *Sturmbannführer* Sepp Kraft's determined youths were fighting well and had been reinforced now by the battle group which had been sent up to support him from the 9th SS Panzer Division. As darkness fell, Brigadier Lathbury suggested to Colonel Fitch that the battalion should halt for a few hours' rest.

Lathbury and Urquhart shared a room in a large house surrounded by a well-kept garden. A message that the rest of the brigade would not now try to reach the bridge before morning was sent off to Colonel Frost and patrols were sent forward towards Arnhem. There was nothing more for the moment to be done. General Urquhart, with his legs over the end of a sofa, wondering what had become of Major Gough and whether Colonel Frost's battalion had got through to the bridge, tried to get some sleep. The men got out their emergency rations and settled down too. It was suddenly very quiet.

A patrol from Major Waddy's company crept into the grounds of the Park Hotel which Field-Marshal Model's staff had left so hurriedly a few hours before. The men moved across the wide and silent lawns to the building they could see quite clearly in the darkness, its white walls distinct and sharp against the black trees behind it and the starless sky above. They entered the house by the cellars, singly or in pairs, waiting for the sudden explosive crackle of machine-gun fire, or the shout of a German voice, touching doors cautiously in fear of booby-traps. 'I was windy', one of them afterwards said. 'I don't mind admitting it. My mate was sick. I felt sick an' all.'

But when they climbed the creaking wooden stairs to the ground floor they found the building deserted. In the dining-room, on a long table covered by a white cloth, places for lunch were neatly laid. The *hors d'oeuvre* – slices of sausage, salame and smoked *paling* on small saucers – were untouched. There was a half-empty bottle of wine on the table, with several glasses and more bottles in a cupboard.

As the men emptied the plates, two officers tossed up to decide who should be first to lead a party out of the relative safety of the hotel to find a way into Arnhem. Even in the dark, they thought, it would be impossible to push on down the road without anti-tank guns; so Major Waddy picked out on his map a path that led through the park behind the hotel.

The party left through the tall sash windows of the dining-room. The others watched them leave until they disappeared into the background of trees. A few minutes later the edge of the wood burst into life as machine-guns sparked and crackled and a flare threw the grounds of the hotel into a sudden glaring light. The men were forced back towards the hotel, and while they ran the machine-guns continued to fire at them and their shadows raced across the turf as the dying light of the flare fell quickly towards the earth.

Meanwhile 'C' Company, which had been detached by Colonel Fitch when the battalion had been held up outside Oosterbeek, had reached the outskirts of Arnhem. After a brief fight with the enemy in the suburbs, their commander, Major Lewis, had led them towards the centre of the town along the railway track.

It was a strangely alarming advance. The town seemed empty. From the railway station they went down a wide street in what they took to be the direction of the bridge. It was difficult to tell whether or not they were going the right way, for the few street plans they had were even less reliable than the maps of the surrounding district. Their route led down narrow streets, past shuttered shops and restaurants. They passed two Dutch police-men but there was no other sign of life anywhere. It was as if they were walking through a plague town or one deserted years before.

Private McKinnon, whose stomach had not been tightened by fear, pushed his way into a butcher's shop to look for something to eat. As he was looking in disappointment at the empty slabs, the butcher came down to apologise for his poor stock. He was, he said, in passable English, completely out of meat but would the Englishman take a little bread and cheese and a glass of wine; and would he kindly wait for a few minutes while his little daughter came up from the cellar to have a look at him. The girl came up and said solemnly in laboured English, 'Many happy returns after your long stay away.'

The whole advance of 'C' Company was like this – unreal and dreamlike. But then, as the leading platoon came into the street leading to the bridge, a German armoured car came out of a hidden turning. A soldier quickly threw a gammon bomb beneath its wheels and blew it up. As soon as he had done so, however, a company of Panzer grenadiers appeared from behind the wrecked car and blocked the way to the river. There was a quick fight with machine-guns and grenades but when it was over only a few men managed to get past the German defences and make their way forward down a side street towards the bridge.

On the northern road the men of the 1st Battalion under Lieutenant Colonel David Dobie had also run up against determined resistance, from artillery units of the 9th SS Panzer Division fighting as infantry, as they advanced into Wolfheze. At first they had moved forward without encountering any serious opposition; and they had begun to feel that it was going to be an easy day for them. Although Brigadier Lathbury had originally decided to keep them in reserve until he saw how the situation developed, 'Intelligence sources on the dropping zones were', as he says, 'so optimistic that I released the battalion on the northern route very early.' Andrew Milbourne, a young soldier from Northumberland, thought it was just like 'on a scheme back in England'. He and the other men in his company heard the firing on the more southerly roads and felt themselves lucky that they had been given the task of occupying the high ground north of the town. Two of them stopped to talk to an old man puffing at his pipe and leaning on a pile of sleepers by the railway line.

They offered him a cigarette and some sweets which the old man accepted gravely and put into his pocket. They felt no sense of urgency or of danger as their battalion moved steadily forward into Wolfheze. And then at about half past four as they approached a crossroads just north of Wolfheze, Milbourne remembers,

> Suddenly the scene changed. Shells began to burst amongst us. Yells and whistles filled the air and machine-guns opened fire. I noticed before I hugged the ground that one of the enemy guns was about 200 yards in front and to our left flank. My officer asked if I had seen anything and, when I pointed this gun out to him, ordered my gun section into action. Grasping the tripod I ran across the road, diving headlong into a very convenient ditch. Cautiously I raised my head searching for a position for my gun. Before having completed my look round, no. 2 landed on top of me. 'You bloody awkward elephant', I began to curse, then stopped. A burst of fire was spraying the ditch . . . Finally I reached my position and slowly spreadeagled the tripod legs. Then, raising it slightly to the required height for a low-mounting, I clamped the legs tight. Shuffling round I yelled for no. 2. Slowly he approached and as he did so I ordered no. 3 to get near enough to supply us with ammunition. At last, after what seemed an age, no. 2 reached my side and mounted the gun.

As Milbourne opened fire 'R' Company moved into the woods beside the crossroads where several old German tanks and half-tracks were milling about in the gathering dusk. Already the fighting was confused; and by nightfall when the other companies of the battalion had moved into the woods, in a blinding downpour of rain, to engage the German tanks, it had become chaotic. A force of German infantry closed in on Dobie's men from behind and began bombing them with mortars, while more half-tracks rattled and screeched through the undergrowth in front. Contact between the various companies was lost, as Piat and mortar bombs, grenades and machine-gun bullets flew and rattled through the bewildering rain-filled air. 'Everywhere we turned or moved,' Milbourne said afterwards, 'we were swept with a withering fire. Dead lay all around, wounded were crying for water. Groans and shrieks of pain filled the air . . . Time and time again they overran our positions and had to be driven out with the bayonet. During this fighting my gun was never out of action.'

By dawn when most of the battalion had fought its way through the woods, past Johanna Hoeve to the northern out-skirts of Arnhem, its casualties were already pitifully heavy. Both 'S' and 'T' Companies had had nearly 30 casualties each and 'R' Company, many of whose men had been driven away from the rest and had stumbled into Oosterbeek, was down to half its strength.

Colonel Dobie could have no doubt now that the Germans held the high ground north of the town in considerable strength; and reconnaissance patrols confirmed his fear that to occupy it as ordered, he would need more support than he could possibly expect. Trying to make contact with the rest of the brigade, his signallers picked up a message from Colonel Frost who was in serious trouble by the bridge. Dobie's mind was made up for him. He need have no further thoughts about whether or not he would be justified in departing from his original orders. He decided he must go to the help of the 2nd Battalion at once. On the set that had picked up Frost, he tried unsuccessfully to reach Brigadier Lathbury to have his decision confirmed; but, getting no response, he gave orders for a change of direction on his own responsibility; the 1st Battalion would move south for Arnhem bridge as soon as it was light. Like Colonel Fitch's men of the 3rd Battalion, his own tried to get some rest before the advance began again at dawn. 'But I couldn't sleep,' one of his men said, 'I couldn't even close my eyes. My mate had been killed and I couldn't stop thinking about the blood coming out of his mouth.'

*

For Colonel Frost and his men at the bridge there could be no rest.

During the fight with the armoured car in the southern outskirts of Oosterbeek several German SS troops – 'boys of 19 and 20 and others of 40, arrogant and sullen' – were captured when the parachutists got round the back of the houses in an effort to out-flank the supporting infantry. On one of them was found the patrol route of an armoured car unit which showed Frost that he was already in danger of being pinned down.

He decided before it was too late to split his force up. 'C' Company, commanded by Major Victor Dover, was given the task of seizing the railway bridge, about three miles downstream from the main road bridge and about a mile south of Oosterbeek, and then of capturing a house in Arnhem occupied as a German headquarters. 'B' Company, under Major D.E. Crawley, was ordered to engage the enemy troops, which were blocking the chosen line of advance, by occupying the knoll of high ground known as Den Brink, half way between Oosterbeek and Arnhem; while Major Digby Tatham-Warter's 'A' Company, with Colonel Frost himself, was to make a dash across the open ground south of Den Brink towards the river on the south-western outskirts of Arnhem and then to rush through the town along the river front.

'C' Company left first for the railway bridge. As they approached it a machine-gun opened fire from the southern bank, 'but there was hardly a pause', says Colonel Frost, 'while they laid a smoke screen' and then some men of the leading platoon, under Lieutenant Peter Barry, began to walk quickly along the sleepers to its southern end. Suddenly an explosion of tremendous force shook the piers beneath their feet. One of the spans, said Corporal Roberts, 'seemed to curl back' in their faces as stones, pieces of iron and splinters of wood shot into the air and splashed into the fast flowing waters beneath them; and when the smoke had cleared away they saw that the 'southernmost span was lying half in and half out of the water'. They had arrived a few minutes too late.

Lieutenant Barry and two of his men were wounded; and 'C' Company, deprived of their first objective, pushed on towards their second – the Headquarters in Arnhem.

Meanwhile 'A' Company had come under heavy fire from an armoured car and machine-guns on Den Brink. But with 'B' Company covering his advance by engaging the enemy on the high ground to his left, Major Tatham-Warter was able to disentangle his men and continue his movement towards the bridge. Leaving 'B' Company to follow on when they could, Colonel Frost hurried on with his Headquarters Company after him. Just before eight o'clock they reached the eastern end of Weerdjestraat and saw through the dusk, almost within their reach now, the big steel girders of the long bridge. It appeared undamaged. And then, as they approached it, they saw that it was still in use; a convoy of lorries was moving south across it against the Americans at Nijmegen.

The men of 'A' Company moved cautiously closer through the dark streets. It was very quiet. They could hear the Dutch inhabitants of the houses by the water front, whispering at their windows and ahead of them the rumble of the lorries on the bridge and, far away, the distant roar of guns.

They crept stealthily forward, their helmets still incongruously covered with their camouflage of twigs and bracken, to occupy the tall buildings which commanded the northern end of the bridge. 'We would knock upon the door of a house', one of their officers said, 'and be instantly met by the earnest prayers of its inhabitants not to billet ourselves on them. Seeing our preparations for defence, they would then say most politely, "Surely you are not going to fortify this house?" To which I would reply, equally politely, "I'm afraid I am".'

The polite and earnest prayers turned to dismay when the British soldiers began to barricade the doors and windows with antique furniture, to tear down the curtains and knock out the windows. 'An old bird was horrified by what we did', a sergeant recalls. 'She began knocking me on the head with a walking-stick. I told her not to make such a fuss. We'd got to do it anyway. I don't think she knew what I was talking about. Anyway she went down to the cellar with a canary and two cats and I never saw her again.'

Through the doorways and windows, the soldiers could now see quite clearly the regular shape of the girders and the great sweep of the semi-circular steel span against the darkening sky. To their right, on the western side of the bridge, there was a row of wooden huts each about 20 feet in length and ten feet wide; and in front of the huts a concrete pill-box. They could see the single slit in its flat and featureless surface. Beyond the bridge they could just pick out the southern bank of the river and the few small houses beyond. Even now it was still strangely quiet.

Colonel Frost 'looked for a suitable building for battalion headquarters . . . We found a house', he wrote afterwards,

> a tall narrow type of house next door to a school on the corner overlooking the bridge and woke up the owner who spoke very good English. He was not at all happy at the prospect of billeting soldiers. The Germans, he said, had gone and he would much prefer us to advance on after them. When I convinced him that the Germans were still very much there and furthermore that we didn't merely want billets but proposed to fortify the house in readiness for a battle, he retired to the cellar quite horrified.

As the men of Frost's 'A' Company (and some engineers of Major D.C. Murray's 1st Parachute Squadron whom Lieutenant E.M. Mackay had brought through with great dash and determination after them) occupied the buildings around him, Major Gough arrived with part of the Reconnaissance Squadron. Gough had tried, with his few jeeps, to make a dash into Arnhem through Wolfheze along the route that the 1st Battalion had chosen; but he had driven into an ambush in the woods beyond the village and had lost several of his men before he managed to extricate the remainder. He had then tried to

Brigadier G.W. Lathbury

Brigadier J.W Hackett

Brigadier P.H.W. Hicks

Major-General R.E.
Urquhart outside his
headquarters

Major-General
S. Sosabowski

Field-Marshall Waelter Model

General Kurt Student

General Willi Bittrich

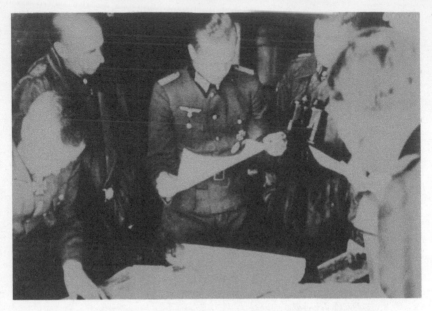

Field-Marshall Model, General Bittrich and Oberst Harmel
at a German Staff Conference

Paratroopers
jumping

Men and supplies parachute to earth

A landing zone

The main
dropping zone

Unloading a glider

Advancing into Arnhem

A Piat gun covering the Arnhem road

The first German prisoners

German troops taken prisoner in a Dutch house

contact Lathbury, but his wireless had failed and he had decided to go back to Divisional Headquarters.

'The General's been looking for you urgently', Colonel Mackenzie told him and sent him off to Brigadier Lathbury's headquarters, where the Brigade Major, Anthony Hibbert, told him that Lathbury and General Urquhart had followed the 3rd Battalion on its march towards Arnhem and had not been heard of since. Major Hibbert added that Urquhart had wanted Gough to get through to the bridge without delay.

Gough left immediately, having failed again to contact Divisional Headquarters to tell them where he was and what he was doing. When he arrived at the bridge, he occupied a building about 50 yards from it belonging to the Arnhem water-works. From the flat roof of this building he had an uninterrupted view of the bridge and could see between the girders right to the southern end. There were no signs of movement on the other bank.

Meanwhile from a window in the house on the corner of Marktstraat which he was using as his headquarters, Colonel Frost had seen a single figure in a uniform which did not seem to be a German one. He sent one of his men to find out if it were, perhaps, a member of the Dutch Resistance.

'Well?' Frost asked the soldier when he returned.

'Oh, he's not Resistance, sir,' the soldier said with refreshing unconcern, 'He says he's Panzer SS.'

It was true.

Less than half an hour before the bridge had been deserted. A Dutch policeman, Constable van Kuyk, who had been on duty there, says that its previous guardians were about 25 old soldiers most of whom had served in the First World War and all of whom had run away as soon as it seemed likely that they might be called upon to fight. But now the Panzer grenadiers from the 9th Division, whom Harzer had sent forward that afternoon, had come up to take over its defence. They had arrived too late to secure its northern end; but they made the capture of its southern end an extremely hazardous undertaking.

At about eight o'clock Frost was soon given evidence of this when Major Digby Tatham-Warter, two of whose platoons had taken up a forward position under the supports of the long ramp leading up to the bridge, decided to send a patrol across to the other bank.

Lieutenant McDermot with about 15 men ran up the embankment and on to the road and began to cross the bridge. They had not, however, taken many steps before the previously silent slit of the pill-box 'burst into flame', so Private Williams said, 'and a cascade of Spandau bullets went clattering down the road', whining as they ricocheted between the girder spars. A moment later an 'armoured car came rolling across the bridge from the far end and opened up too with its powerful turret gun' on the British positions.

Sometime later a second attempt to cross the bridge was made under Lieutenant J.H. Grayburn but this also was driven back by what Grayburn's Victoria Cross citation described as 'a hail of fire from two 20-mm quick-firing guns and from the machine-guns of an armoured car. Almost at once Lieutenant Grayburn was shot through the shoulder. Although there was no cover on the bridge, and in spite of his wound, he continued to press forward with the greatest dash and bravery until casualties became so heavy that he was obliged to withdraw.'

Encouraged by their success in beating back these initial British assaults, the Germans now launched an attack themselves from the southern end of the bridge. After a heavy mortar bombardment, and in the light of illuminating flares of various colours, the Panzer grenadiers ran forward from girder to girder covered by Spandau fire and the fire of the guns of an armoured car; but they, like Grayburn's men, were beaten back. The Germans then tried to rush the bridge in lorries but again the accurate fire of 'A' Company stopped them; the lorries caught fire and the Panzer grenadiers inside them surrendered. Once more the bridge, now brilliantly illuminated by the burning lorries, became a quiet no man's land.

Frost then decided to try and cross the river in some small boats he had noticed on his advance through the town by the dismantled pontoon bridge. He sent back an order to 'B' Company to undertake this task but it was still fighting on the ridge at Den Brink and could not be withdrawn. Frost next thought of 'C' Company which had made for the German headquarters in Arnhem but the officer who was sent to locate them could not get through the cordon of German troops surrounding them near the railway station. And so, Frost reluctantly concluded, another attempt would have to be made on the bridge itself by the small force of men there with him.

If the pill-box on the western side of the bridge could be put out of action, he thought, it might be possible to bring up an anti-tank gun to deal with the armoured car which had helped to push back the two previous assaults. Amongst the equipment which had got through to his force at the bridge was a flame-thrower, and Frost now decided to use this against the pill-box.

Two engineers crawled forward up the embankment and into a firing position beside the girders of the bridge. But just as the sapper operating the weapon was about to open fire on the slit in the pill-box, his companion made a remark which put him off his aim and the flame leaped round his target and splashed on to the wooden huts behind it.

There was a momentary pause as the burning liquid dripped through the cracks in the shed's roofs and walls and then an explosion of tremendous force shook the ground on both banks of the river. 'All hell seemed to be let loose after that', Colonel Frost says. 'Amid the noise of machine-gun fire, a succession of explosions, the crackling of burning ammunition and the thump of a cannon, came screams of agony and fear.' Splinters of wood and glass shot through the air in the suddenly brilliant light; and, in the huts themselves, dumps of ammunition exploded in a series of deafening roars as tracer bullets shot out towards the high steel arch of the bridge in a pyrotechnical display of wonderful brilliance. Soon the structure of the bridge itself was seen to be in flames.

'Now that's a fine thing to come all this way for!' said one of his men to Major Gough.

'It's only the paintwork', said Gough, doubting even as he spoke that he was right. But slowly, as the flames died down, the men could see that the main structure of the bridge was still undamaged.

For a moment, however, until reinforcements came, Colonel Frost decided that he should not make another attempt to cross it that night but that his men should 'snatch what rest they could before the battle which would certainly start in the morning'. He had about 500 men with him now: his own 'A' Company and Headquarters Company, two platoons of Major Crawley's 'B' Company which had managed to extricate itself from the fight on Den Brink, part of Major Gough's Reconnaissance Squadron, and four other parties that had slipped through to him – Major Hibbert with Brigade Headquarters and its defence platoon, another detachment of engineers, a platoon of the Royal Army Service Corps, and part of the 3rd Battalion's 'C' Company.

On reconnaissance in Arnhem that night General Willi Bittrich had been trying to make sense of the conflicting reports that came to him, but the situation was 'completely obscure' and he could not resolve it. And so, relying on the reports which two women operators (both of whom he subsequently decorated with the Iron Cross) promised to pass on to him from the garrison headquarters in the town, he returned to his headquarters at Doetinchem. An hour or two later he decided to visit *Obersturmbannführer* Harzer's command post, but there too 'it was impossible to obtain a clear picture of the situation'. All that was certain was that the north end of Arnhem bridge had been captured by the British and that nothing had yet been reported which led him to doubt that his original orders had been justified. After consultation with Harzer, therefore, he issued new orders to the divisions under his command confirming and extending his original instructions to them. The remaining units of the 10th SS Panzer Division which had not already left were directed to the ferry east of Arnhem and ordered to advance to the south of Nijmegen to 'reinforce and defend the bridgehead there' against the American parachutists and the 2nd British Army; while the 9th Division was ordered:

1. To break the resistance of the British forces at the Arnhem bridge and to recapture the northern end of the bridge.
2. To prevent the movement of reinforcements to the British forces at the bridge from the landing zones in the area west of Oosterbeek.
3. To reduce the enemy sector as soon as the additional troops and armour (which have been requested from Army Group B) arrive in the area and, having reduced the sector, to destroy the troops within it.

The troops and armour from Army Group B, which Bittrich had asked Model to send him, included infantry battalions experienced in house-to-house fighting, artillery and anti-aircraft units and, above all, Tiger tanks. By dawn on September 18th Model had acceded to all Bittrich's requests and orders had gone out, not only to the 191st Regiment of Artillery, two infantry battalions (Knaust and Bruhns) and *Panzerabteilung* 503, which was equipped with modern *Königstiger* tanks; but also to 1 *Brigade Flakartillerie*, several smaller units of the Field Police, *Landsturmbataillons, Heeresbataillons* and a *Pionier-Lehrbataillon* skilled in the use of flame-throwers. As the sun rose on Monday morning all these units had either left or were preparing to leave for Arnhem.

6

Monday

'A grossly untidy situation.'
Brigadier J.W. Hackett

At three o'clock in the morning of the second day at Arnhem General Urquhart was woken from his restless sleep on the sofa in the large house outside Oosterbeek. A few minutes later he and Brigadier Lathbury were accompanying the headquarters of Colonel Fitch's 3rd Battalion on its renewed march towards Arnhem.

Progress was frustratingly slow. 'Occasionally from in front', General Urquhart afterwards wrote, 'came the sound of sharp encounters, brief bursts of fire which brought the entire column to a stop.' He complained to Lathbury but neither of them could force the pace. 'We moved on to the main Heelsum–Arnhem road', a young officer remembered, giving evidence of this general caution, 'and began to move tactically to Oosterbeek and Arnhem. We got about one and a half miles under sniper fire but we couldn't get any further.'

Many of the men in the leading sections were very young and this was their first battle; most of the others had not been in action for more than a year. Only the least imaginative felt unafraid as they advanced at the head of their columns between the neat rows of silent watchful houses that lined the roads into the town. No one, who has had experience of street fighting and knows the feeling of naked insecurity and fearful apprehension which it evokes, can be surprised that the advance was slow. In the circumstances it was inevitable, Urquhart thinks, that the men 'would stop, sometimes unnecessarily, and pay too much attention to the odd bullet'.

'It was a slow job getting along', a soldier confessed. 'We were kept being told to lie low . . . There didn't seem much out in front. Anyway I was glad. I didn't like walking down them streets. You felt Jerry was very close and watching you all the time. I ain't no bloody hero. I just do what I'm told. Nice and easy, that's my motto.'

It was the same elsewhere. A major in the South Staffordshires said that the men 'were much more sensitive at this stage than later on. It took us roughly 13 hours to cover three miles.'

There were other delays too. At dawn, when the 3rd Battalion resumed its march, the Dutch people again came out of their gaily-coloured houses in hundreds to give the British soldiers their encouragement. When they came under fire, so an English officer said, they seemed quite oblivious to it. They were wearing orange arm-bands and favours as on the day before. Men wore orange ties, little girls wore orange sashes round their waists. They brought out jugs of coffee, glasses of *jenever*, bowls of fruit and flowers. Small boys marched importantly beside the English soldiers who patted them on the head and gave them bars of chocolate. Some troops were seen standing 'talking to an attractive blonde through the window'. Others stopped to acknowledge the solemn salutes of an old man in a blue cap whom Sergeant Ronald Gibson of the Glider Pilot Regiment had seen the day before pointing to a ragged hole in the front of his house – the result of an Allied bomb – and saying 'Nix. You here. We free.'

Soon the advancing companies were straggled out for hundreds of yards along the road and moving slower than ever.

On the outskirts of Arnhem the southern road joins the middle one near the Roman Catholic St Elizabeth Hospital, a massive, Gothic building looking down upon the river, and here the battalion was held up again. This time the opposition was much more formidable than before. Tanks and self-propelled guns shot at the advancing parachutists whenever they showed their heads and infantrymen sprayed the streets with machine-gun bullets from upper windows.

Major Waddy's company, which was still leading the advance, was soon cut off and when he reached the river by the Rijn-paviljoen restaurant and came under heavy fire, he decided to withdraw to the main body; but, before he could get his men out of their trap, they were strongly attacked and surrounded. Behind them the other companies of the battalion were also being fired at from the rear, for the whole of the battalion was now surrounded by pockets of German troops.

Tanks and self-propelled guns roamed the streets around them, machine-gunners in the houses watched their every movement. When they replied to the German fire in their rear, not only Spandaus fired back but Bren guns too, for the men were so confused and the units so split up in the maze of narrow streets and conglomeration of buildings in this part of the town, that it was no longer possible to tell friend from enemy or which houses contained British parachutists and which German infantry.

Captain John Rutherford, the Scottish medical officer of the 3rd Battalion and, so one of his men said, 'a cool customer if ever there was one', soon discovered this. The previous night in the large house where he had established his Regimental Aid Post he had looked through the telephone directory and made a call to the St Elizabeth Hospital to arrange for the accommodation of his wounded. On the Monday morning with Captain Phillips, the chaplain, he went over to the hospital where they were both immediately captured 'when the Germans suddenly walked in on them'. Robert Smith now took charge of the 3rd Battalion's medical section and 'there being', as he says, 'no other hospital to which the wounded could be evacuated I had to send them to the St Elizabeth in the care of medical orderlies. The Germans, to their credit, permitted the orderlies to return to us.'

The muddle was further increased when Colonel Dobie's 1st Battalion having, as decided the previous night, left at dawn in a south-easterly direction to try and break through to Colonel Frost at the bridge, arrived in the area of the railway station which is close to the St Elizabeth Hospital and there came under heavy fire from mortars and snipers concealed in the buildings around it. Major Anthony Deane-Drummond, who had come up from Divisional Headquarters to warn Lathbury's Brigade that there had had to be a change in frequency for the main Divisional Command wireless set, found the battalion 'preparing to attack with the aim of reaching the bridge through two miles of enemy held streets'. Hoping that he might be able to do something to improve wireless communications between Divisional Headquarters and the forward units, he attached himself to a company in the 1st Battalion which had been given the task of fighting its way through to Colonel Frost and the headquarters of Brigadier Lathbury's Brigade at the bridge. Soon after the company began its advance its commander was killed and Deane-Drummond took over. 'Street fighting is always a pretty bloody business,' he wrote later, 'and this was no exception . . . We were under constant small arms fire, and at one point the Germans were able to toss stick grenades in our midst . . . Eventually we arrived at a group of houses [almost level with the stretch of river where the pontoon bridge, now removed by the Germans, had once been] but only about 20 men were left out of the whole company.' They had no more than about five rounds of ammunition each and the rest of the battalion was still fighting around the hospital half a mile further back, where repeated attempts to break through to the bridge had been defeated with heavy losses by the fire of self-propelled guns, armoured cars and tanks. Snipers too, reported Major Perrin-Brown of 'C' Company, 'were extremely difficult to locate and inflicted heavy casualties on the battalion.' But by sending up his men on to the roofs of houses, Perrin-Brown was able to give them a chance of meeting these snipers on equal terms and soon they 'were being located and killed in increasing numbers and their bodies could be seen dangling from their ropes in the trees'.

In a three-storey house in the middle of this confusion, the divisional and brigade commanders were completely out of touch not only with their own headquarters but with everyone else's also. On the flat roof of an outhouse, a signaller unsuccessfully tried to make contact with surrounding units; while Brigadier Lathbury, behind a barricade of furniture, fired at any Germans who came into sight.

The streets below them had begun to fill with the debris of war. Several British and German bodies lay on the concrete and cobbles, three knocked-out tanks stood stationary and smoking in the Roemondsplein, flags flapped in the dusty sunlight as wounded were dragged to shelter. Dutch people came out into the streets and risked their lives to drag wounded men, both German and British into the safety of their houses. Occasionally they put their heads out of ground-floor windows to offer the parachutists a sandwich or an apple or a glass of water.

None of them had gone to work that morning. The men had all come out into the streets to discuss the battle and they were all, according to Mijnheer van der Horst 'in the best of spirits, convinced of the successful outcome of the struggle'. They had watched the old German soldiers getting out of the town the evening before and when they had seen the young SS troops coming to take their place and singing war songs as they marched, they had not been in the least disturbed.

'Well let them come, the bloody fools', that's what we thought [says Mijnheer van der Horst]. 'If they want to commit suicide, let them go ahead. What the hell they think they can do against these well-equipped British paratroopers . . . Look at all the airplanes the Allies got! No, these Germans on their stolen bicycles without any tyres can never keep such an army as the British from taking Arnhem . . . ' All of a sudden some kids are running up the street.

'There's a Tommy coming up the road!'

We all run to the corner of the street and there he comes. It's the first Tommy we see. He is dressed in a brown uniform and wears a maroon beret. But he is not alone. He is accompanied by a German soldier with a rifle in his hand . . . There is another cry, 'Some more paratroopers coming!' This time it is a group of about 20 paratroopers but all with their hands up in the air and with German soldiers. In front of them three Dutch civilians. They must have helped the British or hidden them in their homes. We think it is going to be worse for them than for the paratroopers. When they have passed we walk slowly home again . . . Things don't seem to go as they should.

And by mid-morning things had got much worse. By then the metallic rumble of tanks and self-propelled guns was a constant accompaniment to the rattle of small-arms fire, but the 1st and 2nd Anti-Tank Batteries had far too few guns to deal with the armour. Later on the 1st Airlanding Light Regiment's 75-mm howitzers were brought into action but they made poor anti-tank weapons owing to their low muzzle velocity and slow cross-axle traverse. Plastic grenades and gammon bombs were frequently lobbed out of windows but it was rarely that tanks were put out of action and all day long they continued to patrol the streets in a kind of contemptuous immunity. They were obsolete models for the most part, but in fighting ill-equipped infantry this is no great disadvantage. 'The Jerries seemed to have hundreds of tanks', a soldier says. 'You could hear them and see them everywhere. They had more mortars than we did too; and they knew how to fire them all right. Bombs were going off around us all the time.' One of them had just exploded in the yard behind Urquhart's house, when a British Bren gun carrier came rattling down the street and two men jumped out of it and ran up to the General. One of them was Lieutenant Leo Heaps, a Canadian; the other was Charles Labouchère, an extremely tall and excessively thin Dutch Resistance leader. Heaps saluted smartly and told

Urquhart that he had been ordered to try to find him and take back to Divisional Headquarters what information and orders he could. Urquhart was not able to give either. It was difficult enough to say what was happening around him; it was impossible to say what was happening at the bridge. The only request he could make was that Charles Mackenzie, his chief staff officer, should try to do all he could to get reinforcements and ammunition through to the men at the bridge before they were wiped out. Heaps and Labouchère jumped back into the Bren carrier and swinging it round drove out through a storm of fire.

Urquhart realised that he, too, must get out before the enemy closed in.

'We'll have to try and break out', he said to Lathbury. Lathbury agreed and asked him if he would like to throw a smoke bomb.

'Oh, no', said Urquhart. 'You're much better at it than I am.'

Lathbury threw a bomb and, screened by the smoke, the General and the Brigadier ran down the stairs and out of the back door. Major Waddy had already been killed by the blast of a mortar bomb as he ran across the lawn of the house next door in an attempt to find a way through to the bridge by the back streets behind the main road. Now Urquhart was nearly killed as well as he stepped over the garden fence and Lathbury's Sten gun went off in the smoke and a bullet flew into the ground by his foot.

'I'm awfully sorry,' Lathbury said, 'a temperamental weapon at best.' On the other side of the fence, where they seemed for the moment in safety, a Dutchman came out of his house and offered them a jug of *ersatz* coffee. Although it was 'bitter, foul-tasting stuff' they drank it all, before running on through the garden and over a high brick wall and then into a narrow arched passageway between tall houses. 'We ran through the passage-way', Urquhart afterwards remembered, 'where our studded boots made a tremendous echoing noise, and out into a narrow cobbled street.' They turned right in the street, back towards the St Elizabeth Hospital.

As the two men were running fast across the cobbles, Captain Cleminson of the 3rd Battalion, most of whose men had now been killed or captured, saw that they were running towards houses which were occupied by Germans. He shouted at them but they did not hear him. So followed by Captain W.A. Taylor, an Intelligence officer on Lathbury's staff, he ran after them to call them back.

As the four of them were racing down the street, a Spandau opened up on them from an alley to their left and Brigadier Lathbury was hit and paralysed by a bullet which struck his spine. The others managed to drag him out of fire and, pushing him into 136 Alexanderstraat, tumbled inside after him.

'You must leave me. It's no use staying. You'll only get cut off', Lathbury said, but although the others knew he was right, they felt reluctant to go.

'We must try and get some proper medical attention for him', Urquhart said and no sooner had he spoken than the face of a German soldier appeared at the window. Urquhart lifted his revolver, and pulled the trigger. The glass pane splintered and the German, shot in the mouth, fell to the cobbles outside.

The Dutchman, Mijnheer Verschoyn, who had pushed his wife to safety behind the kitchen door, now put his head round it and said that they would look after the wounded brigadier if the others wanted to escape.

Mumbling their thanks and wishing Lathbury good luck, they dashed out of the back door into a small garden. Similar squares of gardens stretched away to right and left behind the terraces of houses; and in front, behind the terraced houses of Zwarteweg, another line of bewildering gardens stretched out of sight. They made for these and rushed through the back door into the kitchen of number 14, Zwarteweg. Anton Derksen pointed to the stairs, warning them in voluble Dutch that the Germans were already coming down the street in front. But they had no need of the warning, for through the landing window they could see the Panzer grenadiers themselves. They climbed up into the attic and waited, pistols in hand, grenades ready primed.

After a few moments, Cleminson said, 'Funny nobody followed us up.'

Urquhart got out a bar of chocolate and a bag of sweets and squatted silently staring at Cleminson's enormous moustache. On such a slightly built man, he thought, 'it looked weird'. He could hear the sound of German voices in the street below. Minutes passed and he felt helpless and absurd hiding in an attic while his whole Division, undirected, fought a battle around him.

'It's time we tried to get out', he said.

'I don't think it's going to be that easy', Cleminson said. 'But we can take a look.'

Taylor climbed down the ladder into the bedroom below and looked out of the window. The crew of a self-propelled gun were immediately below, talking and smoking, two of them engaged on some minor repair to its engine. But even so General Urquhart felt that he must try to escape whatever the danger.

'There's no future in this', he whispered. 'We could lob a grenade down there and make a dash for it.'

It was, he confessed, a big risk but it seemed to him worth taking. The others, however, did not agree with him. They did not have his compelling reasons for wanting to get out, and he did not feel he could order them to do so. And so all three of them remained; and the afternoon wore on, and the sun set.

At Divisional Headquarters, now moved to a group of houses bordering the wood on the Heelsum–Arnhem road, Brigadier Hicks was in command.

His Airlanding Brigade had spent the previous day protecting the landing zones, but now that Lathbury's Parachute Brigade was in process of dissolution the time had obviously come to reinforce it. Lieutenant-Colonel Charles Mackenzie, the G.S.O. 1, had long been aware of this and after discussion with

Lieutenant-Colonel Robert Loder-Symonds, the Commander
R.A., he had decided to suggest to Brigadier Hicks that he ought
to take over command of the Division. General Urquhart had
said before the operation began that, in the unlikely event of
anything happening to both himself and Lathbury, Hicks should
assume control. He was older and more experienced than
Hackett and was an infantryman which Hackett was not. At
nine o'clock that morning Mackenzie had driven off in his jeep
to find Hicks. Charles Mackenzie was, in the words of a fellow
officer, 'a small and neat Scot, with a small and neat moustache
and a large and neat mind. Unhurried, precise and patient, with
a pleasantly dry sense of humour, he was the perfect staff officer.'
Hicks immediately took his advice, agreeing to take over the
Division and to order one of his battalions to abandon its duty of
protecting the landing zones and make for the bridge. Leaving
his second-in-command, Colonel Hilary Barlow, in command of
his brigade, Hicks returned with Mackenzie to Divisional Headquarters.

The situation he took over was an appalling one. There was
little definite news from any of the battalions under his command
and no news at all of Lathbury or of General Urquhart.

Units were repeatedly getting lost or running into ambushes.
A troop of the Reconnaissance Squadron, for instance, on patrol
in the woods to the north-west, suddenly found itself completely
surrounded by the enemy.

The troop commander got his section commanders together
[Sergeant F. Winder recorded], and decided that as we appeared
to be very much in the centre of the enemy our best course was to
make a run for it. We didn't know then just what sort of run it was
going to be. We were ordered to get our jeeps on the main road
and make a dash for it. 'If fired on, don't stop but keep going.'

The troop commander was in the leading jeep, I was in the
second and we had five other jeeps behind us. We started off
down the main road at about 50 miles an hour. We had about

four miles to get back. We went clear for about three quarters of a mile. All seemed quiet and then one of the men spotted about six of our chaps in the wood on the side of the road. These must have been prisoners of war because five or six seconds later we were under Jerry fire and machine-gun fire. We kept going. The drivers started swerving from side to side. The buggy in front of ours turned over into the road. We kept going.

When at last he reached his lines again Sergeant Winder turned round to see how many jeeps had got through. 'There was only one buggy behind us,' he says, 'and in that there was a man shot through the head.'

Colonel Fitch's 3rd Battalion, still fighting around the St Elizabeth Hospital, had also now become completely surrounded. Robert Smith of the battalion's medical section, describes the scene:

The C.O., realising that he was ambushed gave the order to get back to the pavilion – 'every man for himself'. I had turned and was following the C.O. and the adjutant, Captain Charlie Secombe ('Good Time Charlie'), when I was called by one of my corporals who had a badly wounded man in a German mortar-pit. Jumping in alongside them, I found the man's arm was shattered. So I put a tourniquet on it and gave him a morphine injection. Meanwhile the Colonel had been killed 10 to 15 yards beyond the pit and the adjutant wounded by machine-gun fire in both legs. For the next two and a half hours we were pinned down by fire.

Indeed, as Brigadier Hicks soon discovered, there were few units under his command which were not pinned down by fire.

Hicks's difficulties were greatly increased by the fact that there were still virtually no wireless links working satisfactorily.

Our communications back to the base in England [the second-in-command of the Divisional Signals says] were weak and erratic and being constantly interfered with by a strong German station. We had no communications direct to Corps HQ although messages could be sent via England. We had lost touch with 1st Parachute Brigade Headquarters when they were only five miles away from our HQ in spite of every effort on our part to improve the position of our Divisional HQ sets.

The main trouble was that the wireless equipment of the Division was designed for communications over limited distances, not much more in the case of all but the most powerful sets, than three miles. But Divisional Headquarters was eight miles from Arnhem bridge and more than 15 miles from Corps Headquarters which had been dropped at Nijmegen. Moreover the sandy soil, the tall trees and many buildings all combined to lower the range of the sets or in many instances to prevent them working altogether. The problems of communications had been envisaged before the operation began but then it had been rashly hoped that the Division would soon close up on Arnhem and that the initial difficulties would not be insuperable. Suggestions that heavy, high-powered sets capable of transmitting over long distances should be transported had been rejected because to carry these sets would have required a re-allocation of gliders. There was in any event no time to train men to use more powerful sets even if these had been available and, indeed, some operators in the hastily formed Corps Signals unit were not very expert with the ones they already had. 'Further training', it was afterwards officially decided, and 'improved wireless sets' were 'essential'. Apart from the need for more high-powered sets within the Division, the lack of sets capable of communicating satisfactorily with headquarters and bases outside the Division was also sorely felt. It was not only that there was constant interference by a German station and, on one frequency used, by a British station also, but two of the main sets were damaged on landing and never functioned at all.

The aerials of others were constantly being blown over by

blast and the BBC set, which had a 100-foot aerial and was used for many important military messages, was pin-pointed by German 'direction-finders' and was frequently compelled to close down during spells of heavy shelling. Several sets, including Urquhart's Rover set, were put out of action by mortar fire; and operators re-tuning sets in the open by night, or moving about to find positions in which they might work more successfully, were in perpetual danger of being killed by enemy snipers. Most disastrous of all, as the ground-air VHF sets were very heavy and would have needed extra gliders to carry them, the only means of signalling for close air support was by two 'Veeps' (jeeps fitted with VHF trans-receivers and crystal-controlled SCR 193) transmitting on a special communications network. These 'Veeps' were operated by American air support parties, hastily formed at the last moment and insufficiently trained. On landing it was found that neither of the two sets could be tuned to the lower of the two frequencies allotted to them and on the higher frequency no communication could be made. The disastrous consequence was that not until the last day of the operation, when the improvised methods of calling on the RAF with other sets and through different networks were working satisfactorily, was any effective close air support given to the airborne troops. This support, on the first day before the weather had broken, would have been, as General Urquhart said in his official report, 'invaluable. A "cab rank" on subsequent days might have turned the scale.' As it was, the signals failure made it impossible to call for close air support and led him to conclude in the most categoric of all his official comments: 'Signals need drastic revision and improvement. The sets are not satisfactory. The range attributed was always grossly exaggerated.'

The only link between the men at the bridge and the rest of the Division was through Major D.S. Mumford's Light Battery of 1st Airlanding Light Regiment which had established itself in a position by Oosterbeek Laag Church with a forward observation post at the top of Colonel Frost's headquarters overlooking the river. And all that Hicks could gather from the confusing reports which he received from his own officers and from the members of the Dutch Resistance, who had now taken over the local telephone exchange, was that units of the 2nd Battalion with other attached troops were still fighting hard at the bridge and that the 3rd Battalion and part of Colonel Dobie's 1st Battalion were still held up in the densely built-up area around the St Elizabeth Hospital where the Germans had now sited several 88-mm guns. There was some news also that other units of the 1st Battalion were engaged in fierce fighting on the northern outskirts of Arnhem in the suburb of Mariendaal where the enemy were securely entrenched in a large factory by the railway lines.

But nothing was definite. The irregular, faint and crackling messages picked up on the wireless sets had the vague quality of rumours; while the reports provided by the Dutch were scanty, sometimes contradictory and often discounted. Little use, in fact, was made of the Dutch underground at all and not 'nearly enough use', as General Urquhart now believes, of the Dutch telephone system 'at this time working perfectly adequately'. Dutchmen risked their lives to bring information through to the British troops but were received, as often as not, with wary suspicion. 'I was thrown to the ground twice by blast as I was running towards a British headquarters in Oosterbeek', says Paul De Jong. 'I can't remember exactly now what it was I wanted to tell them there. But I remember thinking it was very important at the time. When I got there an English officer wrote it all down on a bit of paper clipped to a map but he didn't seem to believe it.'

'We were told that there were quite a number of German sympathisers about,' an Intelligence officer says, 'and it was difficult to know whom you could trust. General Browning had decided the Dutch should not be told in advance about the landings for fear of a security leak and, as a matter of fact, we didn't even know the names of any reliable Dutchmen with one or two exceptions.' The most trustworthy informants, according to the official Intelligence Report, were consequently found to be 'the Roman Catholic priests, the doctors (especially hospital staffs) and the captured *Abwehr* and *Sicherheitspolizei* agents who seemed only too willing to implicate their associates'.

Despite the scarcity and contradiction of the reports which came to him, it seemed nevertheless clear enough to Hicks that Mackenzie was right and that one of the Airlanding Brigade's battalions should be sent to the bridge. He chose the 2nd South Staffordshires whose 'B' and 'D' Companies had landed with the first lift and he sent them off under Lieutenant-Colonel W.D.H. McCardie. No sooner had they left, however, than Hicks received the news that, in spite of the hopeful weather forecast that had been issued before the operation began, low fog was drifting over the airfields in England and the second lift would not arrive on time. Perhaps, now, when they did arrive the reduced numbers of British troops protecting the landing zones would have been driven off them. This fear prevented him from sending any further reinforcements towards the bridge and, although he has been frequently criticised for not doing so, it is difficult to believe that he was wrong.

By this time the captured plans of OPERATION MARKET GARDEN had, of course, been passed to the *Luftwaffe* who knew when the second lift was due. General Bittrich had asked one of the Channel fortresses, which had been by-passed by the Allied advance, to confirm the time of its passing overhead. Because of the fog in England, he did not get the message when he expected it; but, when he did receive it, he was ready.

Reserves of SS troops were sent towards the landing zones, and anti-aircraft guns, already in use against the parachutists fighting in the town, were taken out of their firing positions and moved westwards. Panzer units in action were withdrawn to deal with the new landings, a squadron of Messerschmitts was sent to strafe the zones and disperse the teams marking the area with their nylon tapes.

The absence of the two companies of the South Staffordshires, which Hicks had sent towards the bridge, was now sorely felt. The whole duty of protection fell on the 7th Battalion of the King's Own Scottish Borderers under Lieutenant-Colonel Robert Payton-Reid and the 1st Battalion of the Border Regiment commanded (in the absence of Lieutenant-Colonel Tommy Hadden whose glider had failed to arrive) by Major H.S. Cousens.

Consequently when units of the *Fallschirmersatzbrigade 'Hermann Goering'* of Colonel Lippert's *SS-Unteroffizierschule* and a reserve police battalion from Ede, as well as Colonel Helle's Dutch SS, tried to penetrate the landing zone's defences, many men got through. Colonel Payton-Reid, whose battalion was taking care of the north-westerly zones over a large expanse of rough land covered with gorse and heather known as Groote Heide, led a determined bayonet charge to drive off several isolated pockets of resistance; but he was only partially successful. Some Germans ran away beyond the marked limits of the zone, but others managed to conceal themselves in drainage ditches and in patches of wood and scrub from where they would be able to open fire when the gliders and transports appeared in the sky.

In the early afternoon the distant hum was heard. Then as the specks in the pale sunlight grew larger, the hum increased to a roar and the air was filled with aircraft. In one of them, a paratrooper says, the men

smoked a bit and some of them sang songs, though some of us wished they wouldn't, because we felt they did it to show they weren't feeling scared . . . Suddenly we saw a couple of planes behind us go down and somebody said, 'There go some poor buggers!' There wasn't so much singing after that . . . Then we heard steel hitting the bottom of the plane but thank God nothing came through . . . My forehead was sweating like anything and my hands were wet through with sweat so I had to mop up with my smock . . . It seemed to take a bloody long time to get to the dropping zone and when the order 'Hook up!' was given we were glad to have something to do. It wasn't long before we got 'Two minutes to go' and we were all ready for it. There was a roar of engines as I jumped and as they died away I could hear the automatic fire from below as I went down . . . Where's this blue smoke we heard so much about? Well I couldn't find any blue smoke and the other chaps couldn't either. So we joined the biggest mob going, and I recognised several blokes from the battalion we were with, so it seemed the best thing to do. We dug in. It all seemed a bit of a shambles. There weren't any lights. There wasn't any smoke . . . One of our lads got wounded in the head, and I was surprised not to feel sick when the blood gushed out of his mouth. We tried to do something for him but he just gave a shudder and went limp, so we took all his grenades and ammunition and left him in a hollow.

Around him the anti-aircraft guns were still firing furiously and machine-gunners and snipers in the woods and ditches were firing too, and many men were hit as they floated to the ground. Several Dakotas were struck by air bursts and exploded into flames. One of them was seen gradually to lose height as the flames licked round its port wing. All 16 of the parachutists managed to jump, although the last one's parachute had scarcely opened out before he hit the ground. The crew stayed in the plane until it crashed into the earth.

And now the wind, which earlier on that day had been little more than a breath, grew stronger and many parachutists were blown away from the dropping zones and into the trees. Some gliders, too, hit the trees and their canvas sides were ripped open on the branches. Soon the dry heather and gorse caught fire and the flames, spread fast by the wind, gave to the scene an added illusion of disaster.

Most of the glider pilots unloaded their cargos with an almost frantic anxiety which made them fumble clumsily as they pulled at the heavy bolts inside the tail. One of them congratulating himself on having got the tail of his glider off and on having unloaded and driven away in his jeep in 20 minutes, looked around and saw 'everywhere groups of men cursing, sweating, and heaving to get the tails off their gliders. Some were even using saws and axes.'

Brigadier Hackett was one of the first to land. He came down close to the place he had picked out on the air photographs as being a suitable one to establish his headquarters. But before making for it, he was determined to find his walking stick which he had dropped during his fall. He felt uncomfortable without it and poked about in the heather, so angry with himself for having lost it that when he stumbled on 10 German soldiers who seemed willing to surrender, he called to them crossly in German, 'Wait here! I'll attend to you presently,' and then continued his search.

At length he found his stick and marching his prisoners in front of him he left for his headquarters. He was still in an impatient mood when he arrived there; and the news that he was soon given worsened it.

Colonel Mackenzie who knew that Hackett's temperament was never mild at the best of times had been apprehensive at the thought of telling him that Hicks had taken over command of the Division. With scarcely a word of preliminary greeting, Mackenzie gave him the information as soon as he arrived at Brigade Headquarters. The protest came as Mackenzie had feared it would.

'Well, there it is', said Mackenzie anxious not to begin a profitless discussion. 'You will only upset the works if you try to do anything about it!'

He then told Hackett that Hicks had decided to take one of his battalions, the 11th Parachute Battalion, away from him and send it in support of the South Staffordshires who had run into strong opposition on their way to reinforce the heavily pressed troops at the bridge. The rest of the South Staffordshires had

arrived with the second lift and had set off to join the two
companies under Colonel McCardie which had left earlier. But
these reinforcements would not be enough; the 11th Battalion
would have to go too.

Hackett's annoyance turned to anger. He was intensely proud
of the brigade which he himself had formed and which he had
devotedly trained to fight as a co-ordinated unit. Indeed his
devotion to it had, many of his fellow officers thought, blinded
him to its faults. It was not merely independent, they considered,
some units in it came close to being undisciplined. Until Hackett
was able to exercise his great gifts upon it in action, this criticism
of its conduct was not apparently unfounded although his loyalty
to it would never let him admit it.

He strongly objected to being told how to dispose his troops,
he said. While he agreed that, if any of his battalions was to be
sent to the bridge the 11th should be sent as it was nearer, he
did not like to be told that one of his battalions had 'already
been nominated'. Eventually he gave in, but with an ill-grace,
insisting that Colonel Payton-Reid's battalion of the KOSB
should be given to him in place of the battalion he had lost.
Mackenzie agreed to this, although to send a whole brigade
under Hackett to fulfil its original task was no longer a satisfactory answer to the dangers that had arisen since the plan was
conceived.

Hackett, himself, had not been in the area long enough to
realise this. But his alert brain soon quickly understood that the
Division was not being managed as it should be and that that
being so the movement of his own brigade would be futile. By
early evening when neither the 11th Battalion nor the South
Staffordshires had managed to get through the defensive area
round the St Elizabeth Hospital, and both of them were only
intermittently linked with the 1st and 3rd Battalions who had
been fighting in Arnhem all day, he had made up his mind to try
and reorganise 'a grossly untidy situation'. He left his brigade
under command of his deputy and drove quickly to Divisional

Headquarters now established in the Park Hotel at Hartenstein. The atmosphere of calm and almost – it seemed to him – of indifference he found on arrival there increased his growing anger. He was well aware of Hicks's personal qualities, but he did not trouble to disguise the fact that he considered that he was now well out of his depth. Although Hicks was a good deal older than he was, Hackett was the senior as brigadier and consequently felt justified in taking a strong line. He felt an understandable resentment that he had not been told beforehand of Urquhart's decision to have Hicks put in command over his head. Urquhart had a bias against cavalry officers and had once referred to Hackett in public as 'a broken-down cavalryman'. The epithet had, of course, been applied without malice but Hackett might have recognised beneath the jibe a latent prejudice.

What orders, he demanded of Hicks, had been given to his 11th Battalion and who was in overall command in its sector? The battalions were fighting individually, Hicks replied. This, Hackett considered, was 'clearly unsatisfactory'.

It wasn't ideal, conceded Hicks, but, as no one knew where Lathbury was and as most of his brigade headquarters were at the bridge, he thought it best that each battalion should try and fight through to Frost on its own. 'It would be absurd', he said, 'not to help the 2nd Battalion in whatever way we can.' Hackett agreed impatiently, but didn't think that the Division was being handled with 'enough drive and cohesion'.

'Well,' said Hicks, 'you can help Frost by driving into Arnhem from the north-west instead of merely occupying the high ground.'

'No,' objected Hackett, 'I think we should first take the high ground east of Johanna Hoeve. I will then see what I can undertake to assist the operations in Arnhem; and I want a series of times so I can relate my actions to everyone else's.'

At that moment Lieutenant-Colonel Henry Preston, the principal administrative officer, came into the room and Hicks said to him, 'Brigadier Hackett thinks he ought to be in command of the Division.'*

Colonel Preston seeing the two angry faces left the room hurriedly and told the duty officer to go upstairs and get Colonel Mackenzie.

'Come down quickly', the duty officer said to Mackenzie. 'The brigadiers are having a flaming row.'

When Mackenzie arrived, Hackett was somewhat calmer. Hicks had allowed him to draw on the map the sort of objectives, boundary lines, centre lines and operational phases that gave some promise of restoring order to a situation with which Divisional Headquarters had been unable to deal. He returned to his brigade having settled that he would move in the morning to occupy the high ground at Koepel and having done as much as he could to create a framework of divisional co-ordination within which his brigade could effectively operate.

As the brigadiers argued how best to help him, Colonel Frost maintained his fight at the bridge.

Earlier that morning several lorries packed with Panzer grenadiers had driven slowly into the area which his troops were occupying. His men held their fire. They could see 'the hesitant look on the faces' of the Germans and knew that they were apprehensive and afraid. Suddenly a British machine-gun opened fire, then another. The Germans leapt from their lorries, firing wildly at the flat walls of the houses. Most of them were

* 'It surprised me very much', General Hackett has since told me, 'to hear "Pip" Hicks say, "Brigadier Hackett thinks he ought to be commanding the Division". I did not really think that at all. What I was trying to do was to get my brigade, which had already had quite a rough time that day, properly applied in the battle on the next . . . I only wanted a tidy job for it to do. What I was told to do was very far from that. It lacked the essential elements of a workmanlike plan and the orders were very confused . . . I had no objection to taking orders from "Pip" if they made sense. But these did not. I was, therefore, inclined to assert my position as senior brigadier of the two and issue the sort of orders for my brigade's operation which did make sense.'

killed; the rest were captured, swelling the number of prisoners in the cellars to well over 100.

Undeterred by this set-back the enemy prepared to assault again. From the tall houses of the northern bank the British soldiers could see right across the bridge to the far side. There seemed little movement there. It was a clear day and rather quiet now.

'Armoured cars are coming across!' The loud, abrupt shout of a signaller sent Colonel Frost leaping up the stairs to the attic. He wondered for a moment 'if this was the vanguard of XXX Corps. From the general air of optimism in high circles which flourished in the planning days this might well be the case. But we were not left long in doubt. The vehicles were obviously German.'

There were 16 in all, mostly armoured cars with a few half tracks, and they came over steadily as if their drivers were conscious that this time they would get through. The leading vehicle passed the still smouldering wreckage of the night before and reached the middle of the bridge. For a moment it waited there while the ones behind closed up towards it. A necklace of mines had been laid during the night by the British sappers who watched and waited for the armoured cars to ride over them. The convoy came on again and the mines did not explode. 'We just sat there waiting', a soldier remembers. 'I had my Piat aimed smack at the leading car. My fingers were trembling. I could see the anti-tank gunners down below and I said to my mate, "We'll let them buggers fire first".'

The convoy gathered speed until the leading vehicles were over the river and travelling fast along the raised approaches to the British position. Suddenly from slit trenches on the embankment, from windows and doorways beyond, from the valley guttering between the gabled roofs, machine-gun bullets, shells from the six-pounders, Piat bombs, the fragments of Hawkins grenades and even mortar bombs tore into the convoy and into the infantry advancing towards the British position from the

landward side. 'All round now the battle raged', says Colonel
Frost. 'There were no exemptions from the firing line, all ranks
and trades were in it – staff officers, signallers, batmen, drivers
and clerks – and amid the din of continuous fire and the crash of
falling and burning buildings even laughter could be heard.'

Opposite Frost's headquarters on the other side of the bridge
approaches, Lieutenant Mackay had established his engineers in
the big van Limburg Stirumschool after heavy fighting the night
before. This school was one of four buildings which were
situated, one behind the other, on the eastern side of the ramp
which led up to the bridge. From its upper windows it commanded both the bridge and the road which ran parallel with the
river in front of it. Its first-floor windows were on a level with the
ramp and less than 12 feet away from it; and during a lull in
the fighting Lieutenant Mackay standing beside one of these
windows, heard a clanking just below him:

> On looking out I saw a half-track. It was about five feet away and
> I looked straight into its commander's face. I don't know who was
> the more surprised. It must have climbed down the side of the
> ramp and was moving down a little path, nine feet wide, between
> it and the school. His reaction was quicker than mine; for with a
> dirty big grin he loosed off three shots with his Luger. The only
> shot that hit me smashed my binoculars which were hanging
> round my neck. The boys immediately rallied round and he and
> his men were all dead meat in a few seconds. The half-track
> crashed into the northern wing of the school.

In all six vehicles were blasted off the ramp that morning,
several others burst into flames; three or four got past the school
but were stopped by sharp bursts from Bren-guns fired at a range
of 20 yards from the upper storeys. It was, said Frost, 'the most
lovely action you ever saw – there they were these awful Boches
with their pot helmets sticking out. When we had dealt with them
they smoked and burned in front of us to the end of the battle.'

It was a heartening victory; but there was no rest. As if in punishment for the destruction of their valuable armour, the Germans increased their mortar fire, which had been intermittent all day, to a furious pitch. Artillery shells, too, came whistling across the river and tore holes in the streets and shattered the roofs of the closely built houses. 20-mm and 40-mm guns fired constantly at the riverside buildings many of which were of wood and were soon burning fiercely. The screams of the wounded grew more intense and pitiful, and through the smoke men shouted constantly for stretcher bearers.

Frost could make no adequate reply to the enemy artillery. The only guns at his disposal were those of the 3rd Light Battery at Oosterbeek which Major Mumford was directing from his attic and the ammunition for these, as for the mortars and the three anti-tank guns in his own sector, was severely limited. He decided that he must preserve the little ammunition he had for breaking up the infantry attacks which, since the armoured assaults had failed, were now launched with an increased vigour.

The first of these attacks came from across the bridge and was driven back by concentrated fire from Mumford's guns and well aimed mortars; but a second attack, made along the river bank, was more successful. It was made in the early afternoon and was one of several which were later to be made from that same direction. In savage house-to-house fighting, with grenades, bayonets and Stens, several parachutists were killed and many more were badly wounded before the enemy were driven out of the area which Frost's men had learned to call 'ours'. The prisoners taken – surly, healthy and contemptuous, a great deal more formidable than the prisoners so far taken elsewhere – were well-trained SS Panzer grenadiers and their captors knew that units which contained men like these would be bound to strike again.

As after the armoured assaults, so now, the enemy gunners opened up in a tremendous cannonade following each infantry attack. 20-mm, 40-mm and 88-mm guns once again joined the

mortars and self-propelled guns in a bombardment of devastat-
ing effect, adding a new danger to the perils of blast and flying
fragments. For the wind that had spread the fire across the
heather-covered expanse of the landing zones, now fanned the
flames that the exploding shells and incendiary bombs started in
the riverside buildings. Before darkness had fallen four houses
were burning fiercely and the flames were crackling out towards
their neighbours. The defenders were forced to leave to find new
positions and as they came out into the smoke-filled streets many
of them were killed or wounded by the blast of bombs and the
snipers' whining bullets that flew from house to house and
ricocheted between the walls in the drifting shadows.

Encouraged by the holocaust the Germans attacked again and
occupied a group of buildings at the western end of Weerdjestraat until in the light of the leaping flames and through the
swirling smoke, the parachutists charged once more with the
bayonet and threw them back.

The cellars below Battalion Headquarters were crowded to
the walls with the wounded now. The two doctors there, James
Logan and D. Wright, worked constantly and tirelessly, their
forearms covered with blood; and only they and Father Egan,
the padre, knew how dangerously low the drugs were running.

But hope was not yet gone. Relief was surely bound to come
soon. In the morning, perhaps, the 2nd Army would come
rolling up the road from Nijmegen; and sooner than that other
units of their own Division would break through the ring around
them. Already during the late afternoon some more men of the
3rd Battalion had managed to find a gap in the German lines by
the railway line and soon others would be sure to follow them.

There was good reason at least to hope so. Colonel Frost had
managed to make contact again with Colonel Dobie who
assured him the 1st Battalion would do all they could to force
their way through to him; his signallers had also picked up a
message from the leading elements of XXX Corps whose signals
were so strong that Frost felt sure relief would come before very

long; and then at eight o'clock he made contact with Divisional
Headquarters and was told that the second lift had landed and
that the South Staffordshires and the 11th Battalion had left for
the bridge some hours before.

Frost felt immensely encouraged. An attempt by two platoons
of Major Crawley's company to open up a path for the other
battalions to get through to the bridge by an attack on the
Germans barring the roads between them, had been defeated by
the heavy fire of German tanks and self-propelled guns, but Frost
still felt confident that a determined assault by the rest of the
Division would force a way through to him and that the leading
troops of XXX Corps would soon reach the river from the south.
His men had survived a night and a whole day against seemingly
overwhelming odds and could hold out, he knew, till morning.
Every attempt that had been made by German infantry to cross
the bridge that day had failed. 'At each endeavour, sometimes
with small numbers and sometimes with large,' he wrote with
justifiable pride in his journal, 'our mortars, artillery and
machine-guns hit them hard and accurately.'

Twenty miles to the south, the bridge over the Maas at Grave
was already in Allied hands. Here American paratroopers of the
82nd Airborne Division had landed astride the bridge and had
captured it within an hour. Six hours later other units of this
Division had advanced far to the east across the Maas-Waal
Canal towards the edges of the Reichswald. The enemy opposition had been rapidly overcome. When he turned north for the
Waal bridge at Nijmegen, however, General Gavin came up
against strong opposition and his men were temporarily checked.

Meanwhile, still further south, the 101st US Airborne Division
had captured all the bridges across the Zuid Wilhemsvaart Canal
at Veghel and although the bridge across the Wilhelmina Canal
at Zon was blown up before they could reach it, one regiment
managed to cross the canal during the night and by the early
morning of September 18th it was in the outskirts of Eindhoven.

Behind the men of this regiment, sappers were repairing the bridge at Zon; in front of them the tanks of the Irish Guards, having blasted their way up the narrow road from the bridge-head across the Meuse-Escaut Canal at the head of General Horrocks's XXX Corps, were rolling north from Valkensvaard. Before nightfall the Americans and British were shaking hands in Eindhoven and the narrow corridor north to Arnhem was open as far as Nijmegen.

7

Tuesday

'As we prepared for yet another night, Arnhem was burning.'

Lieutenant-Colonel J.D. Frost

Knowing nothing of these successes south of the Neder Rijn and nothing even of his own Division, General Urquhart was too conscious of the danger and absurdity of his predicament to take advantage of it and go to sleep. Occasionally he dozed fitfully, only to wake and to worry, to look out of the window to see if the self-propelled gun and its crew had yet moved. But each time he looked they were there; and then at about seven o'clock in the morning he woke from a restless, uncomfortable sleep with a pain in his chest from the grenades in his smock pockets on which he had been lying, and heard shouts from beneath the window and the 'wheeze of the engine of the self-propelled gun and the rattle of its tracks'. A moment later Anton Derksen came up the stairs to the bedroom to say that the English were coming up the street.

Urquhart and his two young companions rushed out of the house to meet them. They were scattered units of the South Staffordshires and the 11th Parachute Battalion making that confused and uncoordinated advance into the town that Brigadier Hackett had so strongly deplored and which, in fact, had led them to fight each other in the dark. Afterwards, regretting that he had not stayed with them long enough to bring a unified control to bear on their movements, General Urquhart took over one of their jeeps and drove as fast as he could for Oosterbeek.

At the Park Hotel, Colonel Mackenzie greeted him somewhat reproachfully.

'We had assumed, sir,' he said, 'that you had gone for good.'

Brigadier Hicks came up and handed back the command of the Division thankfully, and Urquhart listened to his account of the existing situation in growing consternation. There were parties from four battalions apparently – the 1st and 3rd Parachute Battalions, the South Staffordshires and the 11th Parachute Battalion – all trying to advance into the town on their own. Most of the 2nd Parachute Battalion, with various men from other units, still fought alone and unsupported at the bridge. Three other battalions under Hackett – the KOSB, the 10th and 156th Parachute Battalions – were somewhere to the north and might or might not be entering the town. Hundreds of glider pilots had attached themselves to the infantry battalions, while others, from units which had not organised them as well as the 1st Airlanding Light Regiment had, 'were wandering about all over the place without anyone telling them what to do'. The ninth battalion in the Division – the 1st Battalion of the Border Regiment – was the only one left in the immediate area. It was, as Brigadier Hackett had said, 'a grossly untidy situation'. Obviously the most urgent necessity was for the co-ordination of the different attacks in the town.

'Someone will have to get down into the town right away', Urquhart said. 'It will have to be a senior officer.'

Brigadier Hicks's able second-in-command, Colonel Hilary Barlow, was chosen for this duty and left immediately with a wireless set in the back of his jeep. He drove down the road and out of sight and Divisional Headquarters waited for his report. It never came. He never got to the town. Somewhere between the Park Hotel and the fighting in Arnhem he was killed. His body was never found. It was the first of that morning's many tragedies.

The second tragedy was a more fateful one. Now that the operation's progress had been so slow, neither the zones previously arranged for dropping supplies nor, as it was supposed, that allocated for the Polish Brigade due to arrive that morning were any longer practicable ones. Signals were sent informing the RAF that the Supply Dropping Point 'V' north of Warnsborn was not in Allied hands and that the landing area for the Poles would have to be changed as it was inside a strongly-held German sector. These messages did not reach London.

The messages which reached Divisional Headquarters, however, were uniformly discouraging. XXX Corps had only just reached Grave and was already more than 24 hours behind schedule; the enemy were concentrating large forces in the woods to the north; and passing down through these infantry concentrations from the direction of Apeldoorn was a stream of enemy tanks. The day before a Dutch liaison officer, Lieutenant-Commander Wolters, who had arranged with the Dutch operators of the Arnhem telephone exchange that all conversations between German commanders should be tapped, reported that 60 tanks were on their way into Arnhem from the north. Colonel Mackenzie had been sceptical at first but it seemed now that Wolters's information was correct. To make an already bad situation worse, a message came through from Colonel Frost at the bridge that ammunition was now so low that snipers had had to be told to hold their fire until the next large-scale attack. German machine-gunners had consequently been able to establish themselves in commanding positions on the northern bank and were making it almost impossible to move about in the British-held area. The night had been quieter than the men had expected and most of them had been able to get their first few hours of sleep since the landing, but they had woken to the smell of smoke and death and to the growing sounds of battle.

Finally, the news that Urquhart received from the battalions in the western outskirts of Arnhem was totally depressing.

At eight o'clock the previous night the commanding officers of

the 11th Battalion and the South Staffordshires, Lieutenant-
Colonel G.H. Lea and Lieutenant-Colonel W.D.H. McCardie,
had held a conference with Colonel Dobie of the 1st Battalion
near the St Elizabeth Hospital. They decided that they would
make a concerted effort to get through to Frost at the bridge at
four o'clock the following morning. The 1st and 11th Battalion
would try to get through along the river bank, the South
Staffordshires by the main road where part of the 3rd Battalion's
'C' Company had managed to penetrate the German defences
on Sunday evening.

The two advances began as planned on Tuesday morning; but
neither was successful. The South Staffordshires lost many men
in fierce street fighting before being overrun by tanks in the main
street and were forced to withdraw into the outskirts. They then
delivered an attack on Den Brink in an effort to help the advance
of the 11th Battalion which had already been forced to a
halt. Two companies of the South Staffordshires succeeded in
reaching the ridge but they were driven off by the fire of tanks
which kept out of the range of Piats while they knocked down the
houses in which the parachutists sought cover or burned them
down with phosphorus shells. 'We did all we could to get
through', a corporal said. 'But it just wasn't bloody well possible.
An anti-tank gun or two would have made all the difference.'

The 1st Battalion's attack was no more successful than that of
the South Staffordshires. Following the route towards the river
bank that Anthony Deane-Drummond had taken the day
before, they were soon involved in hand-to-hand fighting with
German infantry in the houses near the dismantled pontoon
bridge. Major Perrin-Brown's 'T' Company and Major
Timothy's 'R' Company made heroic bayonet charges and
managed to make some headway against fierce resistance. But
at six o'clock when his battalion had been reduced to less than 40
men, and tanks had begun to open fire at point-blank range,
Colonel Dobie ordered the survivors to take cover in the houses
nearby. As they approached them, German helmets appeared at

the windows and grenades exploded all round them. Eventually Colonel Dobie found shelter in a cellar full of Dutch people. Only two of the men with him were not wounded.

Having sent Colonel Barlow to integrate the town attacks, Urquhart decided to see for himself what could be done with Brigadier Hackett, whose three battalions were in danger of becoming involved in a separate fight north of the town and of being defeated there by German units coming down the Apeldoorn road in rapidly increasing numbers. And it was not only in this sector that the defenders of the town were being strengthened; for now several of the reinforcements which Bittrich had asked for the previous night were coming into the area and being thrown into the battle. All night long assorted and fragmentary units on their way back to Germany had been receiving orders to return to Arnhem from as far east as Koesfeld. And although in response to an order broadcast by the Dutch Government in London, over 30,000 Dutch railway-men had bravely come out on strike and gone into hiding on Sunday evening, this did not unduly affect the speed with which the Germans brought reinforcements into the area.* One of these reinforcements, typical of many, an *Ausbildungs-und-Ersatzbataillon*, comprising recruits of varying ages between 17 and 50 with from four to eight weeks' training, had been recalled from Bochold. It was commanded by Major Knaust who had an artificial leg and hobbled to the front on crutches. Several other officers in the battalion had only one leg or one arm and many of their men were not merely unfit but actually ill. Some of the men were hesitant and frightened and, as many English soldiers had

---

* Eventually this gallant railway strike caused as much suffering to the Dutch people as damage to the enemy, for the Germans as a reprisal stopped all food transports. Thousands of Dutch people died of starvation that winter. Moreover, the Dutch Resistance already fully occupied with helping British prisoners and Dutch victims of Nazi oppression, now had the families of the Dutch railwaymen to care for as well.

noticed by now, talked in unnecessarily loud voices and shouted often as if to keep their spirits up; and once an English soldier saw one of their officers throw his hat on the ground and stamp on it in furious desperation when his men began to argue about who should perform some dangerous mission. But most of them fought well, and a few of them fought with that kind of fanatical determination which characterises the German soldier at his most dangerous, and all of them were encouraged by Field-Marshal Model's promise that they would very soon be reinforced by heavy tanks from the *Königstiger-Abteilung* 503 which had been ordered up from Königsbrück near Dresden.

Urquhart found Hackett's Brigade fully committed and held down on a straggling line between Johanna Hoeve and Lichtenbeek. Colonel Payton-Reid's KOSB were around the farmhouse at Johanna Hoeve to which they had been driven back during the night by heavy Spandau fire around Koepel; the 10th Battalion was preparing to advance to a road junction north of Lichtenbeek; while Hackett with the 156th Battalion was preparing to attack Lichtenbeek itself.

Leaving his jeep on the south side of the railway line, Urquhart walked on to the line and down the grass-covered bank to Hackett's Headquarters which he discovered at the edge of a wood beyond. As he slipped down the steep bank, three Messerschmitts swooped from the sky and forced him to throw himself to the ground. A stream of bullets thudded into the turf but did not touch him.

'I'm delighted to see you're out of it, sir,' Hackett said with polite formality as they both got to their feet. 'As you see, we're pinned down right along the line.' They had made several efforts to get forward, Hackett said, but each time they had been forced back. They were supported by the 1st and 2nd Light Batteries of 1st Airlanding Light Regiment which were firing with great skill, but without heavier support the brigade could not get forward.

Urquhart had already feared that this must be so; but with no more certain information than he had yet been able to obtain from other units of his division he was not yet at all sure what he should do. To order Hackett to force his way forward would certainly be costly and might be destructive; to change completely the line of advance and throw Hackett's brigade in support of the battalions in the town, might mean them becoming involved in an even more costly and obviously more congested fight. He decided that it would probably be best to withdraw the brigade from its present positions and give it a new line of advance along the middle road. Briefly he discussed his plan with Hackett but told him not to carry it out until he had been able to get the whole divisional picture into perspective.

Soon after Urquhart had left to return to his headquarters, however, the position violently altered and made it imperative for Hackett to withdraw immediately.

Behind his brigade, the Border Regiment was attacked by a strong German force, under command of Colonel Lippert, which threatened to cut it off from the rest of the Division and push through to Wolfheze. Colonel Lippert, whose command had now been extended to comprise a heterogeneous and expanding collection of units scattered in a semi-circular line between Renkum and the railway line west of Wolfheze, had his headquarters at Heelsum and was admirably placed not only to penetrate the divisional area from the west but also to drive the British out of Wolfheze. And if Wolfheze were to be taken, Hackett would be unable to get his vehicles back across the railway to the southern side; for the road which led through the village was the only way across the high, steep railway embankment. He would have to send at least part of his force back to seize the vital crossing. He chose Lieutenant-Colonel K.B.I. Smyth's 10th Battalion which left immediately. No sooner had it gone than a message came through from Divisional Headquarters ordering the withdrawal of the entire brigade to the south of the railway line.

It was a fearful and chaotic withdrawal. In their anxiety to get over the Wolfheze crossing while it was still open, the battalions were taken back at a furious pace. 'You can't just get up and rush away from the enemy in daylight like this', one soldier said with disgust. 'You just can't bloody well do it.' But they had to try and the Germans harried them all the way. 'We joined a stream of troops moving back,' a glider pilot whose flight had failed in its attempt to get through to Arnhem wrote afterwards, 'we realised that this was a retreat. We were evacuating the woods and hills we had been about to dig into. It was a long stream of troops of all units . . . Disorganisation started when we had to cross an open field which led to the railway lines . . . When we reached the other side we were not an organised body of men. The men had lost their officers and the officers their men.'

The 10th Battalion came under heavy fire before they reached Wolfheze and in the village itself many men were killed and wounded as they came towards the rendezvous. 'We were given orders', Sergeant Bentley said, 'to leave the wood. It was every man for himself, for by then we were all split up.'

One of the company commanders, Captain L.E. Queripel, had men with him not only from the 10th but from two other battalions as well. He had been hit in the face as he carried a wounded sergeant to the safety of the ditch beside the road; but despite his wound he set off to lead an attack on a German position of two Spandaus and a captured British anti-tank gun which had been holding his company up. He recaptured the gun and killed the men who had been firing it. As his men withdrew before a new infantry assault he was wounded in the face again and in both his arms. But he and some of his men jumped down into a ditch and turned round on their pursuers who were hurling stick bombs at them. Queripel picked several of these stick bombs up and threw them back. He ordered his men to get away while he remained, throwing grenades and stick bombs until the Germans closed in on him and for the third time shot him in the face, and this time killed him.

Other ferocious battles were meanwhile fought around him and when the 10th Battalion came across the railway, there were only 250 men still with it. The 156th Battalion had less than 20 more. Their transport had been almost completely destroyed. Several vehicles, stuck in the soft ground to the north of the railway line, were blasted into wreckage by enemy guns.

In the middle of the engagement, some glider-borne units of the Polish Brigade had begun to land under a furious fire, in a field between the 10th Battalion and the Germans. Several of the gliders, under attack both from Messerschmitts and the ground forces, were in flames long before they reached the ground; others, soaked in petrol from the riddled tanks of the jeeps inside them, exploded into flames on landing; one 'broke up in the air like a child's toy', reported the Polish war correspondent, Marek Swiecicki, 'and a jeep, an anti-tank gun and people flew out of it'. Of the eight urgently needed anti-tank guns only three were unloaded and one of these, which went into action immediately, was destroyed within a few minutes. While the remaining two were rushed away to the area of the Divisional Headquarters, the Polish troops on the landing zone were taken for Germans by some of the 10th Battalion who opened fire on them. The Poles, under fire from both Germans and British alike, cannot be blamed for 'promptly panicking', as Company Quartermaster-Sergeant Turner of the 156th Battalion said they did, 'and rushing round firing in every direction before disappearing'. 'It was a real cock-up', a soldier of the 10th Battalion thought. 'But then it was a real cock-up everywhere that day, I reckon.'

Around the Divisional Headquarters in the grounds of the Park Hotel, the fear which is always most noticeable at the beginning of a battle was beginning to spread. Rifle shots and bursts of Bren-gun fire could be heard at frequent intervals all over the position as nervous men fired at sounds and shadows; slit trenches were seen to be deserted; defensive positions in the open abandoned for the safety of cellars. Dutch people kept running across the road and asking by frantic gestures which way they ought to go so that their families might be safe. Once a tragically incongruous party of children, led by a little girl, came scampering out of the woods and ran away down the road to Wolfheze.

The air was full of rumours – the 2nd Army had been destroyed, the bridge had been blown, Urquhart was dead, Montgomery had said the Division must fight to the last man. Groups of soldiers ran across the hotel lawns and disappeared into the woods. A party of 20 men, including a 'tall young officer', scurried for the hotel shouting, 'The Germans are coming!' And Urquhart and Colonel Mackenzie who went out to stop them were forced to drive them back by blows and threats. In other sectors, too, fear was spreading fast and had to be checked as violently. According to Sepp Kraft, 'in spite of their being the cream of the British fighting forces, a number of cases occurred when certain individuals, to gain relief from battle fatigue, deserted' to the enemy that afternoon.

The atmosphere of despair was increased when the RAF flew in to drop supplies. They were desperately needed. According to a Dutch farmer, Willem van Vliet, over 50 tons of ammunition and other supplies had been loaded into his farm buildings during Sunday afternoon and night. Seven or eight men had been left to guard these stores and when van Vliet protested to an English major that it was madness to leave these few men to protect such valuable material when there were so many Germans about, the major smiled and said, 'The guard we're leaving is perfectly adequate, Mijnheer . . . Our information is pretty good and we happen to know that the number of Germans in the vicinity of Arnhem is negligible.' A few hours later van Vliet's farm buildings and all that they contained were in German hands.

And now there was another disaster. Owing to an error of timing at the rendezvous and the unsatisfactory communications with the fighter bases on the continent, the aircraft bringing fresh supplies flew in without an escort. The fighters had appeared at the rendezvous but as there were no other aircraft there it was assumed that the operation had been cancelled and the fighters flew home again. The unescorted supply aircraft flew in at 1,000 feet, maintaining an unwavering course through an intensive barrage of flak, to drop their canisters carefully on Supply Dropping Point 'V' still well inside the German lines. A new dropping area near Divisional Headquarters was marked with ground strips and a Eureka beacon was set up on a high tower nearby. But, as the RAF's official report puts it, 'the time of drop was uncertain; the beacon could not be left switched on indefinitely as this would have exhausted the batteries. Whenever the strips were displayed, enemy aircraft "strafed" the area. The new supply dropping point was obscured by trees and was much less distinctive than the original [one]. Verey lights were fired, but it appears that most crews failed to see either these lights or the ground strips. During the drop, flak was intense.'

Tired, unshaven men looked up as the aircraft flew over their heads to the dropping zone between Lichtenbeek and Arnhem which they had failed to capture and they watched despairingly as the parachutes unfolded over the German lines. They waved scarves frantically, they poured petrol over the grass and set fire to it, they spread out parachutes on the heather, they fired Verey lights; but the attention of the flyers could not be caught. With magnificent concentration and courage the pilots flew their machines through the flak to their appointed target. Only a few of the 390 tons of ammunition, food and medical supplies fell off target and into British hands, the rest was gratefully picked up by the Germans who distributed most of it to the Dutch. Only 55 aircraft got through unharmed; 97 were damaged and 13 were brought down.

One of those that were shot down was a Dakota whose pilot was Flight-Lieutenant David Lord of 271 Squadron, 46 Group. His starboard wing was hit by flak and burst into flames. The flames spread to the starboard engine but the aircraft came on at 900 feet to drop its first load of supplies. Slowly it turned and circled and went back to drop the rest. Once more it turned and

Lord ordered his crew to bale out. They jumped but he remained. The starboard wing fell off and the Dakota crashed, still flaming, to the earth. The crew of a Stirling of 38 Group also remained at their posts to fly their aircraft through the flak although one of its engines was burning fiercely and all but one of the despatchers were lying dead by the open door. Several soldiers felt the tears running down their cheeks as they watched these crews risk death and die in their heroic efforts to help them.

When the member of a crew baled out, however, they did not always receive the sort of welcome to which their heroism entitled them. One pilot afterwards told Major Cain of the South Staffordshires that he had landed in the divisional area 'rather expecting a sympathetic welcome and perhaps some hot sweet tea. Instead a filthy and bearded sergeant had stumbled over to him and roared, "Whose side are you on?" and when told had thrust a rifle and two grenades into his hands with the words, "Well get —— stuck in then!".'

To the west of Arnhem the bitter battle continued. All day long the fighting had gone on in a kind of savage bewilderment. Houses were lost and retaken time and again. Painful and costly advances were made down one street, while men retreated up others. Some units had given up all attempts to get forward and had, as a young officer in one of them said, stopped outside Oosterbeek where they 'took up defensive positions and waited'. 'It was a bloody shambles', a private in the 3rd Battalion says. 'I never knew what was going on and don't think any of my mates did either.' Anyway 'it wasn't Bank Holiday', another soldier reported.

> There was mortaring and heavy stuff going on. I remember the nasty *shoosh-shoosh-crash-crash* and hoped it wasn't going to be a non-stop performance . . . There were quite a lot of civvies about, though, helping to look after the wounded and getting them off to the hospital and into the shops and houses . . . The

civvies were smashing. No sooner had a chap caught a packet than one of them would come along and try to bandage him up . . . There was bags of muck flying about.

Dwindling elements of the 1st and 3rd Battalions got through in face of tanks and self-propelled guns as far as the western end of Roemondsplein; two companies of the 1st and at least one platoon of the South Staffordshires were at one time within less than half a mile of the bridge. Scattered units of the 3rd Battalion got down to the river by the Rijnpaviljoen restaurant.

But no attack bore relation to any other one; no advance received any support; mortars were fired at point-blank range across narrow streets; British and Germans alike, on more than one occasion, attacked houses occupied by men of their own battalion and often mortared each other until the British learned to recognise each other by shouts of 'Whoa Mahomet!' the parachutists' battle-cry which, so an officer said, 'the Germans for all their cleverness could not imitate'.* Piat ammunition was nearly expended; anti-tank guns were never to be found when needed; enemy tanks roamed the streets at will and inflicted fearful casualties on brave men who tried ineffectually to stop them with Bren-guns and rifles.

'It was impossible to tell how many tanks there were', says Major Robert Cain of the South Staffordshires.

And I don't think we ever disabled one for we never saw the crew get out. At about 11.30 the Piat ammunition gave out. The tanks came up and our men were being killed one after the other. I saw one of our men with only his face left. His eyes were wide open. We could hear the call of 'stretcher-bearer' all the time . . . The German tanks blew up the house next to us and set it on fire.

---

* This cry had been adopted first by the men of the 2nd Battalion in North Africa when they had been in the hills near Sidi N'sir where every message shouted by the Arabs from one village to the next seemed to begin with the words '*Whoa Mahomet!*'

There was nothing we could do about it, so I told Taylor we'd try to get to the anti-tank guns and do a proper job. We moved back about 100 yards. I went through a room which had a picture of Hitler in it and a German on the floor who was wounded but still alive, and he looked very frightened. I suppose he thought I was going to strangle him or something.

Myself, Corporal Perry in my company, and two other chaps got into a trench at the side of the St Elizabeth Hospital. It was a long trench and had been dug some time, probably as an air-raid shelter. I lay low there waiting for another German tank and told the men not to show themselves. Unfortunately the tank came up and stopped within 50 yards of us. The commander was standing up as bold as anything in the turret with black gloves on and field glasses in his hand. Some bloody fool opened up and he quietly got down and turned his gun in our direction. When he did this, the three chaps in my trench panicked and got out and, of course, they were machine-gunned. I said to myself, 'There's no future in staying here with only my pistol!' so I climbed to the top of the trench very slowly, lay down and rolled over and over. The tank was then coming towards the trench. I dropped into the yard of the hospital which was about a 20-foot drop and I lay there for about 10 minutes while I quietly passed out. Then I got up and moved through the back part of the hospital and contacted the 11th Battalion who were some streets behind.

In all those streets around the St Elizabeth Hospital the confusion was as appalling. Robert Smith, of the 3rd Battalion, jumping out of a pit which had once contained a German mortar and waving a triangular bandage on which he had painted a red cross in the blood of a wounded man, found himself confronted by 'a tank manned by Jerries'. 'On my shouting at them in the little German that I knew,' he says, 'they told me to come up on the bank which I did and when I explained to the tank commander that there were many wounded on or about the path he wirelessed the information to his headquarters. Within a quarter of an hour four German ambulances arrived on the scene and as we collected the wounded, they took them to the hospital.'

'It was nightmarish', Andrew Milbourne of the 1st Battalion thought. There was

an utter 'out of touch' feeling . . . Back and forth up and down that road until I knew every inch of the way . . . Back towards Oosterbeek. It was here that I was asked to take a gun in . . . Before I climbed into that jeep a strange, somewhat uncanny feeling came over me . . . I moved forward through this garden just above the river bank . . . My fire must have proved unhealthy because the dull thud and whining rush of shells and mortars began to change the aspect and beauty of our little garden. How long they kept bursting amongst us I can't recall. It seemed as if a thousand devils were raging in our midst . . . 'God this can't go on for ever!'

At the same time, 'Let the dirty bastards have it', I heard myself shouting.

A flash! That's the only way for me to describe it. Just before, I think I remember 'Dob' [Private Doboske] saying something about tanks. I remember saying something about tramcars – then stars. How long I lay there I can't rightly say. My first recollections were of my trying to open my eyes and raise myself up.

'Strange, how strange my hands feel. No pain, yet my hands feel as if they were far away.'

'OK, Geordie,' faintly penetrated my numbed brain. 'OK old son, you're just scratched.'

Milbourne could not know then that he was to lose both his hands and an eye.

Nor in the sudden shock of shattered nerves did his commanding officer, Lieutenant-Colonel Dobie, know at first that he had been wounded. But he, like Lieutenant-Colonel Fitch of the 3rd, Lieutenant-Colonel McCardie of the South Staffordshires and Lieutenant-Colonel Lea of the 11th were all hit that day. Each one of them had lost more than half their officers, and small parties of undirected stragglers came in increasing numbers out of Arnhem, disillusioned and dismayed.

Lieutenant-Colonel W.F.K. Thompson, whose 1st Light Regiment of Artillery had been in action constantly for the past two days in support of the infantry, discovered several of these parties when he left his command post during Tuesday afternoon to visit the front. Colonel Thompson, an extremely able gunner whose light-hearted manner and unsoldierlike appearance concealed an urgent seriousness of purpose, had established his command post with his advanced 3rd Light Battery at Oosterbeek, leaving his 1st and 2nd Batteries in the care of his second-in-command, Major G.F. de Gex. To protect his guns at Oosterbeek he had organised a detachment of Glider Pilots and a troop of anti-tank gunners into a defensive force which formed the nucleus of what was afterwards known as 'Thompson Force'. Now, as he went forward on his reconnaissance he came upon several stragglers from the 11th Battalion and the South Staffordshires coming away from Arnhem. 'Very few officers,' he subsequently reported, 'no means of communication. Major Cain who subsequently earned a V.C. was senior officer, but like others not at his best then. Ordered him to deploy the S. Staffs on left and 11 Para. Bn. on right holding the high ground and covering the railway embankment (west of Den Brink) and the road. Sgt. in Para. Bn said to me, "Thank God someone at last has given us some orders".'

The need for a strong defensive force in the area and for an officer with the authority to organise and control it was, indeed, becoming essential. The evening before Lieutenant J.L. Williams, the Transport Officer of the 1st Battalion, had realised this and had spent the night bringing stragglers and isolated parties into the transport area. By dawn the 40 or 50 men of his Headquarters Company had been joined by nearly 200 more and Williams led this force in a gallant attempt to break through to the bridge. But he was checked, as the rifle companies of his Battalion had already been checked, in the area of the St Elizabeth Hospital where his men held out for the whole of Tuesday in the hope of support which never came. At nightfall, having been joined by some men of the 3rd and 11th Battalions, he decided to withdraw to the railway south of Den Brink where 'Thompson Force' had been established during the day. 'It was pretty bloody having to fall back like that,' a soldier says, 'but I reckon it was the best thing to do. We were not getting anywhere where we were and needed to find a position we could defend before Jerry knocked us off one by one. He knew what he was at, Jerry did. It was best to get back and get sorted out a bit, I think. We all knew by now things were getting desperate like.'

On the far side of Oosterbeek, the officers at Divisional Head-quarters had now come to the same conclusion. For now, out of the 1st Brigade, only those units of the 2nd Battalion under Colonel Frost at the bridge were still fighting as a coherent unit, the 1st and 3rd Battalions having virtually ceased to exist. The South Staffordshires from the Airlanding Brigade and the 11th Battalion from the 4th Brigade had also been irremediably dismembered. And although a few glider-borne units of the Polish Brigade had arrived north of the river, the weather had made it impossible for the Americans to fly in the parachutists to the south of it as planned. Consequently the only troops now available for sending into Arnhem were Brigadier Hackett's two other battalions, the 10th and 156th; for the last two remaining battalions in the Division – the 1st Battalion of the Border Regiment and Colonel Payton-Reid's 7th Kings Own Scottish Borderers – although helped as they were by a gallant but motley collection of men from the Reconnaissance Squadron, the Independent Parachute Company, the Royal Army Service Corps, glider pilots and engineers, all fighting as infantry, were desperately needed to protect what might well prove to be the only bridgehead over the Neder Rijn which the Division would eventually be able to hold. Even this limited achievement seemed by Tuesday night to be a scarcely possible one, as already the men were worn out. Most of them longed for nothing but sleep.

'What a pair I was with in my shell hole!' complained a man in the 156th Battalion.

They lay down straight away, made themselves as comfortable as possible and went off to sleep without a word. I went to the edge of the shell hole to watch for enemy movements, swearing I'd only do it for two hours. Over two hours had passed when I slid wearily back into the hole, hardly able to keep my eyes open after the strain of watching. I shook the nearest shadowy figure into wakefulness and asked him to take over. 'Eh? OK! OK!', he mumbled and turned over again and started snoring. I tried the other fellow – same response . . . I never want to spend another night like that. My eyes would strain into the darkness until my lids were too heavy to stay open any longer and I'd nod off only to wake, startled out of my wits and straining round expecting to see Jerries everywhere . . . When at last morning came, I was fast asleep with my head cushioned on my arms on the edge of the shellhole . . . It was lucky I hadn't had to use my rifle during the night for I couldn't even see through the barrel for dirt.

All night long the Germans played on the men's nerves. Through the rain which began to fall at dusk came the blare of a loud speaker. Now seeming very close, now far away, a disembodied voice called across the lines.

'It is better you should give yourselves up, Tommies', the voice suggested, speaking in careful English without the hint of a German accent. 'Your General is our prisoner. You are surrounded. The rest of the Division has surrendered. If you do not surrender, you will die. Panzer units are about to attack you. Are you hungry, Tommies? Would you like to share the food your aeroplanes have dropped to us. Give up, Tommies.

Why die? You are beaten anyway. Think of your wives, Tommies.'

The voice spoke on, sometimes sharp and clear, at others drowning in the distance. Occasionally before it spoke the Germans would relay a programme of dance music on records – mostly by Glenn Miller. The only reply were bursts of Bren-gun fire and muttered remarks, obscene and cynical. Once Major Wilson's men fired a Piat bomb at the direction from which the voice came and once some men of the 1st and 3rd Battalions shouted back, 'You cheeky bastard.'

Earlier on in the day Major Wilson had ordered one of the several German-speaking Jews in his squadron to call back that they were too frightened to surrender but that they would come out if the Germans sent a party to take them back. In a few moments about 60 Germans came out of the woods opposite them and the men of the Independent Company obeyed with pleasure Wilson's order to fire. All the Bren guns of the Independent Company opened up at a range of 150 yards on the approaching enemy. Wilson said, 'They died screaming.'

The Germans, too, adopted these tactics and groups of them came forward with their hands in the air calling, 'We surrender! We surrender!' As the British troops came up towards them, they threw themselves to the ground and machine-guns opened up behind them.

At the bridge these deceitful tactics, an officer who fought there believes, 'would not have been tolerated. Despite the savage struggle, it was all quite gentlemanly on both sides – chivalrous even. By Tuesday night the place looked like hell but it was a hell we shared and in a way, I suppose, it made us respect each other.'

The number of inhabitable buildings in the area was inexorably diminishing. Tanks and 40-mm guns were pounding constantly at the houses, forcing the defenders to evacuate them. This 'meant, of course,' a company commander laconically recorded, 'that German infantry occupied them. Then, when the tanks had withdrawn, we had to counter-attack to re-establish ourselves.'

In the early morning a heavy anti-tank gun, firing a 20-lb bomb, had blown down the whole of the south-west corner of the van Limburg Stirumschool and part of its roof. The men inside were thrown to the floor or against the opposite walls in the clouds of suffocating dust which billowed up suddenly from the tumbling masonry. In the sudden silence which followed the explosion, German infantry crept forward and, believing that British resistance was ended, set up machine-guns in the open within 10 feet of the shattered building. Soon 60 Germans were in the street below the school. Quietly those defenders who could still move, crept back to their windows and then in a crashing, exhilarating burst of sound they opened fire again. Jumping on to window sills to fire their Sten guns from the hip, shouting 'Whoa Mahomet!' as they dropped grenades amidst the scattering, screaming figures below, they 'knocked off more Jerries', as one of them put it, 'than you could hope to do in a month of Sundays'.

'But we knew', as this same soldier said, 'that when the tanks came back we wouldn't feel so pleased with ourselves.' For, as well as the danger of being blasted out, there was an increasing danger now of being burned out. Tanks were repeatedly firing phosphorus shells into the buildings within the British position and German engineers were systematically turning out the occupants of houses on the outskirts of the shrinking perimeter so that the parachutists might soon be surrounded by a ring of fire. Indeed many buildings by Tuesday afternoon were already charred and smoking shells.

In the large cellars beneath the building used by Frost as his Headquarters the floors were hourly more crowded with wounded and occasionally by German prisoners pushed in to join their companions who squatted in a corner, huddled together in gloomy silence.

In the cellar below the school the tough and enterprising Lieutenant Mackay, himself wounded in the head and with a piece of metal he could not dislodge pinning his foot to his boot, visited his wounded Engineers whom he had put in the care of a sapper who had once been on a first-aid course. One man, he said later, 'was obviously dying with 15 bullets through the chest; and another, shot through the back of the head, was looking a bit grey and snoring. There was another who was a little rocky with one bullet through the stomach and three through the arm. The stomach wound was all right – nothing vital was hit – and I shoved a plug in it. Most of the wounded were suffering from shock and fatigue. I had plenty of morphia and kept them all well doped.'

In the streets above, the mood of the British troops was still curiously light-hearted, almost contented. Some of the men seemed, despite fatigue and hunger, to treat the fighting as a game. They had learned by now that defending a built-up area is much less frightening than attacking in one and when they had got well-defended houses from which to operate they became not merely adventurous but foolhardy. They would follow a tank up a street, jumping over garden walls, their boots tied up with rags to deaden the sound of the hobnails on the cobbles, watching their quarry, excited like schoolboys waiting to pounce, rushing up with Piats and gammon bombs to lie in ambush on the corner of a concealed alley. Others, more consciously histrionic, displayed that courageous indifference to danger, absurd, flamboyant and touching which Englishmen so much admire. One of these was Major Digby Tatham-Warter who led his men in bayonet attacks waving an old umbrella and who affected to seek shelter beneath its tattered canvas during a mortar bombardment.

'Silly sod!' one of his men murmured to a companion as he looked at him. But there was affection behind the amused disdain, and admiration.

All day long more rumours had been circulating – the 2nd

Army had been seen beyond the southern end of the bridge; their own Division was to make a strong attack that night from the north. Megaphones were made out of wallpaper and men shouted down the street *'Whoa Mahomet!'* and then called at the top of their voices:

'What the bloody hell are you waiting for? Come in you lazy bastards!'

Their voices were cheerful as they shouted their good-natured insults. They still seemed hopeful. But there was no one there. And amidst the rubble and the hot and smoking buildings hissing in the rain, with the changeless river in front of them and the flames and smoke behind, they had to fight off their attackers alone. Towards nightfall several Tiger tanks appeared, looking 'incredibly menacing and sinister in the half light', Colonel Frost thought,

like some prehistoric monsters as their great guns swung from side to side breathing flame. Their shells burst through our walls. The debris and slowly settling dust following their explosions filled the passages and rooms. The acrid reek of burning together with the noise bemused us. But we had to stay prepared to meet the rush of infantry. The Battalion Headquarters suffered badly. Digby, Father Egan and others were hit [the second-in-command had been killed the night before]. Then our gunners manhandled a six-pounder round to the front under the very noses of the enemy, while the Piat crews climbed to new positions and so we drove those monsters back, but one remained and could not move again. This last onslaught left us weary. As we prepared for yet another night Arnhem was burning. Two great churches were flaming fiercely and for a little while the shadow of the cross which hung between two lovely towers was silhouetted against the clouds of smoke rising far into the sky. It was like daylight in the streets – a curious, metallic daylight. The crackle of burning wood and strange echoes of falling buildings seemed unearthly. If the wind changed to the west we were certain to be burned out.

And this was only one of his problems. For tired out and hungry as they were, Frost knew that, despite their displays of cheerful vulgarity and brave indifference, his men were reaching the limits of their strength. Some of them had had nothing but apples and pears to eat for 24 hours and during the day the water supply had suddenly failed. The persistent mortaring, the tautophonous rattle of Spandaus, the whine of anti-aircraft shells, the crash of tumbling masonry, the lick and roar of fire were wearing them down. 'We had tablets to keep us awake', one of them said, 'and they were all right; but when you did get the chance to get a bit of a kip – we slept in relays two hours at a time – you felt bloody vague for a long time after it.'

During the afternoon several squadrons of Messerschmitts and Focke-Wulfs appeared overhead and the men ran out into the streets to take in the British identification marks that had been displayed all over the area. The only sign of the RAF they had seen was a single Dakota 'forlornly running the gauntlet' of anti-aircraft fire from across the river.

When night fell hopes of seeing the RAF or, indeed, the 2nd Army had begun to fade. Looking up into the now silent, dull red sky and at the smoke drifting away to the south from the smouldering ruins around them and from the still burning towers of St Walburgiskerk and Eusebiuskerk, many men felt conscious of a sudden despair.

Everywhere there was the smell of war. And the streets were stained with blood.

8

Wednesday

'Almost every building in the neighbourhood seemed to be held by the enemy.'

Major Digby Tatham-Warter

On Wednesday morning it was still raining. Just before dawn the now constricted area of the Division west of Arnhem was subjected to the heaviest shelling and mortar bombardment which it had yet suffered. Many buildings were wrecked and several others set on fire by self-propelled guns firing phosphorus shells. At half past five the bombardment grew less intense and no one could doubt that a new attack was coming.

At about six o'clock a man in the 156th Battalion, whose section had spent the night in the garden of a house in Wolfheze where it had, in his own words, 'been left behind and forgotten' when the rest of the company withdrew in the night to reform in the woods behind the village, went into the house to eat a bar of chocolate for breakfast.

I thought the village seemed strangely quiet and dead [he said afterwards], as if we were the only people in it. I'd only come out of the house a few minutes when I heard a clanking and rumbling in the distance – Tanks! . . . One tank was moving along the road past the station. I couldn't see it because some sheds blocked it from my view, so I waited breathlessly. The first I saw of it was its nose appearing round a shed at the foot of the next garden. Gradually it came into full view. I focused my eyes on the turret –

there was that by now familiar black and white cross! A Jerry! My
heart leapt into my mouth and my eyes nearly left their sockets. I
just couldn't move until the gun started swinging round in my
direction. I waited no longer then but yelling to the boys that it
was a Jerry, I turned to go into the back door. As I did so I glanced
along the back of the next house. In the garden, advancing with
bayonets fixed, were Jerries. Lots of them. I yelled 'An attack' and
dived for the door. They saw me as I saw them and out of the
corner of my eye I saw the leading man drop to one knee and
open fire, and the others flung their rifles to their shoulders. I just
made the door as the bullets began to whistle all round me and
thud into the framework of the door . . . I dashed out of the front.
The rest dashed out, too, into the road. No sooner had they
reached it than a nest of Spandaus opened up . . . Someone
shouted 'There's only one thing to do. Up past the fronts of
the houses!' So away we went. Every house in that street had a
dividing hedge between three and four feet high and there must
have been some 50 or 60 houses on our side of the street. If the
world's champion hurdlers had been there they couldn't have
beaten any of us.

A few minutes later Hackett's whole Brigade was being
heavily attacked. During the night he had been reorganising his
battalions for a fresh advance at first light into Arnhem. He had
wanted to move on the night before. 'I wanted to get integrated
into the Division', he wrote in his diary. 'Div. deprecated a move
but said I was to send recce parties in by night and follow at first
light. I saw nothing to be gained by recce parties in the dark and
it was agreed in the end that I should move the brigade at first
light.' It now seemed doubtful that he would be able to move at
all.

By half past seven all his units were engaged. The enemy were
pressing forward strongly in front from across the railway line,
on his left south of Wolfheze and on his right from Johanna
Hoeve. Several tanks had broken through his lines in various

places and were milling about in his area with predatory watchfulness. Urquhart, dismayed by the now inescapable fact that his last hope of getting reinforcements through to Frost at the bridge had gone, ordered him to abandon his plans for advancing into Arnhem and to close in on the north-east corner of the main divisional area and hold the enemy there.

As soon as these clear orders were given him, Hackett reacted with the skill and foresight of a born tactician. Although completely surrounded by greatly superior numbers of the enemy, he managed by expertly directed movements and well-timed changes of direction to bring his men back towards the rest of the Division. The brigade, in his own phrase, 'handled beautifully'. It was, in the circumstances, an understatement.

Most of the troops had little ammunition left, others had none; some had neither ammunition nor weapons. Using captured German rifles they fought their way back with determination and skill through the open fields and woods. Lieutenant-Colonel Sir Richard Des Voeux was killed as he directed his 156th Battalion; Lieutenant-Colonel K.B.I. Smyth of the 10th was wounded; Lieutenant-Colonel Derick Heathcoat-Amory, with a broken leg and strapped to a stretcher on a jeep which was carrying mortar bombs, was untied just before he was enveloped in the flames that had been shot at the jeep by a German flame-thrower; Major C.W.B. Dawson, the Brigade Major, was killed. In the woods more men of the 10th Battalion were killed by Spandaus firing down the rides and by snipers shooting from the trees; and the rate of withdrawal slowed down. Hackett sent a message to Colonel Smyth to 'pull the plug out'.

Orders were immediately issued for bayonets to be fixed, and the remainder of the battalion cut their way through in a last effort of desperate courage. Less than 70 men got through.

These breathless survivors formed up at the edge of the wood, in which more than that number of their comrades lay dead, and then marched down towards Divisional Headquarters, led by Colonel Smyth, the blood staining the bandages of his wounded arm. General Urquhart, immensely impressed by the discipline of Smyth's 'exhausted, filthy and bleeding' men, directed them to a group of buildings north-west of the main crossroads in Oosterbeek. They knelt down at the windows, already half asleep.

To the north, the remains of their Battalion and the remnants of the 156th Battalion were still fighting in the woods. They had begun to lose hope of getting through when friendly voices shouted greetings to them from the top of one of the long rides between the trees whose thick leaves cast a shadow over the ground.

'Come on Tommy!' the voices shouted. 'Come on!'

'They're the Poles', a cockney voice called out strangely fresh and cheerful. 'Thank God for the old Polaks!'

The British soldiers came out from behind the trees and saw at the end of the ride, in the dim shade cast by the leaves, a group of soldiers in parachutists' smocks waving them on. They walked thankfully down the ride towards them. They were half way there when one of them shouted a warning in a voice which cracked hysterically. It was too late. The figures in the smocks had thrown themselves to the ground and six Spandaus had opened up behind them in sudden long bursts of fire which sent the bullets ripping between the trees until all the British soldiers were dead or wounded or had scrambled out of view again. As the Spandaus fell into silence the German decoys crawled out of sight and into a hollow.

Hackett gave the order to fling them out with the bayonet. Too angry to be afraid, with a kind of desperate fury that made some of them cry as they ran along, the parachutists rushed at the hollow. Taking no chances with such men the Germans sensibly retreated to more favourable ground and left the British to occupy the hollow in their stead.

There were less than 30 men of the 156th Battalion, about 12 from the 10th, 12 from Hackett's Brigade Headquarters and 20 or 30 others – less than 100 men in all, with seven officers.

Hackett decided he could not hope to get them out till dark. And so, for nearly three hours, they fought the Germans off from the lip of the hollow. They were, said Hackett, a 'splendid lot' – particularly splendid in view of the normal work of some of them. For there were clerks and signallers there and men from the Intelligence Section. And Sergeant Dudley Pearson, the chief clerk, turned out to be 'one of the bravest men at really hand-to-hand fighting' that Hackett had ever known. This 'splendid lot' of men rushed out with bayonets when the enemy got close enough to the hollow to throw grenades into it, or with plastic bombs when the grinding rattle of tanks could be heard between the trees. Once Hackett led out his men in a daring counter-attack on a Spandau post about 30 yards away. The Spandau crew were killed with the exception of one man who crouched in his trench, his head pressed close to the earth. Hackett looked down at him and felt unable to drive his bayonet between the high, thin, defenceless shoulder blades.

Leaving the now apparently unattended Spandau where it was, the men withdrew under fire to the hollow to await the next attack. Almost as soon as they had got back to their position the Spandau opened up again, and then another one followed suit. With nearly 30 of his men wounded in the hollow, Hackett decided that he could not wait for darkness to get away. He would have to charge out now if he was ever to escape. The German attacks were becoming stronger and more frequent and he must surely soon be overwhelmed.

At six o'clock he ordered the parachutists to 'make a break for it'. They ran as fast as they could with fixed bayonets for half a mile until they broke through into the area occupied by the Border Regiment. As Colonel Smyth had arrived with less than 70 men so did Hackett. Urquhart sent these few survivors to strengthen the defences on the western edges of the divisional area where the 10th Battalion was already installed.

There were no troops at all now, except those at the bridge, fighting outside the short semi-circular line around Divisional

Headquarters at Oosterbeek. To the south was the river; to the north, to the east and to the west were Germans; and on every side they were trying to close in. In some sectors, in fact, they had succeeded in breaking through the edges of the British perimeter. It was, indeed, becoming increasingly difficult to make any distinctions at all between the German and British lines. And as both Germans and British were using captured weapons it was no longer possible for those whose ears were trained to distinguish between them to recognise friendly or hostile positions by sound alone. A glider pilot sent out on patrol towards Arnhem that day 'heard German voices everywhere' as soon as he began to advance. 'The voices and shouts seemed to be all about us', he says.

> We exchanged fire but it was pretty inaccurate on both sides . . . Then I heard the same engine noise as yesterday, and not long after the same old crash and thud. A tank was moving forward and firing shells into the houses across the road on our left . . . We put a Piat gun in position and lay there waiting. The noise of the tank got nearer and nearer and so did the shells hitting the houses opposite us . . . I was never more frightened than now . . . We only had a little Piat gun just three feet long . . . The feeling of helplessness and fear became stronger and stronger the nearer the tank came. And at the same time the German infantry was working round us, obviously screening the tank. The voices and shouts seemed to be all about us.

Suddenly a man in front of him threw a smoke grenade and, behind the cover of the smoke, some men of the Reconnaissance Squadron, who had been on patrol with him, abruptly drove away in their jeeps; so he decided to withdraw as well. But he had not got far when he realised he was surrounded. There were 'German voices from all directions'. He and his companion thought of going into a nearby house and hiding in the cellar but they feared the occupants might be Dutch Nazis so instead they threw themselves into a shallow rubbish pit in the garden. The Germans came to search the house and garden and then 'just stood about talking in very loud voices and giving each other orders which no one obeyed'. When they had gone away a fellow-pilot rushed out of the back door of a house further down the road, from the attic of which he had shot the whole crew of a tank who were standing in the road below him.

But even though it had now become so constricted, the divisional area could only be sparsely defended; for there was not a single battalion now which had not lost many, if not most, of its best men and once again bad weather had prevented the Americans from flying in the Polish Brigade. Consequently German troops were repeatedly infiltrating between the lines and, although they were as repeatedly driven back, the shape of the perimeter was forever changing and it was becoming increasingly difficult to discover loopholes in the German defences. When the men of Lieutenant Stevenson's troop of the Reconnaissance Squadron were ordered to reconnoitre 'a railway crossing in a northern suburb of the town,' they 'hadn't got very far', Stevenson said afterwards, 'when, coming over the crest of a hill', they 'saw a Jerry self-propelled gun smack in the middle of the road'.

On a visit to the northern sector, General Urquhart and his ADC – Captain Graham Roberts – found themselves driving down a ride in a wood between their own men and the enemy. They jumped out into a ditch and, while Urquhart dashed to a house occupied by some men of the Independent Company, Roberts tried to save the jeep. He climbed back into it, but as he was driving it away at a furious speed down the ride, the steering wheel swung round in his hand and the jeep crashed into a tree. Roberts was thrown clear and limped away through the undergrowth.

On the same day a corporal in the South Staffordshires crawled over to a house which a few hours before had been occupied 'by some blokes of the Service Corps. There was a cellar full of tinned fruit and stuff there', he said, 'and I was after some for my lot.' He jumped through the window and 'landed almost smack in the lap of a Jerry who was squatting on the floor'. 'The Jerry was as surprised as I was', the corporal went on. 'But when I jumped back out of the window he came up to it and shouted something in a laughing sort of voice at me as I ran away. I think it was "*Aufwiedersehen*". When I got back my lot said why didn't I ask him to hand up a few tins from the cellar. I think he would have done. We needed them bad for the RAF came over again soon afterwards and we got nothing from them.'

It was about two o'clock when the RAF flew in that day. 70 Dakotas came into sight from the north and, as on the day before, smoke signals were sent up, troops held out parachutes and waved frantically, squares were burned in the turf by trails of petrol. But again the aircraft droned on above their heads and dropped nearly all their panniers to the Germans, who had by now captured the orders setting out the directions for marking the dropping places and had had them hectographed and distributed to all units, one of which was operating a captured Eureka beacon. Describing the drop, the official report of 38 Group RAF tells a story which the terse and colourless language cannot rob of its pathos: 'Of 33 aircraft despatched 30 (91%) reported successful drops. Two aircraft are missing, but may have dropped. It was later learned that this Dropping Zone was in enemy hands at the time of the drop.'*

Signals had, of course, been repeatedly sent out from Divisional Headquarters to this effect but not one of them had been received. The only sets, in fact, which had any sort of link with the outside world were the BBC war correspondents' set and the set operated by the Independent Phantom reporting unit. There was still no direct contact at all with Airborne Headquarters or

---

* The RAF, for understandable reasons, had always refused to consider soldiers on the ground communicating with supply dropping aircraft. At the Rhine crossing so as to avoid the mistakes of Arnhem, RAF teams wearing maroon berets and smocks went in with the airborne troops.

with the American airborne divisions. All the news which General Gavin of the 82nd US Division had had from across the Neder Rijn since the operation began was contained in a brief and alarming message handed to him by a Dutch civilian who had heard from friends in Arnhem. 'The Germans', the message simply said, are 'winning over British at Arnhem.'

This Wednesday afternoon, however, the Phantom officer in the cellar at Divisional Headquarters was able to give Urquhart news of General Gavin who, with the Guards Armoured Division, was preparing for an assault across the Waal at Nijmegen. Enormously encouraged Urquhart gave orders that the news should be made known to every man in his Division and he went out to tell some units himself. 'He looked as cheerful as anything, the General did', a soldier he spoke to said. 'I even thought we should be joining up with the blokes at the bridge before morning.'

But Frost's long-held grip on the bridge was failing. That morning, as he had been discussing with Major Crawley the formation of a fighting patrol to give himself 'more elbow room to the north', there had been 'the hell of an explosion'.

> I found myself lying face downwards on the ground with fiendish pain in both legs [he wrote later in his journal]. Don Crawley was lying on his back not far away and he started to drag himself into the house, I did the same and Wicks, my batman, came to drag me in under cover. I could not resist the groans which seemed to force themselves out of me and I felt ashamed, more particularly as Don never made a sound . . . I sat on a box in the doorway of headquarters and vainly tried to pull myself together. I felt sick and completely worn out. I tried to swallow the whisky that remained in my flask, but this made me feel like vomiting. The benzedrine tablets had no effect and I could only swallow two of them.

He was taken downstairs into the cellar where someone injected him with morphia and he went to sleep for a little. When he awoke some 'shell-shock cases were gibbering' near him and the German tanks had begun pounding the walls again. 'It was pitch dark down there' and the doctors had to use their torches continuously.

Command of the area now passed to Major Gough, while Major Tatham-Warter took over the remnants of the 2nd Battalion. Ammunition was almost completely exhausted. There were less than a dozen Piat bombs left, only a few more six-pounder shells. Three Bren-gun carriers, loaded with a further supply of shells, had tried to break through, but two were destroyed in the outskirts of the town and the third was forced to turn back.

The courage of the men began to take on a desperate quality. Lieutenant J.H. Grayburn, although the wound in his shoulder was obviously giving him great pain, led several fighting patrols to 'prevent the enemy getting access to the houses in the vicinity. This forced the enemy to bring up tanks', the citation which awarded him the Victoria Cross records,

and Lieutenant Grayburn's position was brought under such heavy fire that he was forced to withdraw to an area further north. The enemy now attempted to lay demolition charges under the bridge and the situation was now critical. Realising this, Lieutenant Grayburn organised and led a fighting patrol, which drove the enemy off temporarily and gave time for the fuses to be removed. He was again wounded, this time in the back, but he refused to be evacuated. Finally an enemy tank approached so close to his position that it became untenable. He then stood up in full view of the tank and personally directed the withdrawal of his men to the main defensive perimeter to which he had been ordered. He was killed that night.

Tanks were milling about in the area in increasing numbers now, but there were few infantry to be seen. For, having successfully sealed the area off from the rest of the mauled Division, the Germans no longer considered it a matter of immediate urgency to wipe out the few obstinate defenders by infantry assaults. They could be burned out. And tanks, at last able to pass across the bridge without fear of being put out of action, rolled up to the buildings and fired phosphorus shells through the broken windows and the gaps in the damaged walls with a kind of insultingly slow deliberation. As each house was made untenable, its defenders blew a hole through to the next one and defended that; but there were becoming fewer and fewer houses now which offered any shelter at all and the paratroopers were being driven back, like animals in a forest fire, into a more and more constricted area and being forced to dig trenches out in the open where the flames from the burning houses scorched the earth around them.

That morning, looking at his men, exhausted and filthy and unshaven, with their shirts cut open revealing blood-soaked field-dressings, but ready even now to go on fighting after more than 72 hours without sleep, after more than 24 hours without food and 12 hours without water, Lieutenant Mackay thought to himself that he would never have to give these men the order – 'This position will be held to the last round and the last man'. He felt instinctively it would be. But now there were no other troops left on his side of the bridge and the school was no longer inhabitable. 'It was like a sieve,' he says. 'Wherever you looked you could see daylight . . . Splattered everywhere was blood; it lay in pools in the rooms, it covered the smocks of the defenders and ran in small rivulets down the stairs . . . The only clean things in the school were the weapons.' The building had begun to collapse and the heat was intense. And so at last he gave the order to evacuate it. Outside he came face to face with 50 Germans beside two yellow Mk III tanks. He stood in line with his men firing from the hip, 'continuously till the ammunition ran out'. The survivors split up into little groups and ran away into the gardens behind the ruined walls. Mackay, himself, removed his lieutenant's stars, destroyed his identity card and fell to the ground completely exhausted. After a few minutes some German soldiers walked up to him. He pretended to be dead.

> They were evidently not satisfied [Mackay says], and a discussion arose. Suddenly a private ran a bayonet into me which came to rest with a jar against my pelvis. When he withdrew it, the most painful part, I got to my feet. They were evidently still very frightened of us and I was forced to walk with my hands clasped on top of my head. I was led past the place where we had our last battle a few minutes earlier. I was pleased to see several still, grey forms, and two more dying noisily in the gutter. There seemed to be masses of Germans everywhere with tanks and self-propelled guns at every corner.

With the death or capture of these last remaining troops on the eastern side of the ramp and with the loss of the school which dominated it, the collapse of the whole position, Colonel Frost knew, could not now be long delayed. For a time there was hope that a last stand might be made in a warehouse further to the north; but at dusk this building was set alight and within a few minutes was burning fiercely. An hour or so afterwards the wireless operator in Major Mumford's observation post, which he had had to move twice already that day, signalled to the 1st Light Regiment's Headquarters at Oosterbeek: 'We have been blown off the top storey. We are quite OK. We have killed three or four hundred Germans for the loss of thirty. We need more small arms ammunition.' It was the last signal which the regiment's operator at Oosterbeek received from Arnhem.

In the cellars the two doctors and their exhausted orderlies were still tending the wounds of over 200 men who 'were almost lying on top of each other' as the suffocating smoke poured down the steps. When the flames threatened to render the make-shift hospital uninhabitable, the doctors told Frost that he would have to ask for a cease-fire unless their patients were to be burned

alive. So two orderlies carrying a Red Cross flag walked out of
the cellars towards the Germans to ask for a few hours' truce.
The Germans immediately agreed; and for the first time in
nearly three days there was a momentary release from the fear of
pain or death as the Germans took the wounded to captivity.
And then the last bandaged body was taken away and the
fighting began again.

A group of men tried to break out to the west to get back to
Oosterbeek but most of them were killed or wounded as they ran
through the smoking streets, and the rest turned back. Every
street was 'well-covered by machine-gun fire and almost every
building in the neighbourhood seemed to be held by the enemy'
who, during the cease-fire, had infiltrated three complete companies of Panzer grenadiers into the British position which by the
early evening was scarcely a position at all. There were by then
only about 150 men still capable of fighting and it was decided
that these should be split up into two parties which, at dawn the
following morning, would concentrate in a group of ruined
buildings by the river bank.

There was no food at all in the area now and no water. There
seemed no longer any hope of relief, no chance of escape or
victory. In the fading light which ended their three days'
defiance, the parachutists looked down the smoking streets,
counting their last rounds of ammunition in stubborn resig-
nation.

In the main divisional area, the quiet that they had become
accustomed to expect with twilight gradually settled over the
position as the enemy's Spandaus and mortars were allowed to
cool down and their snipers crawled forward in their camouflaged cloaks to their positions in the roof-tops and trees and in
the ditches which surrounded the bridgehead.

It was a strange silence, pervasive and alarming, broken
sometimes by the forlorn lowing of unmilked cows in the
meadows by the river. Crawling out of their forward trenches

to stretch their legs or urinate, British soldiers mistook each other for the enemy and challenges would be made in hoarse and nervous voices; and sometimes a shot would shatter the rustling silence and be taken up in a flash of relief all along the line. Often individual German soldiers, either by accident or design, crept forward between the trenches and found themselves within the British perimeter. An unexpected figure was, therefore, always suspect.

Colonel Payton-Reid and one of his company commanders, Major Gordon Sheriff, were standing well inside the area occupied by the KOSB when a soldier walked up towards them in the darkness.

'He spoke German', Payton-Reid wrote in his diary later. 'Before I had recovered from my surprise Sheriff jumped at his throat. After a struggle, while I tried to shoot him but was frightened of hitting Sheriff, Sheriff strangled him. In the middle of this a friend of the German threw a stick grenade. Sheriff was wounded.' The wound was not a serious one, however, and Major Sheriff walked calmly away with his colonel until they were both stopped by the sounds of 'fearful wailing'.

'We'd better go back and put him out of his agony', Payton-Reid said and the two of them returned to the place from which the sounds of wailing had come. They found the body of a wounded goat.

In silence and apprehension, broken by sudden bursts of firing the occasional roar of a motor-cycle, the clatter of an armoured track or a shout of alarm, the night wore on. Towards midnight a company of Germans from Colonel Lippert's force, feeling their way around the northern edges of the British perimeter, were stopped by a cry of '*Halt!*'. At first, a young soldier, Otto Felder, thought that his company had stumbled into the British. 'I stood very still,' he says, 'and my heart beat so hard it hurt my chest. Then there was another shout and I couldn't control my bowels anymore. But as I lay on the ground with my face in the grass I heard a voice calling out words which were really German.'

Felder's company had reached the outposts of Kraft's battalion and the encirclement of the British Division was complete.

An hour later at the bridge the exhausted and isolated British troops were given hope at last. The members of the Dutch Resistance, who were operating a telephone exchange, made contact with Divisional Headquarters where an encouraging signal had been received from General Browning's Head-quarters near Nijmegen. The bridge over the Waal had been captured at last; and the Guards' Armoured Division, so a breathless Dutchman excitedly told one of Major Gough's men, had received orders to race for Arnhem at dawn.

The capture of the Waal bridge at Nijmegen by General Gavin's 82nd United States Airborne Division and the Guards Arm-oured Division was one of the most dashing and brilliant exploits of the whole war. 'I am proud', General Dempsey said to Gavin afterwards, 'to meet the commander of the greatest division in the world to-day.' It was not an exaggerated compliment.

Gavin had intended making an attempt to capture the bridge on Monday, but on the morning of that day the Germans counter-attacked from the Reichswald and overran the landing zones just before Gavin's glider-borne artillery and infantry reinforcements were due to arrive there. After a fierce struggle the Germans were driven back and the gliders, fortunately delayed two hours by the fog, were able to land without serious loss.

The following day, however, the second wave of glider-borne infantry reinforcements were prevented by the fog from leaving at all and, when Gavin was joined on the outskirts of Nijmegen by the Grenadier Guards, he was under such heavy pressure from the Germans in the east that he was only able to spare one of his three parachute regiments for an attack with the British tanks on the road and rail bridges across the Waal. By now the approaches to these bridges were strongly defended and successive attempts by the Guards and American parachutists during Tuesday afternoon to break through the defences were unsuccessful. Indeed, Field-Marshal Model believed that the Waal defences were impregnable and had given specific orders, so General Student says, that the bridge should not be destroyed as it 'could certainly be successfully defended'.

On Wednesday morning, however, a determined effort was made to prove Model wrong. In execution of a plan devised by Horrocks and Browning the night before, attacks were made to clear the Germans from the town and open up the way for the 504th United States Parachute Regiment to reach the river about a mile downstream, to cross it there and capture the northern end of the bridge. By three o'clock the Americans had reached the river's edge and were launching their storm-boats into the fast-flowing water under a furious fire. Although less than half the boats of the first wave reached the far bank, the Americans managed to establish and hold a bridgehead there while the subsequent waves crossed the 400 yards of swirling, bullet-swept water behind them. By the late afternoon they had broken out of the bridgehead, had raised the Stars and Stripes on the northern end of the railway bridge and were advancing towards the road bridge.

Seeing the flag flying through the smoke, the Guards on the southern bank of the river took it as a signal to begin their final attack. Blasting their way through the remaining German stronghold and under heavy fire from German 88s, the British tanks rattled down towards the river while the other parachute regiments in Gavin's Division continued to hold back the enemy's forces pressing in from the Reichswald. Soon after seven o'clock four tanks reached the bridge. Two of them were knocked out by anti-tank guns concealed behind the thick steel girders, but two others reached the other end, smashed their way past the road-block there and linked up with the Americans on the northern bank. An hour later the bridge was securely held and the way to Arnhem was open. The spearheads of XXX

Corps were given their orders to push on to Arnhem bridge at first light.

But already they were too late.

9

Thursday

'Our casualties heavy. Resources stretched utmost. Relief within 24 hours vital.'

Major-General R.E. Urquhart

At dawn, as the tanks of XXX Corps moved north from Nijmegen, the Germans began an operation to clear out the last 150 men of Colonel Frost's force from the houses which they were still occupying by the bridge at Arnhem. The Panzer grenadiers came up the streets, throwing stick bombs through windows and blasting their way into cellars, firing their automatic rifles from the hip. At the end of Marktstraat they were held up for a few moments by fire from the cellars of a house on the corner. But then the British troops defending it ran out of ammunition and two paratroopers came out into the street. While one of them tried to draw the Germans' fire, the other worked his way forward with a knife in his hand. For a moment the Panzer grenadiers held their fire as they watched them and then both the British soldiers were shot, and through the smoke and dust and the rattle of fire and the crash of exploding bombs the German advance continued.

From house to house the Germans pushed through the rubble, surrounding isolated groups of men and forcing them to surrender, missing several who lay hidden in cupboards, under floorboards and in empty water tanks, picking up a few wounded men, leaving others to be collected later. 'The fighting was of an indescribable *Fanatismus*', a German says. 'When the ground floor was taken, the British defended themselves obstinately on the first floor. The fight raged through ceilings and staircases. Hand grenades flew in every direction. Each house had to be taken in this way. Some of the British offered resistance to their last breath. Their casualties rose.' But by nine o'clock the area was cleared. There was no more resistance, and tanks and lorries of infantry were rolling unchecked across the bridge for the south. In the cellars where the wounded lay, the German SS troops came down to their enemies and some of them with rough chivalry offered them brandy and chocolate, congratulating them on the battle they had fought. An exhausted British wireless operator sent out his last signal to report their long-delayed surrender. General Urquhart did not receive it but a German interceptor did. He wrote it carefully on his pad. It was short and matter-of-fact and it ended with the words, 'God save the King'.

In the same hour that the troops at the bridge surrendered, General Urquhart held a conference in the 12-foot-square wine cellar of the Park Hotel.

Now that the 2nd Army was on its way, he told the assembled officers, the horseshoe-shaped bridgehead around Hartenstein, north of the Heveadorp ferry, must be held at all costs. He divided the sector into two commands, appointing Hackett to command in the east and Hicks to command in the west. He had lost touch again with the bridge so that he did not know that the resistance there had finally collapsed, and from the last returns which he had been given there seemed to be 3,000 men still fit to fight. It was little enough, but the men were fighting in conditions which were ideally suited to their native resolution and now that the Guards were on their way north from Nijmegen they would not have long to wait before they were relieved. The bridge over the Waal at Nijmegen was only 10 miles away. A few more hours, perhaps, and the leading tanks would arrive. Also there was reason to hope that the Polish Brigade would be able to fly in that day and enable him to reinforce the weak parts of his perimeter, particularly down by the river where the Germans were making constant efforts to break through.

The encouraging news from the south spread quickly through the Division and many of the men began to believe that they would be 'out of it all by the evening'.

The men's rising hope was given encouragement when, later on that morning, medium shells began blasting targets on the outskirts of the perimeter. They fell with astonishing accuracy, sometimes less than 100 yards in front of the forward trenches and the men cheered in excited satisfaction as they whined overhead and exploded with gratifying force in the fields and woods in front of them. Directed by Robert Loder-Symonds from a distance of rather more than 11 miles, XXX Corps's 64th Medium Artillery Regiment, commanded by Lieutenant-Colonel Hunt, maintained their fire all morning and helped to break up more than one German attack.

The 64th had been contacted by Captain McMillan of 1 Forward Observation Unit shortly after nine o'clock. Colonel Thompson had accompanied General Urquhart on his inspection of the regimental area. The last place to be visited was 1 Light Battery's headquarters in the back of a laundry. 'Entering in the wake of the Divisional Commander,' Colonel Thompson says,

I saw Captain McMillan speaking to the CRA (Colonel Loder-Symonds) and handing him his head-set and microphone. From the CRA's expectant attitude I could see that there was something important in the air. Several times he called up saying that he was 'Sunray' (the code name for a commander) and then, 'Yes, and my Christian name is Robert', then 'Wait!'. For a few moments he looked puzzled and slightly amused and then with great gusto he called up and said, 'Yes. Armitage. Charles Armitage!' Turning to the Division Commander he announced that we were through by wireless to 64 Medium Regiment. The tense atmosphere in the command post relaxed in a sense of elation. It was great news . . . The apparently irrelevant wireless conversation resulted from the efforts of 64 Medium Regiment to establish the identity of our station beyond all doubt. To do this their adjutant had asked our CRA whether he had a friend called Charles in his old regiment who was now a big 'seagull' in a land formation (Charles Armitage was BMRA 11 Armoured Division). We were now linked by wireless to the Corps Artillery . . . Moreover this RA net was the only link between the Division and XXX Corps and over it passed much vital General Staff signal traffic in addition to the fire orders.

The first of these signals was sent while General Urquhart was still out of touch with the situation at the bridge. Believing that the northern end was still in British hands he reported:

Enemy attacking main bridge in strength. Situation critical for slender force. Enemy also attacking Divisional position east from HEELSUM vicinity and west from ARNHEM. Situation serious but am forming close perimeter around HARTENSTEIN with remainder of Division. Relief essential both areas earliest possible. Still maintain control ferry-crossing HEAVEADORP.

This signal contained the first direct news that General Horrocks had had from Arnhem since the operation began. Although its tone was alarming, it encouraged him to hope that with the Nijmegen crossing now firmly in his hands, he would be able – provided he moved quickly – to reach the Neder Rijn at Arnhem while the Airborne Division still held out there. Orders were given for the Guards to turn northwest off the main road if they encountered serious opposition and to make full haste for the southern end of the Heveadorp ferry-crossing near Driel. In this way, Horrocks believed, a base might be formed for XXX Corps to build a bridge and effect a crossing of the Neder Rijn at Heveadorp if a crossing by the existing bridge further upstream at Arnhem was found to be no longer possible.

But, although the tanks of his Guards Armoured Division were already less than 10 miles from Arnhem, they could not push on with that speed which Urquhart had stressed was now so essential. For behind them, on the single road by which they had to be supplied and reinforced, the traffic was chaotic. The ground on either side of the road, for the first few hundred yards north of the Meuse-Escaut canal, was soft and swampy and it was feared that the verges might be mined. Already two three-tonners had been blown up by mines in the verge beside the German road-block about a quarter of a mile north of the bridgehead beyond the canal, and Chester Wilmot, the war correspondent, noticed a sign put up by what he called 'some over-conscientious sapper', who believed that the other stretches of the road would be as dangerous: 'DON'T LET THIS HAPPEN TO YOU. KEEP ON THE ROAD. VERGES NOT CLEARED OF MINES.' Consequently drivers kept their vehicles on the narrow strip of concrete roadway, halting for hours on end rather than move off it when a convoy of trucks with supplies urgently needed at the front tried to overtake them. Moreover, because this roadway was open to both artillery fire and air attack, orders had been given for the vehicles to keep well spaced apart. Movement was frustratingly slow and bottle-necks and jams were constantly occurring. Further north the road narrowed as it passed through villages and over dykes and rivers, and at Eindhoven, where the Germans had bombed an ammunition convoy, it was almost completely blocked by wreckage. In addition, for most of its length and on either side, it was under constant threat from Model's rapidly recuperating and growing army which not only shelled its bottlenecks but made infantry assaults on it in an attempt to cut it altogether.

For these reasons it took three days to bring up the infantry of XXX Corps from the Albert Canal to the Maas and it was accordingly not until Thursday afternoon that the Guards, anxiously waiting to be relieved and supported by this infantry, could push on north from the Nijmegen bridgehead towards

Arnhem. By then the enemy had been able to construct a line of anti-tank defences south of Elst in country deeply cut up and criss-crossed by dykes and drainage ditches which made movement off the roads impossible. Artillery support was limited because ammunition had been delayed in the congestion at the rear, and aircraft support could not be called because the radio sets in the RAF contact car were out of order; and when, as the historians of the Guards Armoured Division report, the only other contact car available within the Division was brought up, that proved 'equally useless'. So the British infantry's attacks on the anti-tank gun sites failed through lack of artillery support while the tanks' forward movement was similarly checked through lack of air support. Nor were there any additional troops which General Horrocks could send forward to reinforce his northward thrust, for Gavin's 82nd United States Division and the Coldstream Guards Group from the Guards Armoured Division were fully occupied in keeping open XXX Corps's corridor between the Maas and the Waal which was under constant threat from the German forces in the Reichswald area. And so, despite Horrocks's orders that the spearheads of his Corps must push north 'as early as possible and at maximum speed', it now seemed unlikely that, for the moment at least, they would be able to do so.

Taking full advantage of the continued isolation of the Airborne Division at Arnhem, the Germans increased the number and strength of their attacks in a determined effort 'to push the British parachutists back into the river before the 2nd Army came up to join them'.

Bittrich believed that he could best end British resistance north of the Neder Rijn by a number of sharp, isolated attacks which would take advantage of the 'British junior commander's lack of initiative'. And so, all along the line on Thursday morning and afternoon, fighting patrols and company attacks kept biting at the edges of the perimeter, giving the defenders no respite and no opportunity for sleep.

In Oosterbeek Laag the attacks were particularly sharp and persistent. Here the men collected by Lieutenant Williams on Monday night, together with a heterogeneous mixture of men from the 1st, 3rd and 11th Parachute Battalions and the 2nd South Staffordshires, some of which had come under the administration of 'Thompson Force' had now all been placed under the command of Major Richard Lonsdale, second-in-command of the 11th Battalion, who had been wounded in the hand as he jumped from his aircraft on Monday. Lonsdale, an Irishman of strong personality and great courage, had assumed command of these and other units (which were thereafter known as 'Lonsdale Force') on Wednesday afternoon in the middle of a battle. His men were then defending the south-eastern sector of the divisional perimeter along a semi-circular line on Hackett's right east of Oosterbeek Laag church, and were in danger of being cut off from the rest of the Division by armoured attacks from the north, east and south. Several times already tanks had infiltrated behind the British positions and had set most of the defended houses alight by firing incendiary shells at them. On one occasion three tanks had come up a cindered track from the river and Sergeant J.D. Baskeyfield of the South Staffordshires had aimed his anti-tank gun at the leading one and knocked it out with his first shot. With his next shot he badly damaged the second tank and was turning to engage the third when his gun was put out of action. He took over another gun, whose crew were all dead, and fired with heart-rending determination at the tank until he too was shot and killed. But acts of heroism such as this could not, as Lonsdale knew, keep back the German armour indefinitely and he decided during the evening that he must withdraw his men to a tighter and more readily defensible line near Oosterbeek Laag church. By nightfall he had extricated them from their isolated positions in the east and had established them around the church on both sides of the road and in the meadow between the church and the river, where on Thursday morning and afternoon they were subjected to violent mortar bombardments from the German positions behind the railway embankment.

Towards evening, while he was standing beside the Rev. R.T. Watkins, the 1st Battalion's padre, 'one of the best', as Lonsdale says, 'a wonderful example to us all'. Lonsdale was wounded again. But soon afterwards he was given news which made his wounds seem unimportant. 'Luck hadn't been on our side', he said afterwards. 'But suddenly it seemed about to change. I could have cheered when Lord Billy Buckhurst, our liaison officer with the 4th Brigade Headquarters, brought me the great news that armoured reconnaissance units of the 2nd Army had reached the far bank of the river.'

There was news, too, that XXX Corps would soon attempt a crossing of the river by the Heveadorp ferry, preceded by a barrage on the low-lying land between the river and the road. It was essential then that the part of 'Lonsdale Force', which for the past 20 hours had been occupying water-logged trenches under the osiers that comprised the hedge running from the church to the river bank, should be withdrawn and brought north of the lower Oosterbeek to Arnhem road.

Sending his brave and intelligent batman, Noble, with his order, Lonsdale withdrew his men from the meadow. As they passed the little church of Oosterbeek Laag they were called inside. Lonsdale had decided to give them some words of advice and encouragement. The constant attacks, the persistent mortaring, the snipers' bullets whining between the trees had driven many of them to the edge of their endurance. They stumbled through the porch, exhausted and filthy, and sat down in the pews in a kind of daze. It was growing dark and it had started to rain again.

It was a rugged, thick-walled, ancient church [Padre Watkins remembers]. And never in all the centuries of its quiet watch over the Neder Rijn had it sheltered such a congregation as now came stumbling in. They sprawled in the pews, they 'brewed up' in the

The bridge at Arnhem, showing the wreckage of the German armour on the ramp at the northern end

A 6-pounder anti-tank gun in action

Defending the Park Hotel at Hartenstein

A re-supply mission

Collecting supplies

Searching a school for snipers

German troops in Arnhem

British prisoners being escorted through Arnhem

A Dutch nurse tending the wounded

Wounded British prisoners

aisle and on the chancel floor, they smoked, they swore. Above all they rested. The crash of shells and the falling of plaster and roof-timbers was nothing to what was going on outside. This was peace.

'The scene as I spoke inside the shattered church lives vividly in my memory', Major Lonsdale says. 'I can still see the tired upturned faces of my congregation, the strangest ever gathered there . . . Yes, I thought, but they're still defiant though, still unbroken.'

This is by no means the first time we have fought the Germans [Lonsdale told them]. We fought the cream of their army in North Africa, in Sicily and in Italy. Now we're up against them here. We defeated them in those earlier campaigns. They were not good enough for us then and they are bloody well not good enough for us now. They are up against the finest soldiers in the world. An hour from now we'll take up defensive positions north of the road outside. Make certain you dig in well and that your weapons and ammo. are in good order. We are getting short of ammo. so when you shoot, shoot to kill. My HQ will be in the area of the church. Good luck to you all.

The men walked out into the rain to join the rest of 'Lonsdale Force' and began to occupy the scattered buildings and to dig their trenches by the uncertain light of distant fires. Including the glider pilots there were less than 400 men left now in the whole of the force but they held on in their new positions till the end of the battle. Buildings were fired and mined over their heads but they kept to the rubble.

'No one, of course,' says Lonsdale, 'had any doubts now as to the seriousness of our position. All hope of breaking through to the bridge had been abandoned.'

'I didn't care by then if I never saw the bloody bridge at all; and I don't think many of us did neither', Private George Wood thought. 'But we dug in and held on. That's how you get. Fed up but flipping stubborn. Those snipers, though. They were a bastard.'

All day long, here as elsewhere, they had been picking out incautious or unlucky soldiers in their telescopic sights and shooting them down. They had strict instructions to respect the Red Cross arm-bands, but anyone else who moved about in the open without an arm-band or flag risked his life every time he did so. 'Padre Watkins did great work in getting in the wounded', one of those he took to a dressing station remembers. 'He was always in the middle of it and didn't seem to care. The snipers didn't shoot at him or if they did they missed him. I don't think they did shoot, though. They were all right like that. There wasn't much firing round the dressing stations.'

The main dressing station was in the Hotel Schoonoord. It was already full on Wednesday morning when Colonel Graeme Warrack, the brave and resourceful officer in command of the Division's Medical Services, left Divisional Headquarters with an American wireless operator who had been wounded in the stomach. He had arrived at the hotel to find a fierce battle in progress around it, and on hearing shouts of command in German, he had torn off his badges of rank and gone upstairs to help with the wounded.

He was hard at work when a shell crashed into the roof and several wounded soldiers in the room that he was in were injured again as the timbers and tiles crashed down upon them. As the men were being moved in the still swirling dust, two more shells hit the hotel and again the plaster and timbers fell into the makeshift wards. At length the hotel was draped with Red Cross flags and inside its battered walls, for the rest of that day and the next, British and German wounded were treated side by side.

A nervous German guard was placed outside it and a German surgeon worked inside it; and, although at first the walking wounded were taken away as prisoners, later on no such rules prevailed. Wounded men walked in past the guard for treatment and were even allowed to go back to their units when their wounds had been cleaned and bandaged. Once a British officer who had called to have an arm wound dressed was told by the sentry that he must consider himself a prisoner of war. 'Nonsense', he said curtly and walked away from the sentry who made no effort to prevent him leaving.

Colonel Warrack, himself, was permitted to leave to attend to his duties and to visit the other doctors in the dressing stations within the British perimeter, at the Hotel Tafelberg and Mevrouw Kate ter Hort's white house near Oosterbeek Laag church.

Kate ter Horst, who for three days and nights had been helping the 1st Airlanding Light Regiment's Medical Officer, Dr Randall Martin, with his growing number of patients, is a woman of remarkable character. Tall and graceful with fair hair and pale blue eyes, she has a serenity of manner and a softness of voice which the wounded found inspiring. In the evenings after she had given her five children their supper in the cellar and had told them a story, she came up to comfort the wounded. Although the house was frequently under heavy fire from both small-arms and heavy mortars she never once showed that she was either afraid or resentful. Nor did she ever appear to sleep or to be in need of sleep.

On his arrival Dr Martin had been optimistic and had asked Mevrouw ter Horst politely for no more than the use of a bicycle shed and washhouse for a 'little Red Cross first-aid post'. 'We don't need much', he had said, 'only the lightly wounded will be treated here and sent on to the hospital in the Hotel Tafelberg, where they can have surgical attention. I hope we won't have many casualties.'

On the first day there was only one, a man with an injured foot. But on Tuesday the rooms began to fill and on Wednesday morning when at dawn Mevrouw ter Horst came up from the cellar she was 'struck dumb with amazement'.

During the night [she remembers] our house had taken on a totally different appearance. The long corridor is filled with wounded, they lie side by side on their linen stretchers and there is just room between them to put down one foot. I get through to the kitchen with great difficulty, where I find a great activity. On the granite floor there are six or seven wounded men . . . Trained orderlies give them morphia injections and in copying-pencil write on the patient's forehead the time and the dose he has had.

'Isn't there any better water?' asks the doctor. 'The pump gives so little and it isn't clear.' I know that there is a good pump at our neighbours, some 60 yards away, and shortly afterwards a few buckets of fresh water are brought in.

I go through the rooms . . . Wounded everywhere, in the dining-room, in the study and the garden-room, in the side corridor and even under the stairs. And in the lavatory. There is not a single corner free of them. Of the panes of glass which yesterday were smashed and partly gone, not a trace to be seen, except of course the splinters which lie like sugar over the wounded. Our rooms are unrecognisable, for the furniture has been thrown out of the windows to make room for the wounded . . . Then I go on to the padre, a Captain, a kind little man with curly hair and spectacles; he is on the job the whole day and only yesterday I saw him cleaning out the indescribably dirty lavatory, while the privates stood round him, watching. A captain and even a chaplain doing such work! You should have had five years of German discipline! – A hurricane of explosions falls around us, the very walls shake round us. I hear the crackling of fire. The house on the other side of the road is ablaze . . . 'Phosphorus'! The thought flies through my brain. The wounded are lying still on their backs, helpless, without a word of complaint . . . In the afternoon even the stairs and landing are full of wounded soldiers. Nobody can get through. The whole top floor is full, Graham, one of the orderlies, tells me . . . Towards the evening I go to the back door for a breath of fresh air and then I see them for the first time: the dead. Most of them lying face downwards with the tousled hair over their muddy faces. There they lie, like forgotten bags which have fallen on the path to the kitchen.

This is the end of a hard day. Can it go on like this much longer? – I read something to the children, some recollections of their infant years, at which they always laugh . . . 'You are very brave children, it won't last much longer and then we shall be free.' And before the night-light goes out everybody gets a cherry from the preserve bottle, to keep them from being too thirsty.

When Colonel Warrack arrived at her house, having visited other houses where the tirelessly working Medical Services under his command were operating in quite as appalling conditions, he found both Kate ter Horst and Dr Martin dealing with several new cases that had recently been brought in, crowding the already congested rooms so tightly that some of the wounded had to be treated in the boiler house.

On a previous visit, Brigadier Hackett on crossing the lawn had been struck in the face by the splinters of a bursting mortar bomb which had killed his acting Brigade Major, D.J. Madden, and badly wounded Colonel Thompson in the stomach. Several other men were also wounded and had been carried into the crowded house for treatment.

Colonel Warrack decided that he must relieve the appalling congestion. He sent several men who were still able to walk to the Tafelberg Hotel and, strapping two men across the bonnet of Martin's jeep and putting two more in the back, he drove to the Tafelberg himself.

Elsewhere at this time other wounded men who could do so were also making their way back to less exposed buildings. One group of these had just left the casualty clearing post in the KOSB's sector which after a heavy bombardment had received a direct hit. They were led by Major Coke, the small, smart second-in-command of the battalion and Captain Devlin, the Medical Officer. They had not gone far when at a crossroads a

German patrol prepared to open fire. The two officers, holding a Red Cross flag, went forward to protest to the extremely young German officer in command.

'Where are you going?' the officer asked.

'We are only going to our regimental aid post', Major Coke replied.

'That may be', said the young officer. 'But you are in our territory and are therefore our prisoners.'

'You can't do that', said Coke. 'We're under the Red Cross. You can't touch us.'

Seeing the officer's doubt, Coke pressed the point.

'You just can't do it', he insisted. 'After all we're only going to *our* house.'

The officer seemed about to give way, but then said, 'I think you'd better come and see the major'.

The major just laughed. 'Of course they're prisoners', he said and sent them further down the road. On the way they met two tanks. Once more Major Coke adopted an attitude of determined self-righteousness. He held up his hand with an imperious gesture and the tanks stopped. A German officer got out and for a few moments Coke spoke to him. Then the tanks turned round in the road and Coke waved his men aboard.

'He's commandeered the bloody thing', one of them said with begrudging admiration.

The loss to their battalions of such men as Major Coke was, however, now sorely felt throughout the Division; for the attacks on the British position were being increased and strengthened. In several sectors the perimeter was becoming dangerously weak where tanks and infantry patrols had infiltrated between the extended outposts and caused heavy casualties amongst the defenders. The attacks were particularly strong from the west along the river line. After heavy fighting the Border Regiment had been driven off the high ground at Westerbouwing and the loss of this commanding position seriously endangered the

Division's hold on the water front. General Urquhart was acutely aware of this and ordered a company of the Border Regiment to retake it. Major Cousens's men, however, were so exhausted that the attack was not put in for fear that, if it were not successful, a disastrous gap would be opened upon that vital corner of the perimeter. And although the defences there and, indeed, on both sides of the perimeter where it led down to the river were now so weak, General Urquhart did not feel he could reinforce them by taking units away from the northern lines which were under increasing pressure from hour to hour.*

Throughout Thursday the Germans had been receiving reinforcements from the west. At noon 45 of the long-awaited *Königstiger* tanks from *Panzerabteilang 503* had arrived in Arnhem. Later came units of another Panzer grenadier battalion from Germany under command of Captain Bruhns, several hastily-formed companies of *Luftwaffe* ground staff fighting as infantry, the 171st *Auffrischung liegende* artillery regiment with over 30 guns from Zutphen and the *Landsturm 'Nederland'* of Dutch SS. By four o'clock in the afternoon all of these units were in action. Five minutes later *Obersturmbannführer* Walter Harzer received a message from Dunkirk: '*Starke viermotorige Verbände mit Lastenseglern in Schlepp haven in sechstausend Meter Höhe um 16 Uhr Dünkirchen in Richtung Südost überflogen.*' This strong force of aircraft which had flown over Dunkirk at four o'clock would soon be over Arnhem

---

* General Urquhart has been severely criticised for not attaching sufficient importance to the high ground which dominates the river at Westerbouwing and for 'choosing a perimeter' which was of no military value. I brought these criticisms to his notice and he told me: 'I hope it will be realised that the perimeter was not a tidy affair set up by itself as such. The last thing we ever intended to do was to sit down on the ground and be attacked, and for the first few days of the battle our only intention was to get forward to the Arnhem bridge with as many units and as quickly as possible. Circumstances decided otherwise and it was only as a result of them that the perimeter was slowly formed – it almost formed itself; at any rate in outline . . . The loss of the high ground at Westerbouwing was a sad blow and it was planned to recapture it . . . It is still a mystery to me how the Germans let us get away with things on the river to the extent that they did, and they failed to make much use of the high ground at Westerbouwing.'

and Nijmegen. There would be about an hour, Harzer calculated, in which to make preparations to receive them. Orders went out to all units of the 9th and 10th SS Panzer Divisions, to all anti-aircraft units and to neighbouring airfields where, at twenty to five, 60 German *Jäger* aircraft were waiting to take off. 'The German commanders looked at their watches', Erich Kern says. 'Soon it would be five o'clock. The artillery fire died down slowly. The barrels of the anti-aircraft guns stared up into the sky from which there came to our ears a slight hum. It was the German fighters . . . Suddenly the first anti-aircraft gun roared . . . and, one after another, other batteries joined in the attack.'

By the time the aircraft arrived in the Arnhem area the flak had become intense and the Poles of General Sosabowski's long awaited brigade jumped out into a cruel fire. Owing to the collapse of the resistance at the bridge it had been decided to drop them not on the polder south of Arnhem but south of the Heveadorp ferry near Driel, the spire of whose church could be clearly seen from the northern side of the river. It was hoped that the Poles would be able to cross over into the Divisional perimeter by the ferry, leaving a bridgehead on the southern bank into which could be driven the spearheads of XXX Corps. The Poles landed at about a quarter past five. They were given, as Bittrich and Harzer had hoped, a savage reception. But Sosabowski himself landed unhurt and was soon skilfully organising his brigade for the river crossing. As he approached the ferry, however, a woman in the Dutch underground, Mejuffrouw Cora Baltussen, gave him some distressing news. The British had been driven off the northern end of the Heveadorp ferry two hours before the Polish landings. The ferry itself was now destroyed and the crossings were dominated by German guns.

Sosabowski moved into a deserted farmhouse to make fresh plans. He was, so one of his officers said, 'in a fearful temper'. He had cause to be. Not only were all his glider-borne units and

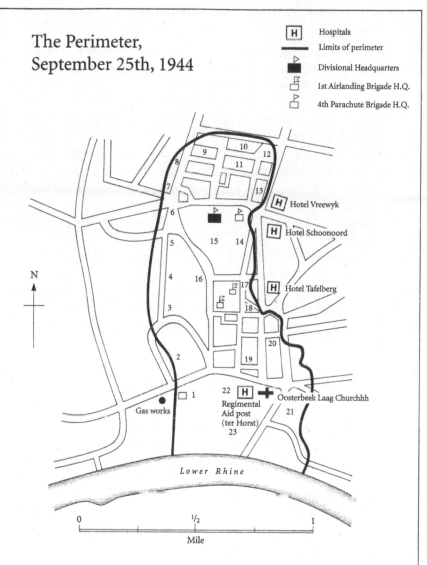

The Perimeter, September 25th, 1944

H	Hospitals
▬	Limits of perimeter
◼	Divisional Headquarters
1st Airlanding Brigade H.Q.
4th Parachute Brigade H.Q.

H Hotel Vreewyk

H Hotel Schoonoord

H Hotel Tafelberg

N

Gas works

22 H Oosterbeek Laag Churchhh
Regimental
Aid post
(ter Horst)
23

21

Lower Rhine

0   ½   1
Mile

Approximate locations of troops

1,2 B & D Companies Border Regiment
3   Units of South Staffordshires
4   Glider Pilots
5   Poles
6   C Company Border Regiment
7   A Company Border Regiment
8   Glider Pilots
9,10 K.O.S.B.
11   Royal Engineers

12   Recconnaissance Squadron
13   Poles and Glider Pilots and remnants of 156th Parachute Battalion
14   Independent Parachute Company and remnants of 10th Parachute Battalion
15   Glider Pilots
16   Div. H.Q. Troops
17   4th Brigade H.Q. Troops
18   R.A.S.C.

19   1st Light Regiment R.A., H.Q.
20   Units of South Staffordshires
21   Lonsdale Force
22   Glider Pilots
23   Units of South Staffordshires

most of his heavy weapons on the other side of the river; but one of his three battalions had failed to arrive. The aircraft transporting it had been forced to return to base owing to bad weather and it was not to reach him for three days. As he was looking anxiously at his maps, the door was thrown open and a naked man, dripping with water and splashed with mud, a camouflaged net wrapped around his face, burst into the room.

'What the hell?' Sosabowski began, but then recognising Captain Zwolanski, his liaison officer at the British Headquarters, he stopped.

'I have just swum the Rhine', Zwolanski said, 'to bring you the latest news.'

'Yes, it looks as if you have', said Sosabowski with an abrupt gracelessness. 'Tell me about it.'

Zwolanski told him that the British would bring rafts to the river bank during the night so that the Poles could cross over to the northern side. But for most of the night Sosabowski waited for the rafts in vain until, two hours before dawn, he felt he could wait no longer and he withdrew his men from the river line so as to be prepared to hold off the German infantry attacks which he knew would not be delayed much longer.

The attack which had driven the British off the northern end of the Heveadorp ferry was one of many which had been made and were to be made that Thursday afternoon on the British perimeter. The Border Regiment was attacked in the west; Major Lonsdale's force was attacked in the south; and the KOSB, after a gallant attempt to halt the onslaught with bayonets, were driven from their positions in the north. They decided immediately to retake them. 'We were delighted to have a chance of having a crack at the Germans', Colonel Payton-Reid wrote proudly in his diary. 'We drenched them with fire first and then with bayonets. They wouldn't stand to the bayonet and made no attempt to fight us. They fired as we came up. We cleared them right out.' But by dusk the strength of the KOSB had been reduced to 150 men and it seemed as impossible for them as for any other battalion to continue much longer to hold their ground.

Soon after seven, the remnants of the 10th Battalion occupying the most easterly position astride the main road through Oosterbeek were attacked by tanks and self-propelled guns firing phosphorus shells. The parachutists had to withdraw from their houses which were soon burning fiercely, and in the withdrawal Colonel Smyth, their commanding officer, was wounded again, this time fatally, and the last of their officers was killed.

It was getting 'a bit chaotic', a soldier records with characteristic understatement. 'Everybody was all over the shop and we just looked for Germans to knock out . . . Then the Tigers arrived and I heard a chap say, "We can't do much against these bastards!" We still had Piats but the ammunition was getting scarce and fresh supplies didn't arrive. We took three prisoners who had Players and Woodbines on them, so we might have guessed that the supply drops had misfired.'

South of the now German-held ferry crossing, the Poles took up defensive positions around Driel and General Bittrich, so as to prevent their opening up the road from Nijmegen, sent Major Knaust's battalion with a Panther tank company south across Arnhem bridge to support those units of the 10th SS Division in the area of Elst. The disappearance of this tough battalion from the edge of the divisional perimeter made, however, only a slight and temporary improvement to Urquhart's position which by dusk was, in the words of one of his staff, 'extremely precarious'.

But, although German patrols were constantly infiltrating between the various units of the thinly held British lines, they continued to be pushed back by the determined fire of the defenders who were learning to use captured and unfamiliar weapons with great skill and ingenuity and to perform tasks for which many of them had never been trained. When, for instance, two tanks rattled into the divisional area from the north-east, one of the 1st Light Battery's guns was man-handled by a detachment including the Officers' Mess Sergeant Roullier and an RASC clerk into a position from which the tanks could be engaged at close range, while Major Cain of the South Staffordshires fired at one of them with a Piat and an artillery sergeant, J. Daly, fired at the other with a Bren gun. No sooner had this danger been averted than a company of enemy infantry infiltrated between the lines of the Border Regiment and E troop of the 1st Airlanding Light Regiment, occupying a gas works from which snipers were able to fire into the heart of the divisional area. Captain C.A. Harrison, E troop's commander, led a hastily collected force of men from various regiments against the gas works and drove the Germans out of it.

Despite the bravery and enterprise of the British troops, however, as soon as the enemy were driven back in one place, they broke through again in another and Urquhart decided that he must constrict his perimeter still further. He pulled back the KOSB, sent the Independent Company with a squadron of Royal Engineers and the remains of the Reconnaissance Squadron to fill a growing gap in the north-east; and withdrew the forward units of the divisional RASC and sent them to fill another large gap in the south-east just north of 'Lonsdale Force'. Even so the defended area was still too large; it was rather less than a mile wide where it ran parallel with the river at the south and about three quarters of a mile wide at the north. In this ceaselessly bombarded area of 450 acres, the 1st Airborne Division struggled to survive. The Germans found an apt name for it – '*Der Lessel*': 'the Cauldron'.

The men's most pressing need was for water, for the Germans had succeeded in cutting off the main supply to Oosterbeek on the first day of the battle. There was little for drinking, none for washing, far from enough for the wounded. Storage tanks, central-heating systems, even fish bowls were drained. The supply drop on Thursday included canisters of water but, whereas a few cases of food and ammunition (disastrously and shamefully including the wrong sort of shells for the 75-mm guns) were dropped inside the British lines, hardly any water was. It was, moreover, the most costly and hazardous supply mission which the RAF had yet to make. Because of the bad weather, the later waves of supply aircraft had to fly in without fighter protection.

> The result [38 Group RAF reported afterwards] is reflected in the casualties. For the first time enemy fighters were in full evidence, and 10 Focke-Wulf 190s, in particular, took heavy toll, shooting down 7 out of 10 aircraft from one squadron in the third wave. A total of 23 aircraft (20% of the force) are unaccounted for; a further 7 were damaged by fighters and 31 by flak which was more intense than ever along the route and in the target area. A total of 52% of the force was lost or damaged . . . Very little was retrieved from this drop.

Colonel Preston, continued to watch the aircraft until only two Dakotas remained in sight.

> And from somewhere in both of them [he remembers] a slow flame started to curl, gradually enveloping each fuselage. Flying lower and lower they continued to drop their panniers whose parachutes showed for a moment, red and blue and yellow against the dark green of the trees. I could not get rid of the impression, which was strengthened by my being unable to hear their engines, that this was no living scene I was watching but something out of a silent film. Soon they disappeared and for a short time there was a strange silence. Then the 88s, freed from the task of dealing with the aircraft, turned once again to us. The rain started again and the crowd in front of the hotel broke up. I exchanged a few words with Michael Packe, just setting out on his forlorn task of trying to locate the few panniers that had fallen within the perimeter. Then, carrying a useless Verey pistol and an incongruously gay yellow handkerchief, I walked slowly back to

the hotel, feeling more futile than I had done since the operation began.

'Bloody few rations there', Colonel Packe had said to him after a previous supply mission, complaining bitterly that what had got through was 'damn useless stuff' and that all the things the Division really needed had 'gone down the drain'. 'Do you know what these are full of?' he added, kicking viciously at some panniers against which Preston was leaning, 'Berets! Red, bloody berets! And that one. That's full of stationery!' And now when the men of the Division desperately needed food and ammunition and water – above all water – they got soap.

'It was bloody awful looking up', a soldier in the 3rd Battalion thought, 'and seeing all that stuff dropping down. I thought to myself maybe there's a bottle of beer in that lot. God, I was thirsty!'

Men risked their lives, in fact, crawling out into the open towards the wells and pumps which were all marked by snipers. The nearest supply to Mevrouw ter Horst's house was from a pump in a garden 60 yards away and the dash towards it was a perilous one, lined with the bodies of the dead. From Divisional Headquarters, General Urquhart's batman, Private Hancock, and a Dutchman crawled into a field towards a well with water bottles and kettles. But when they reached the well, the Dutchman lost his grip on the winding handle and the bucket clattered noisily against the brick sides. Rifles opened up on them from every direction. It was three hours before Hancock returned to Headquarters with the precious water. Another soldier was shot and killed as he crawled in search of water past a trench occupied by some Polish parachutists who 'always believed', so one of his officers said, 'in shooting first and asking questions afterwards. The trouble was they couldn't understand the answers so they shot again.'

It was a cold night and a hungry one. During the early days at Arnhem, men had been able to supplement their rations by the

sides and legs of pork which they had cut from the pigs they
had found in unattended styes and even by venison from the
frightened does which ran out of the woods. But there were
hardly any animals to be seen now. And although some men,
lucky enough to be occupying houses whose store-cupboards
were stocked with tinned food and preserves and whose gardens
were full of vegetables, fed well enough, the only food available
for many of those others out in the trenches was a handful of
boiled sweets or a few sardines and biscuits, and when the
biscuits and sweets and sardines had gone the thirst remained.
'There was a dead cow lying in the meadow near me,' a soldier
in the KOSB said, 'a great big fat-looking bugger, with its legs in
the air, but I couldn't fancy it. It was a drink I wanted. I was
dying for a drink.'

The men longed for cigarettes, too.

They had no cigarettes [says Major Cain], and I hadn't any to
give them, though they used to ask me for them when I visited
them. They'd say 'Where's the 2nd Army? What's the news from
the other side? We haven't had anything to eat for some
time . . . !' There just weren't any rations after the first day. The
troops got vegetables – tomatoes, potatoes. The difficulty was
cooking, though they did a bit in mess tins in slit trenches. My
batman cooked a few meals in an outside lavatory. There were
several hutches of tame rabbits one of which I fed. He used to
scratch at the wire of his hutch as I went by and I'd give him some
lettuce. One day a parachutist came round and I saw him walking
away with my rabbit, dead. I asked him what he was doing with it,
and he said he was on the scrounge. I made him hand the rabbit
over and I left it between my batman's trench and mine and it was
blown up by a shell.

In an upper floor of the Park Hotel a canary, whose cage a
kind-hearted signaller had put behind a pile of books, was also
killed that day by the flying fragment of a shell. 'I went up to give

it a drop of water,' the signaller said, 'and it was lying against the wall with its head off. I felt more upset by that than by all the dead outside. I was jumpy already. But this made me worse somehow. I nearly cried. In fact, if you want to know the truth, I did cry. Of course, we were all jumpy. Or nearly all. The General wasn't. He never got rattled.' Indeed, as Urquhart came out each morning, having shaved with a dry razor blade, and walked quickly across the lawn from the hotel with its scarred walls and shattered windows he contrived to look as composed and confident as ever. 'His calm and cheerfulness', a Polish war correspondent reported, 'are really the sole cause of our optimism.'

It was a calm, in fact, which he found it increasingly difficult to simulate. At the end of this bitter day he called Hicks and Hackett to Divisional Headquarters. 'I want you to read this', he said to them, holding out a signal which he had drafted. 'They ought to know across the river that it's not too good here, but I don't really want to overdo it. Do you think this is going too far?'

'We read it slowly and quietly', Hackett says, 'sitting in wicker garden chairs and we reckoned that no, on the whole, that was fair enough . . . I said I thought it was about right. Pip (Hicks) said so too. Roy (Urquhart) thanked us and handed it in for transmission.'

> No knowledge elements of Div. in ARNHEM for 24 hours [it read]. Balance of Division in very tight perimeter. Heavy mortaring and machine-gun fire followed by local attacks. Main nuisance SP guns. Our casualties heavy. Resources stretched to utmost. Relief within 24 hours vital.

Friday

'Everything possible will be done to get the essentials through.'
Lieutenant-General Brian Horrocks

At dawn on Friday General Urquhart received a reply from XXX Corps Headquarters:

43 Div. ordered to take all risks to effect relief to-day and are directed on ferry. If situation warrants you should withdraw on or across ferry.

Despite the tone of this signal Urquhart did not feel that XXX Corps were fully aware of his predicament or that 'all risks' were, in fact, being taken to relieve him. And his doubts, so it has afterwards been suggested, were justified.

Accepting the fact that he could not now expect to force a passage through to the Zuider Zee but still hoping that Urquhart's bridgehead west of Arnhem could be held until the opportunity came to exploit it, Horrocks had ordered his 43rd Division, commanded by Major-General G.I. Thomas, to push forward at dawn to the Neder Rijn. But, although one of Thomas's brigades reached Nijmegen on Thursday, its leading battalion was held up by a traffic block in the town, and was later directed over the wrong bridge. 'Night had fallen', the brigadier subsequently reported, 'by the time the battalion commander had regained control.' Friday's dawn found the brigade split in two by the Waal. By half past seven armoured cars of the Household Cavalry were on the other side of the village of Oosterhout and had joined up with the Polish parachutists south of Elst. It was not until two hours later, however, that the leading battalion of the 43rd Division reached Oosterhout. By this time the Germans had become aware of what was happening and were able to check the advance almost as soon as it had begun. Two attacks failed and only at five o'clock that afternoon, after a third attack supported by over 100 guns, was a gap made in the German defences through which a mobile column of tanks, infantry and machine-gunners raced away towards the Neder Rijn.

Almost a whole day had been lost. And to the Airborne Division these lost hours had been vital. The 43rd Division has, consequently, been severely criticised for its slowness and caution and, despite a generous and heart-felt defence by Sir Brian Horrocks in his book, *A Full Life,* and a detailed and well reasoned account of these events by Major-General Essame in his, *43rd Division at War,* the criticism is not without foundation. There were, as Horrocks says, good reasons for the delay and ample evidence of individual heroism but it is nevertheless impossible to escape the conclusion that 'all risks' were not being taken. 'I rather think it is our fault', General Thomas's chief of staff, Lieutenant-Colonel David Meynell, told Chester Wilmot that evening. 'We have been slow.'*

Suspecting this, General Urquhart sent for Colonel Mackenzie early on Friday morning.

---

* In making these observations, I do not want to disparage the conduct of any battalion in this fine Division which had suffered heavier losses than any other British division in the BLA. I am sure that had the commander of the leading brigade and his battalion commanders been made aware earlier of the grave situation north of the Neder Rijn more risks would have been taken. It seems only fair to add that General Essame, who is the leading authority on the events which I have briefly described, thinks that I have been unjust. 'I feel', he has told me, 'that you give undue weight to the opinions of a great war correspondent now

'It's absolutely vital', he told him, 'that Browning and Horrocks should know that the Division no longer exists as such and that we are now merely a collection of individuals holding on. Make clear to them that we're terribly short of men, ammunition, food and medical supplies and that we need some DUKWs to ferry the Poles across. If supplies don't arrive to-night it may be too late.'

Taking Lieutenant-Colonel E.C.W. Myers, the CRE with him, Mackenzie set off immediately. 'Do try and make them realise there what a fix we're in', Urquhart called after them. Myers had already studied the problem of ferrying the Poles across the river and could give XXX Corps an accurate estimate of what craft and equipment were required. After a previous visit to the Poles he had concealed an inflatable dinghy near the river, south of Oosterbeek Laag church, and the two officers made their way towards it.

They inflated it and then carried it down towards a small ditch which led to the river.

We started in the ditch [Mackenzie says], but eventually had to get out because it is full of horrible things. We then walked down the hedge towing the rubber boat behind us. We had another chap, Storrs, with us; and he saw us into the boat and we rowed across. I rowed and Myers swore at me for splashing. There were one or two shots fired but they were a long way above our heads. We got over. We parked the boat in a little dip and crawled away from the bank. There was a flap on this side too. We had got through to the Poles on the wireless to meet us. There was a battle going on; and we couldn't make out which were Poles and which were Germans.

dead who did not actually see the battle at the bottleneck before Oosterhout, and to the comment of a Chief of Staff on the point of relinquishing his appointment and who anyhow was miles away from the scene . . . Sixteen years have now elapsed. I suggest therefore that no harm will result if a word of commendation is given to the German commander on the spot for the skill with which he exploited the ground and inspired his men to fight with normal German efficiency. We could not use our tanks, but he, having an excellent concealed lateral road, could use his and did so with effect.'

They climbed up the steep walls of the bank and then down on to the wide expanse of open polder beyond it. They moved across it cautiously towards Driel. Occasionally there was a muffled burst of machine-gun fire in the damp air, but they were not touched. The Polish Brigade had been warned of their arrival but there were no Poles to be seen; and they walked across the wet ground feeling alone and isolated in the cold morning light. And then at last they caught sight of two steel helmets. It was impossible to say at this distance whether they belonged to Poles or Germans.

Mackenzie and Myers jumped into a ditch and lay there for two or three minutes watching and waiting. Eventually they persuaded themselves that the two half-hidden figures must be Poles. Mackenzie got out of the ditch first, waving a white handkerchief, while Myers remained behind to cover him in case they were wrong. Myers watched Mackenzie go forward and then jumped out of the ditch, overwhelmed with relief, as he saw him wave his arm cheerfully over his head.

One of the two figures was a Polish parachutist, the other a British liaison officer. They had each brought two bicycles with them to the meeting place and so the four men rode off to General Sosabowski's Headquarters where they found the Polish Brigade under attack by German troops from Elst, supported by guns north of the river. The Poles were still, as they had been all day, holding their ground; but the constant pressure had made it impossible for Sosabowski to think about anything but the problems of keeping the Germans back.

'General', Mackenzie said to him, 'every man you can get across the river to help 1st Airborne will be invaluable. Even five or ten might make a difference.'

But what could he do, Sosabowski protested, without rafts or boats?

'I think we can help', Colonel Myers said. 'There are some small three-man rubber dinghies which can be pulled backwards and forwards across the river by hawsers.'

While the Polish engineers discussed this with Myers, Mackenzie signalled General Horrocks with the news of the Airborne Division's plight. Using the wireless set belonging to the troop of the Household Cavalry which had pushed through Oosterhout ahead of the 43rd Division and had now reached Driel, he transmitted a message which read: 'We are short of ammunition, men, food and medical supplies. DUKWs are essential. Two or three would be sufficient. If supplies do not arrive to-night it may be too late.'

'Everything possible will be done', Horrocks replied, 'to get the essentials through.'

In the morning rain the shattered Airborne Division still fought back.

Renewing their tactics of the previous day, the Germans threw in continuous, isolated attacks on various points of the perimeter. Self-propelled guns tracked down the roads firing their explosive and phosphorus shells at defended houses. 'These SP guns', Lieutenant Stevenson of the Reconnaissance Squadron recorded,

hit every house in our area at least once and at very short range. We always heard the creaking of their tracks as they came along and it wasn't pleasant. In fact, we decided we must do something about it, so one NCO and a trooper were put with a Piat in a slit trench at the crossroads to wait for the next SP gun. About half an hour had gone by when she came creaking up. The trooper let fly and hit it first shot from about 70 yards. Unfortunately the shot immobilised the vehicle but not its guns. The crew must have recovered very quickly and they brought machine-gun fire to bear on the slit trenches killing and wounding two glider pilots who were in the next trench to our chaps.

Louis Hagen, a brave and enterprising Jewish glider pilot who had been born in Germany, was in this sector helping to throw back the constant attacks made by tanks and self-propelled guns against the houses in the street which he was defending. He had read Wintringham's descriptions of street fighting in Spain and advised the other pilots in his flight how to barricade the windows so that the Germans could not throw grenades through them, how to conceal the communicating trenches dug in the gardens between one house and another so that, if one house fell, the men could crawl away unseen into the next one. He discovered, as Lieutenant Stevenson had done, what an effective anti-tank weapon the Piat was, despite its small size and crude appearance. He had helped to site one in the attic of his house and a 'wave of disgust' came over him when one of his officers came up to offer to fire it because he had once fired a practice shot whereas Hagen, himself, had only 'once been shown how to load it'. He felt they had 'wasted weeks, even months, with drill and kit inspection' and wondered in exasperation why 'instead they hadn't been taught about house-to-house fighting and the Piat gun'. The officer fired it against an approaching self-propelled gun and was thrown, covered with dust, against the wall by the recoil; and the bomb fell 20 yards short. He fired four or five more shots but missed each time.

Around Oosterbeek Laag church the attacks on Friday were particularly sharp and wearingly persistent. Held off by Lonsdale's still gallantly fighting but rapidly dwindling force, the Germans would withdraw for a time and then come back again, sometimes supported by Focke-Wulf 190s which, although the weather was 'too bad for any flying from England', were in action intermittently throughout the day. One group of parachutists, commanded by Major Alan Bush and Captain Cleminson (now the only surviving officers in the 3rd Battalion) and encouraged by Sergeant Callaghan in an absurdly tall Dutch top hat, destroyed a self-propelled gun. Another self-propelled gun was put out of action by the Polish crew of an anti-tank gun who ran down the road as fast as they could, straight at any German vehicles which came into view, pushing their gun in front of them. These Poles, indeed, attacked anything which looked as if it might be German and an English officer told them only to fire at tanks as 'it drew down all sorts of things'. But the Poles took no notice and their officer said, 'Sometimes I fire. Sometimes I do not fire.' 'Eventually they fired once too often,' according to the English officer, 'and were all killed. We weren't sorry as a matter of fact, though the gun was smashed.'

The tanks and self-propelled guns had then to be stopped by Piats. Major Cain lobbed bombs over the roof of a house behind which a gun lay concealed, while an artillery officer, Ian Meikle, directed his fire from behind a chimney stack.

I fired about 50 bombs from this weapon, which blew my left ear drum in [says Major Cain]. Meikle was shouting at me, giving me instructions, when the chimney pot from his house fell into the trench I was in. Meikle was killed. The other man in my trench got out screaming and scrambling. I told him to come back but he wouldn't and I never saw him again. Just after this a tank came up the road. The chaps told me about it. I crept to the corner and there it was coming up the road. I put the bomb into the Piat and fired at the tank. The range was about 100 yards. I think it must have struck the track. The tank fired immediately in my direction and this raised a huge cloud of dust and smoke. As soon as I could see the outline of the tank again, I let it have another. This also raised a lot of dust again. The tank gun fired back straight down the road. Then I looked again and watched, and through the dust I saw the crew of the tank baling out. They opened up with Schmeissers, but I got a couple of Brens onto the road and told my men to keep up continuous fire and the Germans were killed.

Cain then fired at another tank, but the 'bomb went off in the Piat', he said. 'I got bits of stuff in my face and two black eyes. It blew me over backwards and I was blind. I was shouting like a hooligan. I shouted to someone to get on to the Piat because there was another tank behind. I blubbered and yelled and swore. They dragged me off to the Regimental Aid Post.'

Within half an hour, however, this courageous man had regained control of himself and was back in his trench again.

There were some, of course, who were by now unable to control themselves. After six days of continuous fighting their nerves had completely broken. Two young privates in the 3rd Battalion were seen on Friday at about noon to run away screaming towards the enemy lines, their hands in the air, tears streaming down their cheeks. And Alexander Johnson said that 'a whole company' of another regiment ran away shouting, 'Tanks! Tiger tanks! Dozens of them!'. 'We were mortared steadily', Johnson went on. 'Our numbers decreased. One officer's nerve cracked nearby. The situation grew tense. We were very dirty and hungry now. I took over a platoon belonging to the Airlanding Brigade. Temporarily. I think I was viewed with hostility, as an intruder.' But one man found the spirit to march up to him, salute smartly and say, 'Sir. It's my 21st birthday to-day. May I have the day off.' Encouraged by demonstrations of cheerfulness such as this, General Urquhart felt able to report to Corps Headquarters that morale was high. He reported also that the perimeter was unchanged, but unless reinforcements could be got across the river soon, the chances of holding on would be negligible.

When he had received Horrocks' message of encouragement which had been relayed to him by the Poles, Urquhart had asked for a strong mobile column with DUKWs, as well as supplies and two companies of infantry riding on tanks to be sent to Driel. It was already dusk, however, when the column arrived at the river and because the night, which quickly fell, was so dark it was impossible to find a suitable launching place beneath the steep and crumbling banks. The men then made rafts out of cans and boards and anything else they could lay their hands on, but crossing the fast flowing water on these improvised craft proved a cruelly hazardous undertaking. Many of the men drowned as their rafts overturned, others were swept downstream and into captivity by the strong currents. The rubber dinghies which Colonel Myers had mentioned to Sosabowski were not much more useful than the rafts. One of Myer's officers, David Storrs, rowed across the river and back 23 times in one of them but it only carried two men. And by three o'clock in the morning only one rubber dinghy was still undamaged. Soon afterwards General Sosabowski gave the order that any further attempts to get his men across the river should be abandoned for the moment. By the time the night had passed less than 50 Poles and a few cases of ammunition and supplies had entered 'the Cauldron'.

Saturday and Sunday

'Never was darkness more eagerly awaited.'
1st British Airborne Division
Diary, 24 September 1944

It was still drizzling with rain at dawn on Saturday as the bombardment, known as the 'morning hate', opened as usual. And then, in the early mist, the prodding attacks began again. At seven o'clock, Lieutenant Stevenson remembers, 'we came under a terrific mortar barrage – first it came down directly on us, then it lifted three hundred yards back, smack on Squadron HQ. The SP guns came up again and began systematically destroying every house which might give shelter. All this time in the cellars of almost every house were Dutch civilians, women and children who had been caught by the battle. By now we were rather losing count of time. More SP guns and some shell fire.'

Further to the south, Lonsdale's men were heavily attacked by a German force which was making yet another attempt to cut the Division off completely from the river. And in the west the Border Regiment, which had been heavily shelled during the night and by nine o'clock had lost all its vehicles except two jeeps and a motor-cycle, was also strongly attacked again. One of its companies was overrun and surrounded and another, 'B' Company, was driven back to the outskirts of Oosterbeek.

A counter-attack failed [Major C.F.O. Breeze recorded], and so reinforcements in the shape of two platoons of HQ Company under Major Morrissey were sent to assist 'B' Company. This composite force succeeded in regaining some of the lost ground, but in the course of these operations Major Armstrong was severely wounded and captured. The enemy made repeated attempts to break through in this area but the indomitable courage of the soldiers, led by Major Morrissey and later by Major Stewart, despite considerable odds and heavy casualties beat them back time and again.

There were strong attacks in the north and the north-east too, and all day long the mortaring and shelling continued, dying down into a temporary lull only to open again with stronger force than ever. Flame-throwers came rattling down the streets through Oosterbeek to burn the men out from their forward strongholds, and numerous snipers slipped through into 'the Cauldron' to shoot them down as they withdrew.

The smell of the battlefield hung about in the damp air, constant and inescapable. Ammunition was running dangerously low and many men had had nothing to eat for 24 hours and only the rain to drink. 'Rations as such', Major H.S. Cousens wrote afterwards, 'were non-existent and men were living on potatoes and any other food they could find.' They looked at each other with red-rimmed, bloodshot eyes asking 'what the hell had happened to the 2nd bloody Army, and what the devil the RAF thought they were at'. No one blamed the transport crews whose bravery was evident to all. 'The cold-blooded pluck of the pilots was quite incredible', a soldier who watched them thought.

They came on, in their lumbering four-engine machines, at 1,500 feet, searching for our position. The ack-ack was such as I have only heard during the worst raids on London but concentrated on one small area. The German gunners were firing at point-blank range, and the supply planes were more or less sitting targets . . . It made you feel terribly small, frightened and insignificant . . .

One could do nothing but stare awe-inspired at the inferno above . . . The Americans were included in our boundless admiration, for they came along in their unarmed, slow, twin-engined Dakotas as regularly as clockwork . . . Hardly any of their supplies reached us.

In fact less than one-seventh of the total tonnage dropped during the operation was collected by the Division and the sight of the Stirlings and Dakotas flying unhesitatingly into the German barrage where sometimes, although hit and on fire, they continued to circle above the German lines while the Royal Army Service Corps despatchers threw out the supplies before the aircraft crashed into the earth, was so moving that for many of those who witnessed it no more poignant memory of Arnhem remains.

Grateful as they were to the transport crews, however, the men of the Airborne Division could not feel a similar gratitude to the RAF as a whole. For the fighters of the 2nd Tactical Air Force had scarcely been seen. One or two sorties had been flown by rocket-firing Typhoons on Saturday and Sunday and a flight of Spitfires made a brief appearance on Saturday, but there was nothing more than this. And although Allied aircraft flew 10,600 sorties in indirect support of the operation in its entirety (over half of these were by aircraft of 2nd TAF) the Airborne Division received little support which they could witness for themselves.

Apart from the difficulties of calling for close air support, without the use of the two unserviceable American sets which had been specially dropped for this purpose, the lack of help from fighters was also due to problems of liaison.

While American 8th Air Force fighters [the Airborne Corps's report explains] were escorting the various lifts of airborne troops and their supplies in the battle area, it was not possible for technical reasons, for aircraft of 2 TAF to operate there at the same time. Consequently available air effort was wasted and the troops on the ground could not receive the direct air support they required against normal ground targets; this was emphasised by the weather as there were, in any case, only quite brief periods when any air force could operate. British Airborne Division received practically no close support at all.

Even when a request did reach 2nd TAF at a time when 8th USAF fighters were not on escort duty, it was often refused on the grounds that the targets were not pin-pointed with sufficient accuracy. Although the Army was prepared to accept the risk of pilots attacking Allied positions, the pilots themselves, under-standably, were not; and of 95 requests made for air support, during OPERATION MARKET GARDEN, so General Browning subsequently complained, only 49 were accepted.

Throughout Saturday the attacks on the British perimeter continued and at a quarter past eight General Urquhart sent off the following signal:

> Many attacks during day by small parties infantry, SP guns and tanks including flame-throwers. Each attack accompanied by very heavy mortaring and shelling within Div. Perimeter. After many alarms and excursions the latter remains substantially unchanged, although very thinly held. Physical contact not yet made with those on south bank of river. Re-supply a flop, small quantities of amm. only gathered in. Still no food and all ranks extremely dirty owing to shortage of water. Morale still adequate, but continued heavy mortaring and shelling is having obvious effects. We shall hold on. But at the same time hope for a brighter 24 hours ahead.

Their hopes were not to be realised. For the whole of that night and for the whole of the next day, they had to fight on unsupported.

It was fortunate that they did not know that already the chance of an immediate full-scale assault by XXX Corps across the Neder Rijn – now their only hope of success – had already gone by noon on Saturday when the Germans managed to cut across the narrow corridor between Eindhoven and Nijmegen. It was not until Sunday afternoon that the 32nd Guards Brigade, sent back to help the American parachutists reopen the road, had succeeded in this task. For over 24 hours the road was closed and the convoy bringing the assault boats up to the Neder Rijn was held up south of the Waal.

Saturday night was a clear one. The rain had stopped and the sky was full of stars. At about seven o'clock as usual the mortar fire had quietened and in several sectors it was 'almost uncannily quiet'. To the west and south the horizon was a dull red after attacks by Bomber Command; and closer at hand the flames from the burning gas works poured out of the black smoke and cast a flickering light over the ruined buildings and the waters of the river.

After midnight, however, the prodding attacks began again. *Obersturmbannführer* Harzer, knowing how close the 2nd Army was now to the Neder Rijn, had given orders that the British Division must at all costs be destroyed before the relieving force arrived. The KOSB and the Reconnaissance Squadron were obliged to pull back in face of tanks and flame-throwers rolling forward across the lines to their trenches and blasting their houses into ruins from less than 50 yards range.

For the wounded it was another night of pain. And for the Dutch, waiting in their cellars for the battle to end, it was another night of thirst and squalor, fear and uncertainty. That morning, during a lull which had led them to believe that the fighting was over, many of them came up into the light for the first time in five days. 'Pale, quiet, frightened people appeared from the cellars,' a glider pilot says. 'They enquired timidly where they could get some water, and if it would be possible for them to venture into the house proper to collect some blankets and food. There was something like 10 people in each cellar . . .

In our house there had lived, unnoticed till now, a grandfather, father, mother and three children, besides some other people who had moved down from a devastated house. None of them complained and they seemed to be quite apathetic to the destruction of their beautiful houses and furniture', many valuable antique pieces of which had been used to barricade the windows and doorways and were by now riddled with bullet holes or smashed by fragments of mortar bombs.

The Heijbroek family, whose house was on the edge of the British perimeter and was, therefore, repeatedly changing hands, had been in the cellar since Monday night. They had since been joined by others and there were now 22 people there covered by the dust and chalk which fell in clouds upon them every time the walls were shaken by a new explosion. There was no water until it began to rain and then it poured through the holes in the shattered roof and floors and the people in the cellar thankfully collected the gritty, dirty liquid and preserved it with infinite care. The children were given two sips each morning with the 10 bottled beans which comprised their breakfast.

One night, Mijnheer Heijbroek wrote afterwards, 'a large German force stormed the house above our heads. We heard people shouting "*Sieg Heil!*", the exploding of grenades, the rattle of machine-guns and, through it all, the groaning of the wounded . . . After this attack nobody knew if our house was now British or German. The next minute the cellar door was opened as usual. This had happened every day. Then a nice young British soldier appeared and asked us, "Everything all right in the cellar?" We wished him good luck and then the door was closed with the words, "Stay in the cellar. It's dangerous up here!".' The following morning there was another attack and afterwards the cellar door was opened and the Heijbroeks suddenly saw the form of a soldier standing in the almost blinding daylight. 'Hullo Tommy!' one of them said. '*Was Tommy!*' a German voice shouted back as the door was slammed shut again.

Later on three British soldiers came down the cellar steps to hide and were quickly concealed behind the central heating boiler. A German who followed them down told the Dutch people that they would all be shot if they were discovered harbouring the enemy. But the British soldiers were not betrayed.

Not all the Dutch, of course, were so helpful and some of them were openly hostile. A few members of the Dutch National Socialist Party, indeed, offered their services as snipers to the German command and others provided the Germans with information about the strength and dispositions of British troops. Most of the important Dutch quislings had, however, already gone, like the man who had lived in the house next door to Louis Hagen's, and who 'had fled with the Germans the moment the first glider appeared in the sky', leaving his wife and daughter in the cellar. 'The wife had given birth to a boy on the first night of the British occupation', Hagen says. 'In the rooms of their house we found many photographs of German officers, arm in arm with Dutch girls in uniform, giving the Hitler salute. There was also a gold-framed picture of the owner of the house shaking hands with the Gauleiter.'

Men like this, though, were rare. Most Dutch people were friendly and many risked their lives to help the British soldiers. 'The Dutch were marvellous', Major Wilson reported. 'We had a very nice civilian with us. We brought him from a house. He was a big business man. He came down to Hartenstein with us and lived with us till the end. He was about 52. He disappeared into the woods when we left. He spoke perfect English. There was also a good-looking girl who wanted to join us and was very anxious to have a suit of battle-dress.' A Dutchman, who kept the crew of a Vickers machine-gun supplied with water, regularly crossed over into the German lines to fill his bucket, until one night on his return both his legs were torn off by a mortar bomb.

At the white house by Oosterbeek Laag church the foundations shook as the shelling increased and to calm the nerves of the wounded men, lying in packed rows on her blood-soaked carpets, Mevrouw ter Horst made her cautious, weary way from room to room reading the 91st Psalm by the light of an electric torch. The windows had all been smashed long ago and part of one wall had been blown out, killing several wounded men who were lying near it; and, because of the mass of bodies, it was no longer possible to close the doors, so that the cold night air blew through the house. But not even the rushing draughts could remove the stench of ordure and sweat, of bleeding wounds and the sweet and sickly smell of death.

At the Schoonoord Hotel and at the Tafelberg and at another hotel now used as a hospital, the Vreewyk, it was the same, for there was hardly any water. And in the forward RAPs the conditions were even worse. At the Tafelberg, when a shell had burst on the roof smashing the pipes and a cascade of rust-coloured water had poured down on to the wounded men, an orderly mopped up the valuable liquid with a blanket and squeezed it into a bucket. All the rain water he had been able to collect during the day had long since gone and not a drop, wherever it came from, could be wasted.

There were not enough blankets, either, not enough morphia, not enough bandages. Operations were performed under conditions of appalling difficulty or not performed at all. But in every makeshift hospital, dressing station and RAP the doctors and their orderlies although reaching the limits of their endurance, still continued doggedly and with great skill and courage to do all that they could for the wounded men in their charge.

At the RAP near Oosterbeek Laag church, Mevrouw ter Horst asked Dr Martin if there were many dead.

'Thousands of them', Dr Martin said.

His hands hang between his knees [she says], an elbow leans against the table, he is very tired. Slowly he looks up with an expression of melancholy in his dark eyes. I say calmly, 'This house won't be smashed.' He nods, 'I prayed for that.' And then suddenly: 'And if we are hit again, I hope it will kill them all right off.' He pointed to a figure under the stairs with hair matted to a bandaged head.

'He just banged his head against the radiator and he was gone . . . We can't do anything.'

During the night Colonel Warrack decided that the men under his care should not be expected to endure such treatment any longer. He went to Divisional Headquarters to see General Urquhart.

'If you don't mind,' he said to him; 'I'd like to go and see the German commander and arrange for the evacuation of our wounded to his hospitals in Arnhem.'

Urquhart not wanting to give the Germans any cause for encouragement agreed on condition that Warrack represented himself purely as a doctor concerned for his patients and not as an officer on the staff of Divisional Headquarters.

With Lieutenant-Commander Wolters and a Dutch doctor who had been working at the Tafelberg Hotel, Warrack went to put his proposal to the senior German doctor at the Schoonoord Hotel early on Sunday morning. He had little doubt that his request would be granted; for the Germans had already displayed a regard for the rules of war, which was not merely punctilious but sympathetic.

Brigadier Hackett was given evidence of this. He had been called out from his headquarters to meet a German officer who had driven up to the British lines in a half-track flying a large white flag.

'We are about to deliver an attack on this side of the perimeter', the officer had said with stiff politeness looking towards the building used as a casualty clearing station on the main road running through the perimeter. 'I intend to put down a mortar and artillery concentration on your forward positions. We know that you have wounded there and we do not wish to put down a barrage that will hit them. I am asking you to move your forward positions 600 yards further back.' The withdrawal would have entailed the abandonment of the whole Divisional Headquarters area and neither Hackett nor Urquhart to whom the decision was referred for confirmation could agree. But, when the expected bombardment came, it was delivered further south and the casualty clearing station was left outside the barrage area. On the same day when a tank opened fire at close range on the ter Horst house in Oosterbeek Laag, Bombardier E.C. Bolden, the courageous medical orderly and the Rev. S. Thorne, the chaplain, went up to it carrying a Red Cross flag. Furiously shaking the flag and giving 'the most comprehensive display of East London invective' that Padre Watkins had ever heard, Bolden demanded that the tank commander immediately withdraw, as the house was in use as a Regimental Aid Post. The German commander drove his tank away.

On another occasion a self-propelled gun fired two shells through a dressing station window. A British surgeon came out angrily waving a Red Cross flag and asked the German officer in command, 'what the hell he thought he was up to'. The German said, 'Oh, sorry', and he also drove away.

The German doctor to whom Warrack now made his request treated him with similar respect. Although he was the senior medical officer at the Schoonhord, Dr Egon Skalka was an extremely young man and he listened to Warrack with marked deference. Warrack told another Doctor that he thought he was 'quite a decent chap'. He had already been told by *Obersturmbannführer* Harzer, who had long been in possession of the British wireless codes and knew well how the enemy wounded were suffering, to be as helpful to the British doctors as he could be.

Skalka took Warrack and Wolters into Arnhem in a captured jeep flying the Red Cross flag, past charred and twisted tanks, festoons of tram wires, piles of wreckage and rubble and crumpled corpses. In the centre of Arnhem they stopped outside the German Headquarters and were taken up to a room where several officers looked at Warrack curiously.

The acting Chief of Staff, Hauptmann Schwarz, came in and placing a map on the table asked Warrack to be good enough to point out the British dressing stations. As he was doing so, Harzer himself entered the room and walked up to Warrack, greeting him with grave courtesy.

'I am extremely sorry', he said, 'that there should be this fighting between our two countries. Of course, we will help you with your wounded men.' It was agreed that in a restricted area near the Tafelberg Hotel there should be a truce of two hours so that the British wounded could be taken into the hospitals in Arnhem.

When Doctor Skalka had telephoned instructions that all available ambulances should assist in the immediate evacuation of the British wounded from '*der Kessel*', Warrack was offered a glass of brandy which he refused on account of his empty stomach and a plate of sandwiches which he and Wolters ate with relish. Then, presented with a pocketful of morphia and a bottle of brandy, Colonel Warrack returned to '*der Kessel*', paying on the way a visit to the St Elizabeth Hospital which had changed hands more than once during the course of the battle. Here Warrack found the British wounded lying in bed between clean white sheets attended by Dutch nurses and British surgical teams. All the civilian patients had been removed to the upper floors with the help of the senior Dutch surgeon, Dr von Hengel, and although at the beginning of the week when the streets outside were the scene of such bitter fighting, German soldiers had twice broken into the wards and fired over the beds of the patients, the hospital was now relatively quiet and orderly. German surgeons occasionally walked through the wards to offer their help and advice.

'You've got it pretty cushy here by comparison', Colonel Warrack told the South African doctor, Lipmann Kessel, who had been working there with little rest for several days. 'We have eight houses full up to the rafters. There must be 1,500 wounded, many of them sharing a mattress, and there's not an awful lot we can do for them. The situation in the forward RAPs is, of course, much worse . . . They can't stick much more.'

While the wounded were evacuated from the dressing stations west of the town the shelling and mortaring died down. But owing to the difficulties of ensuring that everyone knew that an unofficial truce had been agreed upon and owing also to the Poles' refusal to acknowledge that such an unsatisfactory state of affairs could exist, the fighting did not entirely stop. By mid-afternoon, however, nearly 500 men had been moved out into the safety and relative comfort of Arnhem.

But as soon as the Jeeps had driven away with the wounded, the fighting started again. The Border Regiment was again heavily attacked by a German force trying to break through the divisional perimeter from the west.

> The main brunt of the attack [Major Cousens says] was borne by 'A' Company who lost all their officers, either killed or wounded, and were reduced to some 20 other ranks. The Germans then began infiltrating through the north end of the Company area . . . But some 25 men of the mortar group, whose mortars had by now been knocked out, were led in a counter-attack and by 15.30 hours the position had been stabilised. Half an hour later the divisional ammunition reserve blew up and that evening a check of stores revealed no food, only 2,500 rounds of small arms ammunition, two out of the original 12 three-inch mortars still in action with 20 bombs left, all vehicles destroyed, and the evacu-ation of casualties to the main station, which for the past two days had been in enemy hands, impossible. We were now using 50 per cent captured German arms, ammunition and equipment.

The first line was scarcely distinguishable anymore. Officers when going on their rounds would come across a house until recently occupied by their own men and now taken over by the Germans and when they returned to their headquarters would find Germans there too. The two armies were inextricably interlocked. Men in one trench were never sure who might be found in the trenches out of sight. Captain J.W. Walker, of the 1st Light Regiment, for two days manned an Observation Post at the top of a house forward of the KOSB's front line with German troops in the garden below. Colonel Payton-Reid, when visiting one of his positions, found Germans where his own men should have been and jumping in alarm through the window of a nearby house landed in the cellar as the ground floor had been blown up. It was for him, as it would have been for other battalion commanders, an unremarkable experience.

Nothing seemed quite real any more. Men could no longer feel surprise. They had reached the limits of their strength and were dazed with exhaustion. Many of them fought on as if in a dream; others sat down in their trenches crying silently; some muttered incoherently or stared in front of them with vacant eyes. 'There were times when I got the impression that no one's face was relaxed or normal', Colonel Preston said later.

> Some emotion seemed frozen on each; each face possessed its own permanent 'look'. The looks of dumb, uncomprehending, uncomplaining pain on the faces of the wounded, the bewilderment on the faces of the Poles, the eternally questioning look on the batmen and orderlies grouped outside the cellar door, the terror in the faces of our prisoners – all these seemed to possess a horrid permanency. One began to wonder what one's own 'look' was like and I found myself stealthily examining my face in someone's shaving mirror. I was no different to the rest, I found. And thereafter I endeavoured to adjust my face before leaving the cellar.

A group of soldiers ran for shelter into Mevrouw ter Horst's house and began 'to talk of their fear of the snipers'. 'They hit you in the back', they told her indignantly. They were so cleverly camouflaged, 'you could not discover them anywhere'. She could see how completely unnerved by the sniping they had become. A young lieutenant was brought into the house. 'I was on top of the school over there', he said. 'An explosion took the roof right away from under me and I fell into the school.' He laughed as if on the verge of hysteria; and every time there was an explosion outside he gripped his head convulsively.

In the cellar a group of soldiers were huddled, sheltering from their fear.

> Must I send these soldiers away, [Mevrouw ter Horst wondered]. I cannot decide to do so. We must get through this night; it is the last perhaps. But if the Germans come to the cellar hole and see the British soldiers? Won't they throw hand grenades in? . . . The hours creep on . . . It becomes more and more suffocating around us. The children sleep heavily as if they were drugged. When dawn begins to break I must go upstairs, outside for a moment. I feel quite sick . . . The soldiers in the cellar are awake but they make no indications of leaving . . . as if they were dazed and rigid in their horror at this fight.

A medical orderly came down and told them to go away. They got to their feet and moved about a little but they would not leave. 'Come on boys', he said sharply. 'Get on. You've got to defend the place.' Reluctantly they climbed the cellar steps and went back to their trenches.

But some soldiers by now could stand no more and could not be made to return. Although General Urquhart had reported to Corps Headquarters the day before that morale was still high, in fact the nerves of many men had broken. The mortar bombardments, often so intense that 50 bombs fell in a minute, had shattered the resistance and self-control of men, tired out and hungry, who could no longer, as one of them said, 'even think straight. You found yourself muttering under your breath and when you began to talk out loud you couldn't get your words out, or, if you could, you stuttered.' To escape from the frightening effect of inactivity men crawled out of their trenches to hunt for snipers, competing with each other, notching their rifles for each confirmed kill, trying to beat the record of a man in Major Wilson's company whose notches numbered 18. But some men could not bring themselves to leave their trenches at all and a few of them when they did leave them crawled over to the German lines to give themselves up. 'Towards the end of the fighting', Sepp Kraft subsequently reported, 'many soldiers surrendered because of hunger and other privations, including breakdown of morale.' These breakdowns and surrenders were, in fact, less common than Kraft's comment indicates and the great majority of the men – indeed practically all the men in well-led units and formations such as 'Lonsdale Force' which contained a high proportion of seasoned soldiers of strong character – were of course fighting still and prepared to go on fighting with the stubborn determination which characterises the British soldier in adversity. It is true, though, that even in those units where this virtue was most evident 'people', as an officer in the Reconnaissance Squadron said, 'began to do mad sorts of things'. In his own area 'an SS tough had been wounded in the street and was kicking up the hell of a row about it. Our chaps – gave him a lullaby through the window. We had had no rations since we moved into the house on Tuesday. We lived mainly on fruit.'

Louis Hagen, the glider pilot whose fluent German had led to his being asked to go on several patrols beyond the British perimeter, noticed the 'drawn white faces and unsteady eyes' of the men in the trenches around Divisional Headquarters when he came to make a report. 'These', he felt, 'were the real heroes of Arnhem. It looked very brave to volunteer for patrol and to defend a key position like our row of houses . . . but I knew full well that it was not daredevilishness, hate of the Germans or a sense of duty that made me volunteer so readily for the first patrol on Thursday – but the simple fact that I was afraid of being frightened by the slow rain of mortars. I soon found that others might have fared better had they acted as I did. Not all had stood up to the strain.' In the darkest part of the cellar at Headquarters and in a storage room below the gardener's cottage he found men 'who had lost all their nerve and self-control. They looked like people who had been seasick for days. Nothing in the world would coax them up. Down there they vegetated; ate, slept and relieved themselves in a world where only their fear was reality. There were men and also a few officers, of all ranks and regiments and of the most varied types' and they made Hagen realise that being frightened or not 'was a matter of luck, like being musical or short-sighted'. And he admits that he was momentarily pleased when he recognised one of these frightened men, a superficially tough staff-sergeant who was always boasting of what he could do when he got his hands on the Germans and how he would tear their children in half because the only good Germans were dead ones. He had called Hagen 'Miss Hagen' because he wore pyjamas and didn't swear; but it was Hagen who was the real soldier now and being a real soldier he didn't taunt the terrified bully, as he was tempted to do, but left him alone with his pitiable fear.

For the captured Germans who had lost their nerve there was not even the squalid safety of the cellars. They had been put in the tennis court of the Park Hotel, like animals in a cage, for there was no room for them elsewhere. The men were in a long zig-zag trench, the officers in smaller, separate dugouts. And one officer, in an attempt to set an example to the men, refused to squat down even in the heaviest mortaring but kept his head and shoulders erect and motionless above the level of the upturned soil. When, during a lull, the men began to shout for food and water, another officer got out of his trench and shouted at them to keep quiet. The British had had no food and little water for days, he told them, but were nevertheless showing a discipline and courage which should have shamed them. The efforts of these

and other officers to instil in the men the quiet fortitude of their
ideal were, however, unavailing.* The stronger of the youths
and the more controlled of the older men sat still in silence,
uncomplaining and stubborn; but many of the others shouted
hysterically or wept without shame and when interrogated were
submissive and co-operative and pleaded, with a kind of apology,
that they had been forced into uniform and made to fight.

'You had to feel sorry for them', a soldier says. 'They were
such a miserable-looking lot but, at least, they could go to sleep. I
would have given a month's pay for a good kip.'

Indeed, for almost every man in the Division exhaustion
was overwhelming. That evening at a battalion conference of
the KOSB, Payton-Reid was talking to his acting second-in-
command, Captain Walker of the Royal Artillery. There was
one other officer present and Sergeant R.F. Tilley of the Glider
Pilot Regiment who had taken over from the battalion's
wounded RSM to become in Payton-Reid's words, 'one of our
most active members'. As Payton-Reid spoke, he noticed without
surprise that Captain Walker had gone to sleep. Soon the other
officers dropped off and then Sergeant Tilley's head dropped to
the dusty table. Payton-Reid remembered, as he recorded later
in his diary, that they had had an average of two or three hours
sleep in 24. 'There were no rations at all . . . There wasn't much
water and we hadn't any tea. Hardly any cigarettes.' Above all
there was this appalling tiredness. Payton-Reid's voice mumbled
away into silence and then he, too, fell asleep. He had been in
the middle of a sentence.

At Divisional Headquarters, the diary was being filled in with
its usual laconic record of the day's events:

---

* These prisoners included some girls of the Wehrmacht's Women's Services all
of whom were quiet and controlled. An officer of the Divisional Staff came across
one of them while walking across the tennis court one evening. A mortar bomb
exploded nearby and he jumped quickly into the trench she was occupying. 'Oh,
Major,' she said, in a voice at once reproachful and provocative as she pressed her
body close to his, 'this is not a time for fear, but for love.'

24 September 19.00 hours. A day of heavy shelling and mortaring
and desperate fighting on all sectors. Many attacks at first
achieved some penetration, but the situation was almost always
restored, and by nightfall the perimeter was substantially the
same. Never was darkness more eagerly awaited.

On the southern bank of the river more men of the Polish
Brigade and the 4th Battalion of the Dorsets from General
Thomas's Division, ably supported by Lieutenant-Colonel B.A.
Coad's 5th Dorsets and Lieutenant-Colonel George Taylor's 5th
Duke of Cornwall's Light Infantry, were preparing to cross over
into 'the Cauldron' as it was felt that unless a firmer grip were to
be obtained on the northern bank, it might well prove impossible
to extricate the Airborne Division.

Indeed, it seemed impossible at first that even a company of
the Dorsets would be able to cross the river. The crossing was to
have been made at half past ten on Sunday night but that
afternoon the road from Nijmegen had been cut, preventing the
convoy bringing up the boats from reaching the Neder Rijn. In
fact, even if the road had not been cut it would no doubt have
been found impossible to get the boats up to the river in daylight
owing to the loss of the high ground at Westerbouwing. Eventually when the road was opened again and the lorries crossed over
the Nijmegen bridge, two of them took the wrong turning and
drove into the German lines at Elst, and two others skidded off
the slippery road in the rain and became irretrievably bogged
down in the dykes. Men pulled the boats off the lorries and
struggled to carry them across the mud flats in the rain and the
increasing German mortar fire. But by the early hours of the
morning only nine boats had been dragged to the river; and it
seemed impossible that any of them would be able to cross it.
'The whole world', General Sosabowski writes, 'seemed to be
exploding around us.' But nevertheless the attempt to reach the
Airborne troops had to be made. 'Hour by hour all through the
night', Sosabowski 'received messages of boats being sunk. Every

time' he went out to 'have a look around, files of stretcher-bearers trudged past bringing back the wounded'.

The apprehensions he had always felt about the British attitude towards the operation were now being proved well-founded. Consequently his own attitude, at a conference with Thomas and Horrocks held earlier that day, was not immediately co-operative. 'I am General Sosabowski,' he had said. 'I command the Polish Parachute Brigade. I do as I like.'

Thomas and Horrocks exchanged glances, and then Horrocks said, 'You are under my command. You will do as I bloody well tell you.'

There was a pause.

'All right', Sosabowski said grimly. 'I command the Polish Parachute Brigade and I do as you bloody well say.'

An engineer officer was crouching on the start line next to Lieutenant-Colonel Gerald Tilly, the Commanding Officer of the Dorsets. As Tilly prepared to take his battalion to what seemed 'to be certain death', the Engineer heard him say, 'Good-bye. Tell the brigade that everything is OK and thank them for what they have done.'

On the river bank [the engineer said afterwards] sappers took the boats and rowed men and supplies across. It was pitch dark. On the far bank were two burning factories illuminating a rising forest of trees at the water's edge. The swirling current drifted the boats downstream on the crossing and further downstream on the way back. Men wading in mud and water dragged them back along the water's edge for more trips. The mortar fire eased up a bit but was replaced by automatic fire. Someone [the Poles] had launched a DUKW about 200 yards upstream. As this swirled down across our front a Spandau opened up on it. The man on my right – a sapper corporal – was shot through the head and another on my left got a bullet through his arm. The ferrying went on until daylight. It was a bad night.

Most of the Dorsets, crossing in their few boats a platoon at a time, were borne downstream by the fast currents and landed well beyond the edge of the perimeter. Many of them were killed or wounded as they clambered on to the bank and the others having got ashore were so disorganized and found it so difficult to find their bearings that the Germans had no difficulty in containing them within a small perimeter west of the divisional one.

Further upstream Colonel Myers, returning to the Division with two letters from the south, got to the other side of the river and then scrambled along in the water until he was sure he had reached the base of the perimeter. He climbed out and walked up to the Park Hotel to deliver his two letters to General Urquhart. One was from General Thomas; the other from Browning. Urquhart opened Browning's letter first:

Dear Roy,

Sosabowski will be bringing you this, I hope to-night. I will not labour your present position, and it may be little consolation to you and the 1st Division when I tell you that the opinion held this side of the river is that the action of the 1st Division has, apart from the killing of the many Boche it has undoubtedly achieved, enabled XXX Corps and the Airborne Corps between them to capture the Nijmegen Bridges and to break clear through the main German defence line on the Waal.

From the information at our disposal, the German undoubtedly moved back the bulk of his forces from Nijmegen to Arnhem just before our airborne attack took place; and instead of the Nijmegen crossings being an acutely difficult problem, the Arnhem crossings have become most acute in consequence.

You can rest assured that XXX Corps are doing their maximum under the most appalling conditions to relieve you. As you know, I am responsible from inclusive Nijmegen down the narrow corridor back for approximately 40 miles, and the road has been cut between us and the main body for 24 hours, which does not help matters much. It is now through again, and the Army is pouring to your assistance but, as you will appreciate better than I do, very late in the day.

I naturally feel, not so tired and frustrated as you do, but probably almost worse about the whole thing than you do . . .

It may amuse you to know that my front faces in all directions, but I am only in close contact with the enemy for about 8,000 yards to the south-east, which is quite enough in present circumstances.

Yours ever,

F.A.M. Browning.

The letter from General Thomas told Urquhart that the plan to form a bridgehead west of Arnhem had been abandoned and that the Airborne Division was to be withdrawn at a time to be agreed. A few hours earlier Horrocks had decided that a final attempt to get across the Neder Rijn should be made on Monday night. But immediately after he had come to this decision, the Germans once more cut across the road. There were reports too from air reconnaissance that Panzer reinforcements were approaching the northern banks of the Neder Rijn where the enemy infantry was digging defences; and neither VIII nor XII Corps operating on the flanks of XXX Corps had been able to make the headway that had been expected of them when it was not known what troops Model had at his disposal. Having got so far, Horrocks found it difficult to accept the fact that he could get no further. But eventually he was forced to conclude that everything possible had been done and he agreed with Browning and Dempsey that the time had come to get what still remained of the Airborne Division out. Montgomery gave his approval to the withdrawal which was to be known as OPERATION BERLIN. It was just after six o'clock in the morning that Urquhart received General Thomas's letter. He could smell the stench of battle and around him lay the swollen bodies of countless unburied dead. He walked for a moment in the grounds of the hotel. The trees, which had once surrounded the hotel on three sides, were now nearly all down.

> The others [Colonel Preston thought], stripped of their leaves or with branches trailing or with the torn canopies of parachutes adding to their disorder, looked for all the world like women whose clothing had become ripped or torn in some primitive orgy. To me they had a faintly obscene air. At the foot of the trees could be seen the mounds of earth which were the slit trenches of those who lived in the open. Dotted about, here and there, were vehicles, some wholly burnt out, some seeming to be perpetually burning like Indian funeral fires.

Through the mist of the early morning, General Urquhart walked, passing these desolated ruins of war and the anxious, careworn faces of his men. Some of them kept awake by benzedrine stared across the scarred landscape and shook their heads as familiar objects changed their shape or glided drunkenly up the sky. Some of them had been given double vision by too much benzedrine and others saw nightmarish shapes that swayed and swelled then disappeared like smoke sucked up a chimney. Major Cain, squatting in his trench wondered if the gold cock on the church's weathervane would still be there in the morning. 'It had stayed there through all the bombing' and had 'become a sort of symbol'. And then it occurred to 'someone who', so he says, 'didn't seem to be me that my trench was rather like a grave'.

Urquhart returned to the cellar at Headquarters and sent a message to Corps Headquarters.

> I consider it unlikely that we can hold out any longer. All ranks are now completely exhausted as the result of eight days' continuous effort. Lack of food and water and deficiency in arms combined with high officer casualties rate has had its effect. Even comparatively minor enemy offensive action may cause complete

disintegration. Should this become apparent all will be told to
break out, rather than surrender. Controlled movements from
present position in face of enemy is out of the question. We have
done our best and will continue to do our best as long as possible.

Half an hour later Urquhart told the signaller to call General
Thomas. Soon after eight he was speaking to him. Outside the
shelling had started again.

'OPERATION BERLIN', Urquhart said, '*must* be to-night.'

Monday

'Oh, God! Give us a moment's silence. Give us quiet – if only for
a short moment – so that at least they can die.'

Mevrouw Kate ter Horst

Urquhart called a Divisional conference for half past ten.

When Brigadier Hicks arrived he was out of breath. German
infantry had occupied several houses between his headquarters
and the Park Hotel, and when they had been thrown out by a
squad of glider pilots, a Tiger tank had driven up to the gate of
the headquarters. He had had to wait for it to be put out of
action before leaving. He ran across the churned lawn of the
Park Hotel, which for days had been carefully watched by an
expert sniper and was now covered by a Spandau that raked it at
the least sign of activity; and he came down the cellar steps,
'looking a good deal more dishevelled than usual but calm as
ever'.

Lieutenant-Colonel Ian Murray, Commander of the 1st Wing
of the Glider Pilot Regiment and – as Brigadier Hackett had
been badly wounded in the stomach on Friday – now commander also of the eastern side of the perimeter, was already
there. Within a few minutes Loder-Symonds, Mackenzie and
Myers were also sitting round the map-covered table beside the
empty wine racks and the piles of dusty, broken bottles.

'We are to clear out to-night', Urquhart told them. 'We will
move back on a timed programme by two routes. In general
those farthest from the river will start first. I don't expect that

either of the routes will be free from enemy interference; but they are the best available to us.'

Glider pilots were to act as guides along the routes which in difficult places would be marked by parachute tape. Colonel Myers's Engineers would be responsible for the last stretches across the open meadows by the river and Myers was also to be responsible for the ferry service. Men would march with their boots muffled and cross the river in boatload parties of 14. They would not be told of the evacuation until the last minute. All doctors would stay behind with the wounded.

It would be an operation of appalling difficulty for the river frontage left in their hands was already reduced to little more than 600 yards; and if the withdrawal were to be detected the troops would be at the mercy of German gunners. It was essential that artillery support from XXX Corps across the river should be extensive and well directed; and that the Germans, not merely in contact with the paratroopers but interlocked with them, should learn nothing of the Airborne Division's plans.

Even before the conference had broken up, however, the Germans made a determined effort to cut the Division's tenuous hold on the river frontage as if they had already discovered the British intentions. Down by the church the 1st Light Regiment's troop positions which had been part of the front line since Thursday, were overrun and the enemy poured into the perimeter and across the western withdrawal route, cutting the divisional area almost in two before being driven off by the few remaining 75-mm guns fired at a range of no more than 50 yards over open sights. In 2 Battery, now completely overrun by enemy tanks, there was only one 75-mm howitzer still serviceable. Lieutenant A. Donaldson and Lance-Bombardier J.H. Dickson managed to reach it when their 6 pounder anti-tank gun was knocked out by a Tiger tank. The howitzer was then also knocked out, but not before Donaldson and Dickson had hit and broken one of the tank's tracks. Crawling away from the smoking

howitzer these two young men found a Piat and with the last
rounds of ammunition left in the area they engaged the tank for
the third time.

> The Germans' attacks that morning were of a most violent nature
> [Alexander Johnson reported]. They threw everything at us
> except Big Bertha. Half way through the battle Peter yelled at
> me, 'Take over Mike's flight. He's wounded.' I did and found
> myself commanding – two men. Shortly after I found myself at
> the wrong end of a submachine gun and having no ammunition
> with which to argue, was forced to obey the screeched words of
> command of my captor, a spotty-faced creature of about 12 – or
> so he looked.

There were countless other infiltrations elsewhere that day,
and on one occasion a company of Panzer grenadiers occupied a
wood less than two hundred and fifty yards from the Divisional
Headquarters in the Park Hotel. And although they were so
close, Loder-Symonds called for a barrage against them by the
155-mm guns of 419 Heavy Battery and directed these guns,
which were several miles away, from the mouth of his dug-out at
Divisional Headquarters. For the rest of that day and night
'there seemed' to Padre Watkins, 'as many of their shells landing
in our area as outside it. We did not enjoy it, but it certainly sent
the German tanks home.'

'About three o'clock', Lieutenant Stevenson says, 'things
began to get really hot. There was really heavy sniping from
close range coupled with extremely heavy mortar fire which
made our positions practically untenable. After considerable
casualties we decided we must move further back still. We
began to move and were caught in the open by savage fire from
self-propelled guns.

Everywhere that afternoon the fire seemed heavier than ever.
The Tafelberg Hotel was hit three times and a nurse and two
orderlies were killed as well as several wounded. The place

became uninhabitable and Colonel Warrack ordered the rest of
the wounded to be taken out. As they were trundled out on
wheelbarrows and trolleys the building was burning fiercely.
Snipers had by now crawled through the hedge of Mynheer ter
Horst's orchard.

> They fired shamelessly into the house [his wife remembers], into
> the rooms and corridors, crowded with helpless people. Nobody
> dares leave the house, two medical orderlies have been shot down
> while they passed the windows with a stretcher between them –
> from outside the wounded are calling . . . More wounded come
> in and . . . all around they are dying – must they breathe their last
> breath in such a hurricane? Oh, God! Give us a moment's silence.
> Give us quiet – if only for a short moment – so that at least they
> can die . . . On the cellar steps there are again a few soldiers. The
> Germans are all round us, everybody knows it now, it is only a
> question of hours . . . 'Will you please go upstairs now?' We ask it
> after a long hesitation; but if the Germans find them here, then it
> is all up with us . . . In the cellar opening we have put a cushion
> against the shells, the door to the stoke hole is closed. And then it
> happens – a tremendous shock. Over our heads we hear the
> thunder of bricks rolling down, stifled cries from all sides, the
> cracking of timbers.

Some men lying above her were wounded for the fourth time.

In one of the dressing stations behind the German lines,
General Urquhart's ADC, Captain Roberts, and another
officer, Captain Murray, were asked by Colonel Warrack to
try and get a message through to the British XXX Corps
gunners not to drop shells in the area while this and another
dressing station in German hands were being evacuated. They
walked out past the guard, Roberts with his leg in a splint and
Murray with a bullet hole in his neck, and found a Red Cross
jeep beyond a house full of corpses of men who had died
from their wounds. They got into it and drove unchallenged

to the British lines to hand Warrack's message in for transmission.

As the long day wore on and the shelling continued, preparations for the withdrawal went on. When darkness came at
last, guides made sure of their routes, tapes were pulled out from
hedgerows and placed in position, the last pigeons were released,
the wounded who were strong enough were given guns to fire so
as to give the impression of a still occupied position, and the men
tied up their boots and any equipment which might rattle with
rags and sacking and the torn trousers of the dead. Those whose
faces were not already concealed by dirt and a week's growth of
beard, blackened their skin with soil or soot. And at ten o'clock
they began their silent march to the river. 'Somebody went
round distributing little packets of sulphanilamide and morphia',
a soldier remembers. 'The password was "John Bull". If we
became separated each man was to make due south for the
river.'

It was a dark night and the rain poured down through a strong
wind, muffling other sounds. The men opened their mouths to
let the water drive in. From across the river the heavy guns of the
2nd Army began their comforting barrage. The CRA had sent a
fire plan for covering the withdrawal to XXX Corps; and the
guns of a battery of 7 Medium Regiment, a troop of 84 Medium
Regiment, 43rd Divisional Artillery, 419 Heavy Battery and 64
Medium Regiment were all firing before the night was over. So
heavy, in fact, was this fire that the German command believed
that the 2nd British Army were going to make an assault across
the river that night. Four field companies, two of the Royal
Canadian Engineers and two of the 43rd Division, were waiting
on the other side of the river to ferry the men across. The
Canadians had wooden storm boats with outboard motors;
the British collapsible assault boats which had to be paddled.
'The river did not look inviting', one of the British sappers said
later. 'The current was swift and the water black and deep. The
far bank was out of sight.' He had come up 300 yards from the

forward assembly area over two high embankment dykes and a waste of mud flats. 'It was a dark night. The din of our own fire was terrific . . . Away to the left the factory by the Dorset crossing was still blazing.'

The survivors of the Airborne Division stumbled through the darkness down to the river, holding hands or each other's smocks, feeling their way along the lines of tape fastened between the trees, hearing gratefully the whispered instructions of the guides. Some parties got lost and stumbled into German patrols; others waited while a man, disobeying orders, went off to offer a wounded man a chance to escape. All those unable to walk had been ordered to remain behind, but many bandaged figures were carried down to the river's edge. Padre Watkins had collected 30 'bloody, ragged wrecks of men' from the ter Horst's house and with two medical orderlies took them across the garden 'strewn with the unburied dead' who had been removed to make room for new casualties, and then down to the river. 'It did not seem possible that they could get far', Watkins says. 'They were so weak. But Bolden (the medical orderly) had chosen well. They were soldiers, every one. By dawn they were south of the river and not one of them was lost.'

As he approached the river Louis Hagen 'began to see human bodies lying all along the path'. All day long his fellow glider pilots had been so desperately tired that 'they seemed to be sleep-walking' and twice as they stumbled about in the dark they had got lost and once they had been saved from walking into the fire of a Spandau by an officer all of whose men had been killed or wounded by it. Hagen had kept his head up to now but at the sounds of groans and cries for help from wounded men and a low voice muttering in delirium, at the sight of 'feverish, pleading eyes' looking up at him out of the darkness of the meadow and at the feel of arms frenziedly clutching his legs, he panicked. He dragged limp bodies along towards the beach; he ran round, close to hysteria, asking uninjured men to help him; he vomited and felt faint. Then someone came up from the river and ordered him in an authoritative voice 'to leave the wounded where they were'.

In the cellar of the Park Hotel, a padre was saying prayers. When he had finished, the papers of the Division were burned. The sergeant-major handed out benzedrine pills and General Urquhart passed round a bottle of whisky he had found in his pack. They left in single file, Mackenzie leading.

> We were the last section out [an Intelligence officer said]. A fair spraying of bullets came down the road at intervals, so we ran across singly or in pairs . . . There was plenty of halting and crouching down . . . It was very slow moving. The night was black and wet, making it impossible to see the helmet or body of the man in front. Then about 21.30 hours a clatter of mortar bombs came down – lighting the woods and roads with a queer blue light. The men scattered like demons in a pantomime. I was lifted off my feet with the blast of one bomb and I came to, lying against the foot of a tree. There was no one about so I pushed on quickly and eventually contacted two of my section . . . A machine-gun was firing at us . . . After much blundering about we hit into the tail of an enormous snake of men. Every unit seemed to be there but our own. Utmost confusion, no one caring whether he showed over the sky line or not. We went on, finally contacting the end of our section near the river. Again the Hun tossed over mortar bombs and many men were wounded. There was plenty of screaming. A boat turned over too – terrible cries. Shortly after I contacted Captain Allsop who was wounded in the left thigh. We got into the same boat together squatting near the bow. We shouted to the others to move down.

All along the meadow now, men were squatting down in the mud under fire, wet and shivering, waiting for their turn to get into the boats. A few men could not bear the agony of waiting and pushed past the others to the river bank. General Sosabowski records that about 100 of them dashed down to the water and were sent back by an officer who shouted at them furiously, 'Behave like Englishmen!' But most of them were quiet and controlled. A young officer thought of Dunkirk and felt that this was what it must have been like. He had been at school then. His father had been killed there. He felt suddenly proud that he was English and that Englishmen could behave like this, quiet and patient, trying to comfort the wounded with grim jokes and a rough tenderness and, without realising it at first, he began to cry. He put his face in the mud so that his men should not hear his sobs and one of them put his hand on his shoulder and squeezed it.

Colonel Myers at the river's edge stood up to his ankles in mud as the red tracer shells flew over his head marking the withdrawal routes. The river was splashed with rain as the storm boats crossed and recrossed over the fast-flowing water, their engines chugging loudly above the distant roar of the guns. Some boats were swept off course by the swirling currents; the engines of others failed and the men tried to row with their rifle butts; many of them sank and sent the soldiers floundering into the water. Colonel Preston watched a boat come into the bank and the men

scrambling and heaving themselves into it from all directions. Some, the walking wounded, were helped and hauled over the side to lie in the bottom amongst the boots of the others. The air was full of whispered curses and mutterings of those getting aboard and of the blasphemies of the crews who had the two-fold task of preventing the boat being swamped by its passengers and being holed by the boulders on the bank. In a moment the boat had filled with men, and those still trying to clamber in were prevented from doing so by those already there, or failing to climb aboard were falling into the water or onto the shore.

'Let them go. You'll capsize it,' he whispered urgently and immediately those who were still trying to struggle aboard

abandoned their efforts and moved back to wait for the next
boat.

The Germans, quiet at first through ignorance of what was
really happening and deceived by a brave and skilfully executed
diversion by the small force of Dorsets which had crossed the
river the night before and by another diversion carried out
further west by 129 Brigade, had understood by now what was
happening. 'Since darkness', Otto Felder says, 'we had been
listening to the roar and crash of shells in the streets and fields
outside and we thought that the British had reached the river in
force at last and would soon be coming across. Then word came
that the parachutists were retreating. We cheered with happiness. And then my unit was sent out to try and stop them getting
away.'

By midnight mortar bombs were falling heavily on both sides
of the river and Spandau bullets were spattering into the water,
while from the high ground at Westerbouwing heavy German
guns were dropping shells amongst the boats which chugged so
slowly back and forth across the wide expanse of water.

At half past two in the morning, the British guards left their
prisoners and came down to join the rearguard parties. The
wounded were firing into the darkness and sending out mis-
leading signals on the few still serviceable wireless sets. The Light
Regiment, now commanded by Major J.E.F. Linton, fired their
last shells and then took the breech blocks off the guns to throw
into the river. The rest of the ammunition was blown up. The
rearguards reached the river at dawn.

But by now the crossing was no longer merely dangerous, but
impossible. The current had become so strong that the crews of
the assault boats had to be increased from four to six and then to
eight and, even so, the boats were swirled downstream beyond
the embarkation points. Machine-gun bullets spattered into the
water and mortar bombs sent up fountains of spray. Many more
boats were hit, and struggling, screaming men thrown into the
river. Smoke bombs were fired in an effort to screen the crossing-

places but the Germans themselves took advantage of the cover
to bring their machine-guns through the roads right up to the
water's edge. A Canadian officer made two crossings to take over
some German life-belts, which had been found earlier in a
supply depot, and left them on the far bank and brought back
as many men as he could. On the first crossing five men in his
boat were hit and on the second scarcely a single one escaped.

Several men jumped into the water fully clothed and tried to
swim to the other side, with their Sten guns across their backs,
but for most of them the current was too strong and they too
weak to resist it. Their clothes and equipment pulled them down
and they could be seen frantically struggling to disentangle
themselves from their laces and straps before sinking for the last
time under the water. Others undressed and dived in half-naked
and most of those who did so got across and staggered dripping
and covered in mud to the houses on the far bank where they
wrapped themselves in whatever clothes or blankets they could
find.

Already German tanks were rolling into the perimeter and for
the first time in more than a week, they were unopposed.

Over 300 wounded men were taken prisoner inside the ravaged
perimeter; almost 10 times that number were already in German
dressing stations and Dutch hospitals outside it. Hundreds of
these were later sent back to freedom by the Dutch Resistance,
but for many more there could be no return. Over 1,200 British
soldiers were dead, and more than 3,400 German soldiers were
killed or wounded.

At dawn on Tuesday a Dutch girl came out of her cellar at
Oosterbeek and looked down the rubble-lined street into
Arnhem. For six days she had not been out into the open. She
recognised nothing at first, not even her own face reflected by the
water inside an upturned German helmet. There was no roof on
her house now and only two walls were still standing. The light
seemed very strong and she felt dizzy. It was like coming up into

another world, she thought; it was so strange and quiet. It was almost as if the world had ended.

A gentle wind blew across the ruins.

PART THREE

Post-mortem

The Lost Prize

'Heavy risks were taken in the battle of Arnhem, but they were justified by the great prize so nearly within our grasp.'

Sir Winston Churchill

'Heavy risks were taken in the Battle of Arnhem,' Sir Winston Churchill wrote in the sixth volume of *The Second World War,* 'but they were justified by the great prize, so nearly in our grasp. Had we been more fortunate in the weather, which turned against us at critical moments and restricted our mastery in the air, it is possible that we should have succeeded.'

That the prize was, in fact, so nearly in our grasp is undeniable. A Luftwaffe Intelligence report entitled 'Air Landings in Holland', and written at the end of October 1944, admits that had OPERATION MARKET GARDEN succeeded, the Germans would have had 'extreme difficulty' in preventing the Allies from breaking out on to the north German plain. It is clear from captured German documents that this view is one which the *Wehrmacht* shared. And after the war most German generals, including von Runstedt, Speidel, Blumentritt and Student, agreed that Montgomery's plan, if fully backed by Eisenhower, would have been successful. That the heavy risks were justified in the absence of this whole-hearted backing is, however, arguable.

The official German explanations for the British defeat were that the landings were insufficiently concentrated; that Allied Intelligence was apparently unaware of the presence of *II Panzer Korps* in the area northeast of Arnhem; that bad flying conditions not only prevented the resupply and reinforcement of the Allied troops but also prevented the break-up of German supply and reinforcement columns moving towards the battle area; and, finally, that the British Airborne Division was landed too far in advance of the 2nd Army's front and could not be expected to hold out for the time it would take before the tanks of XXX Corps were able to reach the Neder Rijn. To these four explanations, Colonel-General Student has subsequently added two others – that the landing zones west of Arnhem were too far away from the objective, and that the troops lost far too much time in overcoming the relatively weak opposition in the early stages of the battle and consequently arrived at the bridges too late.

It is true, of course, that the landings were not sufficiently concentrated and that, because they were spread out over three days, the Germans never had the full strength of the British Division to contend with. The weather, the lack of aircraft, the understandable reluctance of the United States Air Force to agree to a night drop, are all seen as reasons for this lack of concentration. To find reasons for the lack of reliable Intelligence reports regarding German strength in the area is more difficult. The simple and tragic fact is that the British Airborne Division landed at Arnhem without any clear idea of the German forces it would be likely to meet there, although information on which a reliable estimate might have been made was available both in London and at more than one Allied headquarters on the Continent. And it landed between six and eight miles from the bridge, largely because of Intelligence reports which were found to be exaggerated or, at least, out of date. General Urquhart himself mentioned this in his official report.

We must be prepared to take more risks during the initial stages of an airborne operation. It would have been a reasonable risk to have landed the Division much closer to the objective, even in the

face of some enemy flak . . . Initial surprise was gained, but the
effect was lost because it was four [actually more than six] hours
before the troops could arrive at the bridge. A whole brigade
dropped at the bridge would have made all the difference . . .
Both the Army and the RAF were overpessimistic about the flak.
The forecast about the impossibility of landing gliders on the
polder country was also wrong. Suitable Dropping Zones and
Landing Zones could have been found south of the bridge and
near it.

By not emphasising the stern note of the warnings he had
previously received he does himself, and those who shared his
responsibility for planning, less than justice. The warnings about
the intensity of both light and heavy flak were, in fact, categoric
and uniformly depressing. At a meeting at Bentley Priory on
September 12th, when the forthcoming operation was being
discussed by Army and Air Force representatives, an officer on
the staff of 1st Airborne Army presented the flak position. He
said that there had been considerable strengthening of flak
defences throughout the area chosen for the operation and 'in
particular at Nijmegen, Arnhem and on a landing field in the
area'. The whole area was covered by heavy anti-aircraft fire and
the light flak, being mobile, could be heavily reinforced in any
threatened area. The plotted flak circles were increasing and a
day or two before the operation began had, indeed, extended
over all the dropping and landing zones.

To fly, in broad daylight, over 1,500 British and American
troop-carrying and tug aircraft into the heart of the plotted
danger area and thereafter, perhaps, into additional flak over
Deelen airfield on turning round, seemed to the RAF foolhardy,
and Urquhart cannot be blamed for accepting their decision as
correct and choosing his zones accordingly. The slow-moving
aircraft would present an extremely vulnerable target. Furthermore, about two hours would necessarily elapse between the
time the head of the stream was over the dropping zones and the

time the tail was clear. The route lay over more than 100 miles of enemy-held territory so that German defences would be thoroughly alerted by the time the targets were reached. In the light, then, of Intelligence reports and flak plottings the choice of dropping and landing zones for the first day of the operation seemed inevitable. Not so inevitable, perhaps, was the choice of dropping zones for Brigadier Hackett's Brigade on the second day. Clearly once the first lift was on the ground and it had become obvious that the flak warnings had been exaggerated, it was too late to change the whole plan by dropping Hackett's Brigade close to the bridge south of the river. But should the original plan have provided for this? Chester Wilmot thought it should. It would have been reasonable for Urquhart to argue, he wrote, 'that if the flak defences in this area were subdued by D plus 1, the risk would be small; and if they were not, it would mean that the bridge was not held and, therefore, it would be essential to take the risk of dropping a brigade there in order to secure the capture of this vital objective'. This is a telling criticism, but it presupposes by implication a more certain knowledge of the enemy's strength than Urquhart possessed. Again, in the light of the Intelligence reports which guided him, it seemed likely that the bridge would be in his hands by nightfall on 17th September and if it were not in his hands by then the danger of light flak would have immeasurably increased by the following day when the Germans would have had time to strengthen their defences. If the flak did increase to this extent, there would be time to re-direct the Polish Brigade to another dropping zone on D+3.

As it happened the flak over the zones west of Arnhem on the first day was not severe. But it might well have been had the aircraft been compelled to fly those six to eight miles towards the town. It was painfully clear from the opposition to subsequent landings that the flak potential was there.

The third of the German explanations for their victory – that bad flying conditions interfered with both air support and air supply – needs elaboration. It is certain, as Sir Winston Churchill said, that the 'weather turned against us at critical moments', although the weather forecast issued before the operation began gave no indication that it was likely to do so.* Nevertheless, by D+1 the weather had deteriorated to such an extent that the second lift was five hours late; on subsequent days it had become so much worse that the flight plans had to be seriously curtailed and drastically altered. The failure of both the Poles and General Gavin's gliders to arrive on Tuesday, September 19th, or even on the 20th, was disastrous.

But if the hundreds of tons of supplies, which despite the weather were dropped over the Arnhem area, had fallen into British hands and if the method of summoning close air support had not been limited to two unserviceable wireless sets the British Division might even so have survived. For the failure of supply and adequate reinforcement – as also the failure of close air support – is no less attributable to the bad communications than to the bad weather.

The Division was dropped with signals equipment which, as General Urquhart subsequently said, needed 'drastic revision and improvement'. After the operations in Italy, during which the Division was spread over a 20-mile sector, a report had been prepared which emphasised the need for a re-assessment of the types of sets required for airborne operations but little had been done to implement its recommendations. As the Cabinet Office Papers show, the range of battalion, brigade and divisional sets were nearly all insufficient and the signallers were sometimes inadequately trained. Even if the conditions imposed by the trees and buildings and the sandy soil had been less unfavourable, these difficulties would have remained. Moreover, there were mistakes in planning, some of which might have been avoided if the signals officers had been consulted immediately the operation

* 'Weather forecast at 16.30/16 September (D Minus 1): Period 17–20 September. Suitable for A-B operations with fair weather apart from morning fog. Light winds.' (Cabinet Office Papers).

had been decided upon. 'The Airborne Division did not know the frequency of 43 Division. The tie-up with XXX Corps regarding frequencies, call signs, codes etc. left much to be desired . . . The two air support parties were not briefed until the middle of the night prior to take off . . . Both parties were useless . . . The virtual breakdown of wireless communications hamstrung the swift passage of Intelligence until it had a purely historic interest.' On two of the frequencies chosen, powerful stations (one British and one German) were already operating.*

The failure of communications was largely responsible not only for the tragic disaster of the re-supply missions, the lack of close air support and the difficulties of control within the Division, but also for the lack of reinforcement on those days when flying was possible. On the Wednesday, Major-General Hakewill Smith, commanding the 52nd Lowland Division, offered to take one of his brigades to Arnhem. Browning still out of touch with Urquhart replied, 'Thanks for your message but offer not repeat not required as situation better than you think.' Although on that day the weather would not, in any case, have permitted these reinforcements being taken to Arnhem, the following day it would have done, and there were gliders available.

---

* Major-General Richard Moberly, who as Chief Signal Officer of 1st Airborne Corps tried hard to get the 1st Airborne Division the equipment he felt was essential, writes to me to say: 'When I formed the 1st Airborne Divisional Signal Regiment early in 1942 no suitable rear link wireless sets existed for the airborne role. Furthermore we were restricted to a very small regiment on the assumption we would never fight for longer than three days! We selected the No. 22 set, which had still not come into production. It was fairly successful in North Africa, Italy and Normandy. It turned out quite unsuitable for Arnhem. Meanwhile many attempts to get some better sets had always been turned down by the War Office on the grounds that there was no spare production and they considered that wireless sets for jungle warfare and airborne operations should be the same! Only after Arnhem was a meeting held at Director level and it was asked what I needed . . .

'The position was made worse by the reluctance of commanders to allot additional airlift for bulky wireless sets as this would have meant fewer fighting men.' This, of course, was the main reason behind the Airborne Division's rejection of larger sets the previous January.

The German contention, that the landing at Arnhem was, in General Browning's phrase, a 'bridge too far', should be answered by Field-Marshal Montgomery himself. The battle of Arnhem, so he has written,

> was 90 per cent successful . . . full success was denied us for two reasons; the first weather . . . second, the enemy managed to effect a surprisingly rapid concentration of forces to oppose us. In face of this resistance, the British Group of Armies in the north was not strong enough to retrieve the situation created by the weather by intensifying the speed of operations on the ground. We could not widen the corridor sufficiently quickly to reinforce Arnhem by road.

Leaving aside the weather, on which perhaps more than sufficient exculpatory emphasis has been laid ('We might have held our bridgehead over the Neder Rijn if we had experienced really good weather', General Sir Francis de Guingand sensibly observes, 'but I wouldn't like to bet on it'), the speed and force of the German reaction were undoubtedly remarkable.

Apart from the skill and verve of the counter-measures immediately taken by Model, Student, Bittrich and Harzer; apart from the capture of the Allied plans – which in any event did little more than confirm the conclusions that these Generals had drawn from the information already in their hands – apart, too, from the failure of the Allies to advance beyond Antwerp after the port was taken and thus prevent the reinforcement of the 1st German Parachute Army and *II Panzer Korps* by many thousands of men from the almost trapped 15th German Army, the overriding factor was that by September 17th, 1944 the enemy was already near to recovery, whereas the impetus of the Allies' advance was already near to being lost. And the momentum of the attack which came to so sudden a halt after the fall of Brussels and Antwerp was never regained. To say this is not to belittle the remarkable achievements of the Guards

Armoured Division and the 82nd and 101st US Airborne
Divisions, nor those of many individual units of XXX Corps,
but there is no denying – *pace* Sir Brian Horrocks and General
Essame – that the final stages of the 2nd Army's advance from
the Waal to the Neder Rijn, as the early stages of the British
Airborne Division's advance into Arnhem, were characterised
by a caution which had never before been shown but which at
this stage of the war, it must be added, was wholly understandable.

Montgomery had expected XXX Corps to reach the Neder
Rijn in two or three days. If it had taken twice as long, it would
not have been too late. But by September 25th the bridgehead
on the northern bank had all but collapsed. Even then General
Horrocks thought that, having got so far, a last desperate effort
to cross the river should be made and General Sosabowski
agreed with him. But, in view of the preparations which the
Germans had by then made to resist such a crossing, it would
have been particularly hazardous. It seems, indeed, that without
either the diversionary landing of some 20,000 troops in Fries-
land, which General Fuller had suggested might have turned the
scale, or the second airborne landing east of Arnhem which the
Germans believe might also have tipped the balance by serving
the same purpose of forcing them to operate in two directions
instead of one, the battle of Arnhem was lost by September 22nd.
By nightfall on this day it was clear that the appalling congestion
on the Eindhoven–Nijmegen road and the increasing enemy
pressure on either side of it, had made it not only impossible to
increase and adequately supply the forces in the foremost areas
but had also made it unlikely that, even if a bridgehead across
the Neder Rijn were to be successfully established, it could be
successfully held.

For this reason it does not seem that Sir Brian Horrocks's
regret that he did not order General Thomas 'to carry out a left
hook across the lower Rhine much farther to the west' is a valid
one. He might have been able to relieve the pressure on the

Airborne Division by threatening the Germans from behind, but it is doubtful that the 43rd Division would have had sufficient time to launch an attack before the Airborne's resistance north of the Neder Rijn collapsed, and it is certain that any bridgehead formed would not only have been extremely difficult to maintain but would also have increased the difficulties which R.W. Thompson has shown the failure at Arnhem entailed.

> In the end, Mr Thompson believes, the Allied advance gained so much that many have tried to argue failure into victory. It is, I am sure, a wrong view. Arnhem had to succeed and it failed. For many days the British 2nd Army was dangerously extended and the enemy was able to concentrate re-organised forces in all the area from Nijmegen to Venlo and to flood a large proportion of the land between the rivers. It made a festering sore in the right flank of the British salient and it was a painful operation to cut it out. Six months later XXX Corps, gathering almost the entire reserve of the 2nd Army under command, would be involved in the bitter fight for the Reichswald Forest. Nearly seven months after Arnhem, in mid-April 1945, the Canadians would capture the bridge.

In this historian's view the fundamental fault lay in the failure to realise the supreme importance of Antwerp and the necessity to clear both sides of the Scheldt estuary. It is true, of course, that there was a clear choice between the rich harvest which OPERATION MARKET GARDEN came so near to reaping and the more certain but less immediately rewarding harvest that possession of a usable port at Antwerp would have offered – just as it was a clear choice between the Ruhr and the Saar. But I consider that the campaign to clear the Scheldt estuary would certainly have been even more difficult and prolonged in September than in fact it proved to be later and that there could have been no hope for a swift and successful advance up to the Neder Rijn at Arnhem afterwards. On the other hand a quick and successful conclusion to OPERATION MARKET GARDEN would not have precluded a subsequent operation against the German defences along the Scheldt. It seems to me, too, that the direction of the Allied advance was the right one. I do not, however, believe that OPERATION MARKET GARDEN should have been launched without more intensive support than Eisenhower felt able to give it. This, of course, is written with the benefit of hindsight. No one can blame Montgomery for believing that even without this support the gamble was justified. He had been given hope of good weather on which so much depended; he had been provided with reassuring Intelligence concerning German strength and the likely speed of German reactions; lives would be lost, but less than would have to be expected in fighting an opposed crossing of the Rhine. If conducted with dash and determination the operation would be over before the lack of the priority he had asked for was a determining factor. The decision was not unsound. The advice he and his commanders were given before the battle began was demonstrably so. And as soon as this became clear he wrote a final appeal to the Supreme Commander:

> I have said stop the right flank and go on with the left, but the right has been allowed to go so far that it has outstripped its maintenance and we have lost flexibility . . . I would say that the right flank of the 12th Army Group should be given a very distinct order to halt, and that, if this order is not obeyed, we shall get into greater difficulties. The net result of the matter in my opinion is that if you want to get to the Ruhr you will have to put every single thing into a left hook and stop everything else. It is my opinion that if this is not done, then you will not get the Ruhr.

Montgomery was now painfully aware that, had he been given the priority he wanted from the beginning, the progress of the 2nd Army's two flank corps could certainly have been accelerated, and thus German pressure on XXX Corp's long salient could certainly have been relieved. Not only, indeed, could the 2nd Army have then operated more quickly and on a wider front but the 1st US Army could have made a strong diversion at Aachen.

On September 22nd, at a conference of army group commanders at Versailles, which Montgomery did not personally attend, sending the more diplomatic de Guingand instead, it was agreed that the British should be given 'overriding logistical support'. Eisenhower, more anxious than ever that the approaches to Antwerp should be captured, agreed that Patton should 'sit down on the Moselle'. But by then it was too late. Before Eisenhower's decision could take effect, the battle of Arnhem was lost.

It was not, though, a complete defeat. Montgomery's ultimate claim of 90 per cent success is, as Chester Wilmot has written, 'difficult to support, for the vital strategic purpose of OPERATION MARKET GARDEN had been frustrated. But 'on the whole the Allied Airborne Operation', in General Student's words, 'proved successful in so far as it gave the 2nd British Army at a single stroke possession of vital bridges and valuable territory.' Whether or not the possession of this territory led to the 'festering sore' which R.W. Thompson condemns, it did provide the Allies with 'an excellent springboard from which to launch the final attack upon Germany. Although the operation failed to secure its immediate objective, it cannot, therefore, by any means be accounted a complete failure.'

As for the men who took part in it, Montgomery paid them a fine and justified compliment in a letter to their commander. 'So long as we have officers and men who will do as you have done', he wrote, 'then we can indeed look forward with complete confidence to the future. In years to come it will be a great thing for a man to be able to say, "I fought at Arnhem".'

Four months later Urquhart ended his official account of the battle with the words, 'There is no doubt that all would willingly undertake another operation under similar conditions in the future. We have no regrets.'

'No. No regrets. Not really, I suppose,' said one of the men whom he had commanded when reminded of this verdict.

There were mistakes, of course. There always are in a battle. And you can't help thinking about the men who died because of them. They might have been saved. But then, there would have been other mistakes and other men would have died. The mistakes are not so important now, except when they provided lessons for the future. The important thing is not to forget the dead.

BIBLIOGRAPHY

UNPUBLISHED SOURCES

Account of the 2nd Battalion of the Parachute Regiment's Operations at Arnhem

1st Airborne Division Report on Operation Market, Parts I–V

Airborne Operation Market. Compiled by F/O R.N. Bassarab, Operations Officer, 299 Squadron

Cabinet Office Papers

Canadian Army Training Manual, No. 70

Diary of 2nd Battalion, The South Staffordshire Regiment

Diary of 156th Battalion, The Parachute Regiment

Diary of Events: 1st Parachute Battalion, by Lieutenant-Colonel D.T. Dobie

Diary of Events: 2nd Parachute Battalion, by Major A.D. Tatham-Warter

Diary of Events: 3rd Parachute Battalion, by Major A. Bush

Diary of Brigadier J.W. Hackett

Diary of Brigadier G.W. Lathbury

Diary of Lieutenant-Colonel J.D. Frost

Diary of Lieutenant-Colonel R. Payton-Reid

Field Artillery at Arnhem 17th–26th September, 1944

German Army MS. B-717 (The files of The Office of the Chief of Military History, Department of the Army, Washington)

German Report on British Airborne Operations in the Western Arnhem Sector

Operation Market. Appreciation and Operation Instructions, by Commander Glider Pilots

Operation Market. Administrative Instructions

Operation Market. The History of 1st Parachute Brigade

Personal Stories from Various Theatres recorded at Interviews at Aldershot, Parachute Regiment HQ (The Files of the Airborne Forces Museum)

Report on Operation Market, by 1st Airlanding Brigade

Report on Operation Market, by 1st Parachute Brigade

Report of the Activities of 4th Parachute Squadron, RE

Report on Operation Market, Air and Military, by Commander Glider Pilots

Report on the Organisation and Equipment of Airborne Divisional Engineers, by Lt.-Col. E.C.W. Myers

Report on the British Airborne Effort in Operation Market, by 38 and 46 Groups, RAF

Report on Operations Market and Garden, by HQ, British Airborne Corps

Report on Operation Market, by 4th Parachute Brigade

Reports on their experiences by various Officers and Men who fought at Arnhem, 17th September 1944 to 25th September 1944 (The Files of the Airborne Forces Museum)

Short Diary of the Activities of 7th King's Own Scottish Borderers

War Diary of 1st Airborne Division

War Diary of 1st Battalion, The Border Regiment

War Diary of Headquarters, 1st Airlanding Brigade

PUBLISHED SOURCES

Airborne Forces (Air Ministry: 1951)

Airborne Forces (*The Second World War, 1939–1945* (War Office: 1951) (*Otway*)

BOEREE, Theod A., *Slag bij Arnhem* (1952)

BRADLEY, General Omar, *A Soldier's Story* (Holt, New York: 1951)

BRERETON, Lewis H., *The Brereton Diaries* (William Morrow & Co.: New York, 1946)

BRYANT, Sir Arthur, *Triumph in the West* (Collins: 1959)

BUTCHER, Captain Harry C., *My Three Years with Eisenhower* (Simon & Schuster, New York: 1946) *By Air to Battle* (HMSO: 1945)

CHURCHILL, Winston S., *The Second World War*, Vol VI, *Triumph and Tragedy* (Cassell: 1954)

COLLIS, Robert (with Han Hogerzeil), *Straight on* (Methuen: 1947)

DEANE-DRUMMOND, Anthony, *Return Ticket* (Collins: 1953) *De Slag om Arnhem* (Arnhem Municipality, n.d.)

EISENHOWER, Dwight D., *Crusade in Europe* (Doubleday: New York, 1948) *Report by the Supreme Commander to the Combined Chiefs of Staff on the Operations in Europe of the Allied Expeditionary Force, 6th June 1944 to 8th May 1945* (HMSO: 1946)

Entscheidungsschlachten des zweiten Weltkrieges. Im Auftrag des Arbeitskreises für Wehrforschung (Verlag für Wehresen Bernard & Graefe, Frankfurt am Main)

ESSAME, Major-General H., *The 43rd Wessex Division at War, 1944–1945* (William Clowes & Sons Ltd.: 1952)

FALLS, Cyril, *The Second World War* (Methuen: 1948)

FULLER, Major-General, J.F.C., *The Second World War* (Eyre & Spottiswoode: Revised Edition, 1954)

GAVIN, James M., *Airborne Warfare* (Infantry Journal Press, Washington: 1946)

GIBSON, Ronald, *Nine Days* (Stockwell: 1956)

GUINGAND, Major-General Sir Francis de, *Operation Victory* (Hodder & Stoughton: 1947)

HAGEN, Louis, *Arnhem Lift* (Hammond, Hammond: 1945)

HEIJBROEK, M., *The Battle Round the Bridge at Arnhem* (Translated by Mrs C.R. Bottenheim-Baring-Gould, for the Airborne Museum, Kasteel De Doorwerth, Oosterbeek, n.d.)

HORROCKS, Lieutenant-General Sir Brian, *A Full Life* (Collins: 1960)

HORST, H.B. van der, *Paratroopers Jump* (Privately published, 1946)

ter HORST, Kate A., *Cloud over Arnhem* (Alan Wingate: 1959)

INGERSOLL, Ralph, *Top Secret* (Harcourt, Brace, New York: 1946)

KERN, Erich, *Buch der Tapferkeit* (Druffel Verlag: Leoni am Starnberger See, 1953)

KESSEL, Lipmann, *Surgeon at Arms* (Heinemann)

LIDDELL HART, Captain B.H., *The Other Side of the Hill* (Cassell: 1951)

MACKENZIE, C.B., *It Was Like This!* ('Adremo' C.V., Oosterbeek: 4th Edn, 1960)

MARTENS, Allard (with Daphne Dunlop), *The Silent War* (Hodder & Stoughton: 1961)

MILBOURNE, Andrew, *Lease of Life* (Museum Press: 1952)

MONTGOMERY, Field-Marshal Viscount, *Normandy to the Baltic* (Hutchinson & Co.: 1947)

MOOREHEAD, Alan, *Eclipse* (Hamish Hamilton: 1945)

NALDER, Major-General R.F.M., *British Army Signals in the Second World War* (Royal Signals Institution: 1953)

NEWMAN, Group Captain M., *Prelude to Glory* (1947)

NORTH, John, *North-West Europe* (HMSO: 1953)

PACKE, Michael, *First Airborne* (Secker & Warburg: 1948)

PACKENHAM-WALSH, Major-General R. P., *The History of the Corps of Royal Engineers*, Vol. IX (Institution of Royal Engineers: 1958)

PATTON, General George S., *War as I Knew It* (Houghton, Mifflin, Boston: 1947)

PAUL, Daniel (Lipmann Kessell) with John St John, *Surgeon at Arms* (Heinemann: 1958)

POGUE, Forrest C., *The United States Army in World War II. The European Theatre of Operations. The Supreme Command.* (Government Printing Office, Washington: 1950)

ROSSE, Captain the Earl of (with Colonel E.R. Hill), *The Story of the Guards Armoured Division* (Geoffrey Bles: 1956)

SAUNDERS, Hilary St George, *The Red Beret* (Michael Joseph: 1950)
The Royal Air Force, 1939–1945, Vol. III (HMSO: 1953)

SETH, Ronald, *Lion with Blue Wings* (Gollancz: 1955)

SHULMAN, Milton, *Defeat in the West* (Secker & Warburg: 1947)

SMYTH, Jack, *Five Days in Hell* (William Kimber: 1956)

SOSABOWSKI, Stanislaw, *Freely I Served* (William Kimber: 1960)

ŚWIĘCICKI, Marek, *With the Red Devils at Arnhem* (Max Love Publishing Co.: 1945)

THOMPSON, R.W., *The Eighty-Five Days* (Hutchinson & Co.: 1957)
URQUHART, Major-General R.E., *Arnhem* (Collins: 1958)
VERNEY, Major-General G.L., *The Guards Armoured Division* (Hutchinson: 1955)
WILMOT, Chester, *The Struggle for Europe* (Collins: 1952)

PERIODICALS

Armoured Cavalry Journal, Vol. LVII, No. 3: Hugh Exton, 'Guards Armoured Division in Operation Market Garden'
Au Cosantoir, Vol. IX, 1949: Colonel-General Kurt Student, 'Arnhem from the Other Side'
Border Magazine, Vol. I, Nos 3 & 4: Major C.F.O. Breese, 'The Airborne Operations in Holland in September 1944'
Borderers' Chronicle, Vol. 19, No. 4: 'The KOSB at Arnhem'
British Legion Journal, Vol. 30, No. 9: Evelyn Lister, 'An Echo of Arnhem'
Ca Ira, Vol. XIII, No. 2: Lieutenant-Colonel George Taylor, 'With XXX Corps to Arnhem'
Eagle (The Regimental Magazine of the Glider Pilot Regiment), Vol. II, No. 10, Summer 1954: G.J.S. Chatterton, 'The Glider Pilot Regiment at Arnhem'
Field Artillery Journal, Vol. 35, No. 4: I.P. Tooley, 'Artillery Support at Arnhem'
Fighting Forces, Vol. XXI, No. 5: A.H. Burne, 'Arnhem'
Fuze, Vol. I, No. 10: 'From Gunners to Gliders'
Glider, September 1957
Gunner, Vol. XXVII, No. 5, August 1945: 'The Battle of Oosterbeek'; Vol. XXXIII, No. 1, January 1951: C.E. Best, 'The Mediums at Arnhem'; Vol. XXVIII, No. 7: R. Williams, 'Arnhem and the War Correspondents'
Intelligence Corps Notes of Interest, Vol. 8, 1945: 'With the Airborne at Arnhem'
Illustrated London News, October 27th 1945: Cyril Falls, 'Arnhem – A Stage in Airborne Tactics'

Journal of the RAMC, Vol. XCVIII, Nos 4 & 5: M.E.M. Herford, 'All in the Day's Work'

Journal of the RASC, Vol. LXIX–LXX, 1945–1946, p.51: 'How the Supplies Reached Arnhem'; Vol. LXIX, No. 2: Michael St J Packe, 'The RASC at Arnhem'

Journal of the RUSI, November 1945: Field-Marshal Sir Bernard L. Montgomery, '21st (British) Army Group in N.W. Europe 1944–1945'

King's Royal Rifle Corps Chronicle, 1946: Lieutenant the Hon. Piers St Aubyn, DSO, 'Arnhem'

Marine Corps Gazette, Vol. 35, Nos 4 & 5: Colonel R. McC. Tompkins, 'The Bridge'

Mufti, Vol. 16, No. 6, June 1951: 'An Echo of Arnhem'

Oxfordshire and Buckinghamshire Light Infantry Chronicle, Vol. XLVIII, 1946

Pegasus, Vol. I, No. 2, July 1946: J.A.G., 'Do You Remember?'; Vol. I, No. 3, October 1946: D.O.C., 'Do You Remember?'; Vol. I, No. 3: Alan Wood, 'How Arnhem was Reported'; Vol. III, No. 3: 'News from Arnhem'

Reconnaissance Journal, Vol. 4, No. 1, Autumn, 1947: Lieutenant J. Stevens, 'Arnhem Diary' and Sergeant F. Winder, 'I.O.s Report' and 'Postscript'

Royal Air Force Journal, Vol. 2, No. 12, December 1944: Flight-Lieutenant A.A. Williams, 'I was at Arnhem'

Royal Engineers' Journal, Vol. LXVIII, No. 4: E.M. Mackay, 'The Battle of Arnhem Bridge' (reprinted from *Blackwood's Magazine*); March–December 1946, p.22: 'The Evacuation of the 1st Airborne Division from Arnhem'

Royal Pioneer, Vol. 7, No. 30, March 1952: F.W. Wooding, 'The Airborne Pioneers'

Services and Territorial Magazine, Vol. 20, No. 190, 1951: Alexander Johnson, 'Airborne Operation'

Soldier, Vol. 13

Sprig of Shillelagh (The Journal of the Royal Inniskilling Fusiliers), Vol. XXVIII, No. 322, Spring–Summer 1948: Major H.S. Cousens, 'Arnhem 17th–26th September 1944'

Springbok, Vol. 38, No. 9, September 1955: C A. McCulloch, 'The Epic of Arnhem'

Stand-to, Vol. 2: Robert Smith, 'With the RAMC at Arnhem'; Vol. I, No. 8: Chester Wilmot, 'What Really Happened at Arnhem'; Vol. I, No. 9: Stanley Fijalski, 'Echoes of Arnhem'

INDEX